Walking
to Japan A MEMOIR

Derek Youngs &
Carolyn Affleck Youngs

tellwell

Tellwell Talent
www.tellwell.ca

ISBN
978-1-77302-273-4 (Paperback)
978-1-77302-274-1 (eBook)

DEREK YOUNGS
JUNE 16, 1940 – MARCH 18, 2011

TABLE OF CONTENTS

Part 3

ACKNOWLEDGEMENTS

I thank Carolyn for more than I can ever say, and—for not getting grumpy when I ask, "Does anyone really care about semicolons?" I thank Lin, in spirit, for her unconditional love and unwavering belief in me. Thanks to Lani, for always being there, for cutting my hair, and doing my taxes! And of course, thanks to daughters Pauline and Christine, and grandchildren Kyle and Chamille, for whom I wrote this book. To all of you, and the many others who supported me along the path, whether you pointed the way or pushed me, sheltered me or fed me, hugged me, questioned me or contributed to the many incarnations of these stories, I offer my deep appreciation and love.

Derek Walker Youngs

My thanks to all who encouraged and helped me through the last few years! I must also give special mention to a few. Lani Kaito—for our ever-growing connection as widows and friends, and for the stories you have entrusted to me. Lucile Kerkmeer—for our laughs, and your recollections. Cynthia Monroe—for sharing your unwavering friendship, great ideas, sensitive eye and storytelling ear. Appreciation to readers Carol Zhong, Sue Kenney, and Zachariah Crow. Last but not least, I thank the Nipponzan Myohoji Buddhist monks for their dedication to peace and their gracious hospitality.

Carolyn Affleck Youngs

Walking to Japan

Anyone who has lost a beloved partner will know the debilitating and overwhelming nature of that loss. When my husband died suddenly and unexpectedly, I was knocked off my feet. In the freshness of grief, I waded through the tasks that accompany the loss of a spouse—notifying friends, arranging a memorial service, filing legal paperwork—aware of a more daunting job that lay ahead. I had a book to finish writing.

When I met Derek, I found that he didn't engage in conversation like most people do, sharing casual anecdotes. He rarely answered questions directly, either. This made him seem inscrutable. I learned that he wasn't evasive, but private. He carefully considered his words, which he often delivered in the form of a story, and only if he sensed a measure of readiness from his audience, be it a room full of people, or just one friend. Even me. Otherwise he just wouldn't bother. This wasn't disrespectful; he felt that people's need for quick answers was a reflection of their own insecurity. For him, every story had a spirit, which must be honoured.

Derek put pen to paper and recorded some of his stories. With enough encouragement and goading by folks who wanted to know more about their friend, father, lover or guru, he began to shape this material into a book. I started helping with the project in 2004, and our long, sporadic, stimulating, and sometimes intense working relationship evolved alongside our personal connection: from mentor and student to collaborators, from friends to lovers, and then spouses.

At times I took dictation; at times I honed pieces he'd already written. Derek would read what we were working on aloud, needing to *feel* the words, not just recite them. If a passage felt flat, one of us—or both—would rewrite. We knew we were finished a section when we sat back and marvelled, *Who wrote that*? The stories were still his, but now it was *our* book. After seven years, it seemed that with just a few more short chapters we'd be finished. But then—

With Derek's sudden death, the project was now completely in my hands. And as intimate as we had been, and as often as I'd been able to finish his sentences, I didn't know how to complete it alone. After much contemplation, I sensed he would somehow guide me through the process, but I needed time to regain my balance.

Eventually, when I found my footing, I began to envision the book in a new light. Although Derek never intended to write a spiritual self-help manual or an autobiography, there were lessons in his stories, which I knew would speak most clearly in the context of his life. I needed to paint a more complete picture of this charismatic figure, the peace pilgrim with his larger-than-life calling and very human shortcomings.

I unearthed several boxes from our garage and found a wealth of material: photographs, videotapes and cassette recordings of interviews and workshops, as well as some hastily scribbled notes, a few diaries, and letters filled with tenderly scribed passages. His faded words revealed a younger, more idealistic version of the man I had married, engaging as ever, curious about life, and quick to laugh. As I read, I recognized a spiritual awakening. A hard-working young man's worries about the *doing* aspects of life, the struggles of raising a family and paying the mortgage, were gradually replaced with questions of *being*. He spoke of love, responsibility, letting go, and finding peace—inside and outside himself.

My discoveries were exciting and rewarding but gave me a sinking feeling at the same time. The more facts I accumulated, the more the process felt like assembling a giant jigsaw puzzle that just kept growing. "How far along are you on *Walking to Japan*?" friends would ask, and I'd have to admit that I really didn't know. I had lost perspective. So, I chose to redirect my focus temporarily, and went to live overseas for six months, spending every day walking until I tired myself out.

Gradually, through the rhythm of my feet everything came clear, and by the time I returned home to Canada I was ready to work again. I could hear Derek's voice and put it to paper, though at times I wondered who was really speaking. "Is that really you?" I asked aloud, half hoping for an apparition, half feeling ridiculous for doing so. I could feel Derek's amusement at my dilemma, as if he were giving me a gentle push.

And then I heard: *I trust you, so trust yourself. Besides, is it really that different now that I'm dead?*

I had to laugh. "Easy for you to say!" I shot back.

My process spanned years, and there were times when I struggled. Occasionally I had to weigh Derek's portrayal of an event against someone else's, or against objective facts. I wanted precision. But to my husband, the big picture mattered more than specifics. So I have tried to stay true to his vision and his memories, while being as accurate as possible. However, since life is messier than books can afford to be, some of the names, timelines and details have been altered or merged in the interest of privacy, clarity and flow. And although *Walking to Japan* is Derek's life story, in his voice, you'll find that I appear from time to time, speaking in my own voice (indicated by a different typeface). I hope this is not an intrusion, but adds to the big picture.

When Derek told me, a few years before he died, what he wanted to call the book, I laughed. *How cheeky*, I thought. "The only problem," I told him, "is—what if someone picks it up thinking it's an actual guide to walking to Japan?" Derek peered at me over his reading glasses, one eyebrow raised. Oh, how I miss that look!

So, no, it's not a guidebook, if you're wondering. Derek didn't care about how to get from A to B, but how his mind and heart were opened along the way.

—Carolyn Affleck Youngs

Dreams are important, not because they might come true, but because they take us places we would never dare go, places we can't even imagine. Goals are rigid and planned, but dreams—they're flexible, mutable, unpredictable.

I never dreamed of becoming a peace walker, but I dreamed of *more*. That dream pulled me along like an invisible hand, and it took me from walking for peace to talking the walk, on the radio and onstage, addressing huge groups of people with dreams of their own.

When I tell a tale from the road, there are always questions. Occasionally someone will pique my imagination or make me reflect deeply. But often people ask the same old things: "How many miles have you walked? How fast? How many pairs of shoes have you worn through? Where does your money come from?" I see that these questions are sometimes less about me than the person asking. What's revealed are *their* priorities in life, their concerns, their insecurities. As innocent as these questions are—because of course it's not every day you meet someone who's walked across entire countries—I try to dodge them. I don't mean to be flippant, but I'm not all that interested in the *how manys*, or even the *hows*. The *how* of my journey is just one foot in front of the other. What interests me more is *why*. I walk because it is my life. It's no longer something I do; it's who I am. It's everything: passion, loneliness, confusion, frustration and joy.

The questions I ask myself are the most important. I have a lot of them. Questions can keep me awake, aware of my own motivations and limitations. They keep me engaged in the process of trial and error, and that is how I learn. I've never enjoyed playing by others' rules—religious rules, societal rules, political rules. They seem arbitrary and designed to stop people from thinking for themselves, so I have had to navigate through everyone else's versions of what's right and find my own way. *What do you really believe, Derek? Who is this lover of life? Who is this destroyer? How can you make a difference? What are your dreams for yourself and the planet?*

When I speak in public, I try to get people to think about this stuff. But then it's question time, and I hope to hear something new. One day, I did: "Do you plan to write a book?"

The question both excited and terrified me—a good way to recognize a dream, if there ever was one. So I set out to claim it. I started by penning letters to friends, and then quarterly bulletins which I circulated for several years. This kind of writing came easily. But when I tried to write anything long or serious, my hands froze and my thoughts scattered like leaves in the wind. Every attempt just confused and discouraged me. I wrote poems, researched, and walked around libraries, hoping to soak up the right vibes to get me started. I did everything but write a book.

What was I doing? I wasn't a writer! Frustrated and lost, I accepted help from a screenwriter, Katherine. "OK, Derek, let's start with the basics," she said. "Who are your favourite authors?" I froze. Maybe if I didn't answer, she'd forget the question. No such luck. "Your favourite authors?" she repeated.

Heart pounding as it hadn't since being called up before the headmaster in grammar school, I stammered, "I … uhh … don't have any. I haven't read a whole book in almost, um—25 years." Katherine's eyebrows rose like startled crows taking flight from a nest. "The world was going crazy back then," I blurted. "Just like now, I suppose. Newspapers and books were full of violence—the Cuban Missile Crisis, the Kennedy assassinations, Kent State, the Watts riots, Charles Manson. So much bad news, and I was powerless. I had to stop reading before I lost my mind!" She stared at me blankly, saying nothing. Shame turned me queazy. *No one in their right mind would admit to not reading books,* I thought. Staring at the ground, I shuffled my feet, resisting their impulse to flee. Silence, at that moment, was definitely not golden but pitch-black.

Glancing up at her face, I was certain I could read her thoughts. *Sure, Derek. I'm a professional writer, a literature scholar, and I'm still struggling to get a book published. And you—a guy who doesn't even read books—you're just wasting my time!*

After a long pause, her mouth opened and I braced myself. At last she spoke. "Oh." I imagined all the disappointment of the world in that one small sound.

How can such a tiny word carry so much power? Katherine meant nothing by it, but I let that "Oh" sabotage me. For years I was intimidated by the mysterious world of books.

And then, I met Carolyn.

Now, finally, my stories are here for you to read. I hope they give you a chance to wonder, to laugh, and to think about your own story. I invite you to walk with me, and be part of a dream—a dream that came true and continues to take me to places I could never have imagined.

CHAPTER 1

JAPAN?

The road stretches out from under my feet, curving gently uphill into the mountains. The gentle forests of Épinal blanket the horizon. Craggy stone castles jut out from thickets of trees. Behind me, strewn down the slopes, lie a cluster of tiny settlements amidst undulating vineyards. I have the illusion I could reach out and pick up the buildings, like children's toys scattered in a garden.

My beautiful white pony walks beside me, her hoofs the heartbeat of our journey; the steady *clip-clop* gives a rhythmic counterpoint to the jangle of cowbells in the distance. Our constant companion, the long and placid Moselle River, travels with us though this fairytale land. The air is fresh, layered with delicate floral scents. Lanky, white storks perch on the rooftops of half-timbered houses, gazing out from nests the size of boulders. Songbirds crowd the trees and burst from bushes at our approach. Their sweet music lulls me into a reverie, as I recall the cool milk and crusty bread a farmer's wife offered me the early that morning.

"*Bonjour monsieur, excusez-moi!*" My pastoral interlude evaporates as a car pulls up beside me, windows rolled down. Two pretty young women peer at me, grinning from ear to ear. "Why," they ask me in French, "are you walking up this road with a pony?"

Unable to resist the temptation for a little flirtation, I smile innocently. "I'm walking to Japan," I answer. "Er … *je marche au Japon!*"

With huge saucer eyes, they look at each other, giggling. "*Japon? Mais non!*"

"*Ah, mais oui!*" I counter.

"*Pourquoi?* And with a pony? How is this possible?"

"Well, I walk for peace," I continue in a mixture of English and simple French, "and it's my dream to reach Japan. I know that sounds strange, but let me assure you, it's true."

"But *monsieur*," they reply, staring in amazement, "Japan is an island, *non?*"

I chuckle, knowing I have them hooked. "An island for certain, but I will walk there. And if you have time, I will explain. Can I tell you a story or two?" They look at each other, laugh, pull their car over to the side of the road and get out.

"Please, tell us," they prompt me.

And so I begin. "Once upon a time…."

CHAPTER 2

BEGINNINGS

There was a bustling English coastal town called Redcar. Can you imagine its streets of identical red brick row houses, with white-framed bay windows overlooking the road? Their jolly chimney pots line up like soldiers against billowing clouds in an azure sky. Next, picture a backdrop: a great long stretch of sandy beach, with striped towels, folding chairs and bathing-suited bodies blanketing the sand, tucked right up to the tideline. Couples stroll lazily down a promenade and children laugh in a nearby playground. Out on the gently rolling white-capped waves, fishing boats bob merrily up and down. It's like a picture postcard.

Suddenly, the scene changes. The sky is full of bombs and real soldiers line the streets. The beachfront is strung with barbed wire, land mines lie buried in the sand, and huge concrete barricades block access to the roadways. Townspeople huddle indoors behind blackout curtains. It's World War II, and Redcar, with its steel refinery, is vulnerable to German attacks from sea and air.

It was during an air raid that I came into this world, on a dark morning in 1940. A dramatic beginning, to be sure. My pregnant mother, bless her brave heart, was alone in our little house on Sandringham Road when an air raid alert sounded. Her water broke. Unable to call for help or get out of the house, she delivered me herself, cutting the umbilical cord with her teeth. As I imagine that moment, I feel myself propelled into a world of screaming sirens and the eerie drone of bomber planes.

A neighbour's keen intuition sent her dashing across the road to our house. Jean found me in an upstairs bedroom, nestled in my mother's weak embrace. As my mother rested, Jean cleaned and bundled me up, then rushed outside to hand me down into the underground womb of the air raid shelter, where a small group of neighbours sat hushed in the damp space, only one small candle illuminating the fear on their faces.

Jean ran back towards the house, but flying shrapnel pierced the air, forcing her retreat. My mother sat up and crawled downstairs to the back door to try to reach the shelter. Exhausted and bleeding profusely from the labour, she couldn't open the door. She lay there alone and frightened, waiting for the *all clear* signal. A few hours later the horn whined its message of safety to the town. The planes had passed and everyone could return to their daily business.

My neighbours carried me out of the shelter, uncertain whether my mother would still be alive or whether the houses would still be standing. But she was, and they were. My mother and I were reunited and our weary friends returned home.

Years later, I told a friend this story. "Good grief, Derek," he said. "You were being bombed from the moment you took your first breath. No wonder you've chosen to walk for peace."

CHAPTER 3

INVITATION

So how did I become a peace walker? Perhaps the best way I can explain is by jumping right into the middle. Maybe that's not the usual way to do it, but I've never been one for convention.

In 1985, I was living on Galiano Island, a little chunk of paradise off Canada's West Coast. My two daughters, Christine and Pauline, had flown the proverbial nest and were testing their new-found wings. My partner, Lani, was on a sojourn abroad, following her own life's path as a healer.

With everyone gone, I took time off from my work as a massage therapist to enjoy some solitude. Every day I hiked up the steep wooded trail to the peak of Mount Galiano, where I sat on a rocky outcropping, gazing out across the water. In the distance, a fringe of snow-capped mountains met blue sky. Below me, eagles circled lazily, their outstretched black wings tipping into each updraft. The sun warmed me, and I felt flooded with light.

As my intimacy with nature deepened, and my awareness broadened, I remained lit with an inner glow. But the thing about light is that it reveals shadows.

One morning I turned on the television and happened upon a news story about protesters blockading a logging operation of old-growth forest in northern British Columbia. Trees that had been standing for hundreds of years were being threatened with destruction. Men and women were camped out in and around the trees, chanting and yelling and crying, while workers with chainsaws and heavy equipment drew nearer. Tension and emotions ran high. The scenes were so intense that I couldn't watch. I changed the channel but landed on a cops-and-robbers drama. This turned my stomach. With only a few channels to watch, there was only one other option.

Over the next half hour I learned about the Doomsday Clock, a symbolic device "started" in 1945 by concerned scientists as an indicator of the risk of nuclear disaster. As the dangers increased, the hands moved closer to midnight, the final hour. There was now the equivalent of two tons of TNT weaponry on Earth for every living person, and this fact was barely registering on our emotional radar. Our culture had been systematically desensitized to the violent truth. The time was now almost three minutes to midnight.

I'd been born during the Second World War. The atomic bombs that destroyed Hiroshima and Nagasaki should have been the first and last of their kind. But they weren't. Technology was way beyond that now. What did this mean for my children? And my children's children?

I turned off the TV, walked out the door, and went up the mountain. But I didn't find solace there. I couldn't hear the songbirds for the sounds that filled my imagination: the roar of chainsaws, the screech and splintering crash of falling giants, the whiz of bullets, and the sickening roar of a nuclear detonation.

I lay on the ground, tears sliding down my cheeks onto the damp earth. I think I may have even screamed out loud. But I know no one answered. I was alone, my beautiful world crumbling, along with my idyllic life.

Days of introspection stretched into weeks, but no amount of self-searching yielded answers. I saw only humanity's evils: greed, violence and apathy. Darkness spread through me like an inkblot. Trapped by my own negativity, I felt impotent, powerless to change even my bed linens, let alone change the world. At times I worked myself into a fury and then lapsed into lethargy. "This situation is dire," I said in despair to a friend on the phone. "Why the hell doesn't somebody do something?" As I said the words, a thought surfaced. *I am somebody.*

For my future grandkids to have good lives, I would have to stop wondering *what* and *how*, and just do something—anything—NOW. I recalled an anti-war statement I once read: *I will not preoccupy myself with an enemy. I* recognized that I had been doing just this. I had created an enemy called "world destruction" and now my own thoughts about it were destroying me. My passionate anger had rendered me blind and lame.

Passion is life's essential fuel. But it must be tempered. Remembering this, I vowed to stop shaking my fists at the sky, stop hiding in denial, and to use my passion more productively. Anger would keep me alert and motivate me during the times when all I wanted was to crawl into bed and hide under the covers. I needed a healthy outlet for my rage, one that would serve both me and the planet. But what was it?

I asked for guidance—from Spirit. I was not a religious man, but I believed in something, and that this something would help me. Not everything is always a sign, but when our intentions are true, I believe that the universe somehow conspires to show us the way. One day, I was flipping idly through a magazine on the kitchen table and something caught my eye—a promotion for something called the Great Peace March for Global Nuclear Disarmament. In the past I wouldn't have noticed the slick advertisement, but now I had goose bumps. A little voice in my head whispered, *You can do this*!

CHAPTER 4

SUPPORT

The Great Peace March blurb described some lofty goals: a nine-month commitment to walk almost 6000 kilometres from Los Angeles to Washington, DC. Walkers would spread the message of global disarmament and a ban on nuclear weapons.

Without thinking twice, I wrote to request a registration package, and when Lani returned home, we spent days discussing practical matters. Was I physically capable of walking that much? I was fit, certainly, but I'd never done any long-distance hiking. That didn't seem as big an issue though, as what might happen to our relationship if I were to go away for nine months. Neither of us liked the idea of such a prolonged separation.

Lani understood that I had to follow my heart, and that it was crucial for me to have her support and blessing, just as it had been for her to have mine when she travelled to pursue her calling. Ultimately, we would not let the physical distance drive us apart. We would continue to make each other a priority, and deal with our lives day by day. If something came up and Lani, or my kids, really needed me, of course I would come home.

Weeks later I received an application form in the mail. It was so detailed that I doubted whether I'd be accepted. "Come prepared," it announced:

You will need:
1. *Active medical insurance coverage with policy number*
2. *Sleeping bag (rated to 5ºF), rain gear, and proper walking shoes*
3. *Money to cover personal expenses*
4. *Money and/or travel arrangements for returning home*
5. *Completed medical exam and release forms*
6. *Tetanus vaccination or recent booster*

My most daunting task was to raise money. Each walker required a minimum of $3,500— a huge sum for me. I was working again at my massage practice, but saving that much would take too long. How would I come up with the rest in time? After brainstorming, Lani and I came up with an idea that required me to swallow a large amount of pride. I wrote a letter to all of my friends, printing in large letters at the top of the page: "I AM NEEDED, I AM WORTHY, AND MY ACTIONS MAKE A DIFFERENCE TO THE WORLD."

Below, I talked about my desire to join the Great Peace March—the GPM. This surely felt like the most courageous letter I'd ever written:

> *The path this is taking me along leads to home, our home,*
> *the Earth…. I am asking first for you to join with me in*
> *spirit, and secondly if it is possible, to send a donation*
> *to support me during those nine months. Whatever the*
> *decision it would be an honour to carry you in my heart.*

I dropped dozens of envelopes into the mailbox and then waited. Would friends understand my decision to walk away from everything I cherished? Was I an idealistic, escapist fool? Imagining the worst, I could almost hear my friends grumbling: *Who does he think he is, Gandhi? This is just a nine-month vacation he wants us to bankroll! Six thousand kilometres? I don't think he even walks to the grocery store. You know what, Derek? Get lost. Take a hike!*

Ha ha, I thought to myself. But it wasn't funny. I was really worried about what people would think. A couple of agonizing weeks crawled by, and then—my mailbox began to fill up. Too afraid to open the letters, I stacked them on the kitchen table, and stared at the growing pile. When the day came that I couldn't stand it any longer, my hands fumbled to open the first reply. The words sank in. Ripping one letter open after the next, I bathed in a stream of affirmation. My friends actually GOT it.. I wasn't walking away; I was walking *towards* something. They thanked me, expressing their own fears for the future and longings to do something. I realized that my concerns about their judgments were really my own fears of failure. I really had no idea whether I could walk that far.

Three months later, emotions still running high, I made a tally. I'd received more donations than I'd asked for—almost $5,000! But during all this heady excitement I had completely forgotten the acceptance letter. I never received one. But why? Maybe with my history of asthma they thought me unfit to walk. Maybe their roster was full, or maybe I had been too vague about my thoughts on nuclear weapons. *Maybe,* I thought, *I should phone them.* So I dialed the organizers' office in Los Angeles. My mouth went dry, but I managed to squeak out my inquiry. On the other end, a harried but friendly voice chirped, "Of course you're registered. Sorry! Guess we forgot to mail your acceptance letter. See ya soon!"

I hung up the phone, stunned. *Now you will have to walk.*

CHAPTER 5

LEARNING TO WALK

My bag was packed. Yet as my departure day approached, my initial *yes* became more and more shaky as I confronted doubt after doubt. And I hadn't even left home. But whenever I make a change in my life I imagine all the horrors, dangers, and impossibilities of pursuing any new challenge. This fear in itself is good, for it keeps me awake and aware of dangers. What is not good is when fear freezes me. When this happens, it's a sure sign I need to get closer to what I fear, to loosen its grip. And once I take the first step, it becomes easier. One step leads to the next. Honestly, the hardest thing sometimes is just getting out the door.

On March 1, 1986, I stood outside Los Angeles City Hall. Buses, cabs and cars pulled up, and people emerged with backpacks and placards. Walkers streamed in from all directions, and soon I was engulfed in a sea of bodies: children, hippies, elders, Buddhist monks, folks of all colours and costumes—nearly 1,200 people in all. I was full of anticipation, apprehension, joy, and bewilderment, and I could tell everyone else was, too. The air felt electric.

Below the stairs of City Hall was a huge stage. Celebrities spoke and then officials from Japan took the podium to present us with the eternal flame of Hiroshima. We would carry this living symbol with us to Washington.

Then the musician Holly Near came onstage and sang a new song she'd written just for us.[1]

> *We will have peace*
> *We will because we must*
> *We must because we cherish life*
> *And believe it or not*
> *Daring as it may seem,*
> *It is not an empty dream*
> *To walk in a powerful path*
> *Neither the first nor the last …*

As I sang along, it felt like the words came straight out of my heart. I looked around and realized that all of these strangers and I were not just going on a peace march, we *were* the Great Peace March. And now, amid thunderous clapping, singing, cheers, and tears, we took our first steps.

The press were everywhere. A gang of reporters followed us, bristling with microphones that they thrust into our faces. Planes and helicopters swarmed us, diving down for aerial close-ups. The March was off to an exhilarating start.

Towering skyscrapers slowly receded as we entered the suburbs. The initial euphoria waned. The enormous cheering crowds were replaced by small groups of young students, waving to us as we passed. The weather ahead looked dark and foreboding, and our huge grins shifted to looks of determination. Long periods of silence—more exhausted than contemplative—punctuated our cheery songs.

After a few days on the road, our deflation became more evident at the rest stops. Instead of huddling into little groups like chattering school children, we went off alone to tend to our aching, blistered feet. Although there were some experienced trekkers in our midst, few of us had walked for longer than a stretch of an hour or two. By the end of the first week almost everyone was in pain, many complaining of shin splints, swollen knees,

---

1   *The Great Peace March* Words and music by Holly Near ©1978 Hereford Music. Printed by permission.

and heat exhaustion. My hip joints felt like bone-on-bone, and I had lost a toenail. I had also been ravaged by ant bites. The reality of walking like this for several hundred days began to feel physically impossible. Could we really do this? Could *I* really do this? I'd never left my friends and family for such a long time. I began to miss Lani terribly. But I couldn't turn back now. No way.

In less than two weeks and 175 kilometres into our walk, we were snaking along through the freezing, rain-drenched, wind-blasted Mojave Desert. Suddenly, the sky roared and from out of nowhere came a helicopter, scattering dust and sagebrush everywhere as it landed. A figure emerged, silhouetted against the haze. It was like a scene from a Francis Ford Coppola film. As the debris settled, we found ourselves face to face with David Mixner, the head organizer of the walk. He waved us in closer. We encircled him, pressing together, sensing that something serious was going down.

In a slow and trembling voice, he spoke. "I'm sorry. The walk is over. You'll have to go home." Puzzled at first, we thought it was some kind of a cruel joke, until he continued. "We're bankrupt … there's no money … so please … you must go home." He was serious. People in the back of the crowd had to rely on those up front to pass the words along, and eventually we all heard the news. The words tore into my heart. A year and a half in planning and now my dream was shattered. We were all in the same boat; we'd given up jobs, homes and relationships to be here. We'd worked hard fundraising, and now—in an instant—it was all over. How could this be?

What had happened to our money? There are many stories.[2] Some suspected that members of the Reagan administration had an interest in seeing the walk stopped. After all, during this time, peace activists were considered as evil as communists. We also had detractors scouting ahead in the communities that wanted to offer us services and shelter. They warned business owners and town councils about purchasing adequate insurance when 1,200 hippies came to camp in their backyards. *What kind of insurance?* I wondered. *Hippie insurance?* One by one, communities began to rescind their offers and a few scattered seeds of fear grew into a blight

---

2   David Mixner would later state that the GPM was was a success partly because of his own administrational failure, and that his ego had played a significant role in its collapse.

that spread across the country. Our support began to disappear, leaving organizers scrambling.

After the initial shock subsided, however, marchers instinctively formed two large concentric circles. They chanted passionately, "We're still here, we're still going!" Inside me, another more subdued voice cried, *But how?*

This circle in the desert began a series of long, painful days and nights of arguing, crying and questioning. We had all started off in LA with a linear perspective: walking from A to B. There had been an organizational hierarchy and a clear goal: to bring the missiles down. But now, that clarity had disintegrated. Feeling disempowered, we watched as repo men swooped in like vultures picking meat from the bones. They drove off with our support vehicles, carrying away medical supplies, food and water. "No money, no trucks," they said. Why did THEY now hold the power? In a bid to stall for time we grabbed their ignition keys and threw them into the desert. But like robots, they continued with their repossession and we lost our hold on the stream of vanishing supplies. It seemed hopeless.

The media returned. Now they had an even bigger story, for failure is apparently more newsworthy than peace. The press announced to the world that the GPM was dead and the remaining corporate sponsors pulled out. No one wants to back a loser.

About 700 people returned home and I did not fault them. But 500 of us stayed. Stranded in the desert, we looked around at each other. We were a living expression of "all walks of life," a genuine microcosm of society, united with a common purpose. And before we knew it, swiftly and organically we formed sub-circles. There were activists, feminists, musicians, gays and lesbians, seniors, Christians, and even an anarchists' non-group! This is a natural response. Prehistoric humans found it easier to live in smaller, more manageable tribes. Scientists can even describe this phenomenon with mathematical formulae. We were all creating new comfort zones, circles of familiarity, kinship and shared values. On the flip side, we also found it convenient to have another group to blame when something went wrong, which took place on a daily basis. It was all too easy to create enemies within the ranks.

Each group thought they knew best. Everything would be OK if only we'd all just pray, or sign more petitions, or eat more vegetables, or—you name it. But tribes need to cooperate and we would get nowhere unless we learned to get along. So we called a meeting and huddled into the largest tent we could find. One man put up his hand, saying, "What we need is Robert's Rules of Order."

"Are you kidding?" someone chimed in from the back. "We need Parliamentary Procedure!"

"Guys, guys!" a woman yelled, "Haven't you heard of consensus?"

The irony of arguing about how to talk was lost on many, but we made a genuine grassroots effort. We learned to how to talk, how to listen, and we learned that we just needed to keep talking and listening until everyone felt heard. The solution would often emerge much later. The process wasn't perfect, but it worked.

During the reorganization process, we'd accumulated sufficient donations of money and supplies to head out for a few more weeks. People still believed in us. A farmer gave us a milk truck to convert into a water truck. Someone brought us a kitchen on wheels. The Organic Producers of America donated food and Native American Indian bands offered their land for us to rest on. On March 28, 500 naïve but determined people picked up their gear, buttoned up their jackets and left California for the glittering lights of Las Vegas.

We inched our way across the next bleak stretch of land, where local old-timers popped out of nowhere to warn us of the desert's serious dangers. Joining us around our evening fire, they shared accounts of hypothermia, terrifying us with tales of scorpions and poisonous snakes, and suggesting our only protection would be to wrap layers of plastic bags around our feet. The stories spread like wildfire in the community. They'd been right about the hypothermia: the desert got cold at night, and several underdressed walkers succumbed. I hoped they were teasing us about the rest.

Ordinary folks continued to appear from nowhere to offer support. One individual anonymously donated $18 to each walker and a luxury ski resort provided lavishly furnished condos. The gifts poured in, and we were able to purchase new support vehicles, portable toilets, and cooking supplies. Celebrities, including Paul Newman, Yoko Ono, Jackson Browne, Ron Howard, Reverend Jesse Jackson, Leonard Nimoy and Carl Sagan supported us with their presence, their talents, and their money. The Shivwit Paiute Indians cooked us dinner, as did the Hare Krishna devotees. One afternoon, an impoverished family invited me and a friend to dinner at their house, and we dined like royalty on canned soup and Kool-Aid. They had so little, yet they were willing to share it all. The next morning as we walked past their house, the two little girls stood in the back of a neighbour's pickup truck holding a sign saying *God Bless You*. We ran to hug them goodbye.

One scorching day after almost six hours of walking we were nearing delirium as we reached the peak of a short hill. Down the other side was a little van parked in the barren valley. As the mass of us approached, I saw a man step out of the vehicle. He lifted the hatch and proceeded to dish out ice cream cones. *Aha,* I thought, surveying the absurd scene. *I know what this is—a mirage.* I remembered one of the old-timers warning me about optical illusions in the desert. I stood back and laughed as the others obediently stood in line for their cones, wondering how everyone could be so easily duped by this vision. But when I saw strawberry ice cream running down 500 grinning faces I ran to the line, receiving my cone just as he scraped the last drop from the bucket. *Not a mirage, but a miracle,* I thought. It was not the first or the last.

Peace City, as we called ourselves, was a small town on the move and we all took on volunteer work. Jobs included: cleanup, first aid, fundraising, promotion, mail, kitchen duty, school and daycare, and we even had our own radio station on wheels.

With infrequent access to shower and laundry facilities, *cleanliness* was a relative term. In the few towns that had a single public shower in a laundromat or gas station, we'd have to line up around the block. As well, each of us had only one or two changes of clothing, so instead of waiting in line for washing machines, hordes of us would descend on the local thrift stores to purchase new outfits. For fun, some of us bought the most outrageous items we could find. We'd emerge looking like a circus act, with sparkly scarves, striped bellbottoms, capes, gaudy beads, bow ties and top hats. And wouldn't you know it? Those were the marchers who ended up on the front page of the newspapers.

How we dressed and presented ourselves sparked heated discussion and eventually a vote on a dress code (defeated). So we had to let go of the judgments and worries about our image, which was all just ego stuff. The impact we would make collectively would undoubtedly be more than just one single person could effect, positively or negatively. We had to hope so, anyway. At times it was hard to believe our message would come through, especially when news coverage became sparse, and when so much focussed on *how* we walked, and *who* walked, but not *why we walked*.

Even from the inside it could be hard to keep the *why* in sight. We found we weren't always the peaceful happy people we thought we were. The walk not only stripped away our professional roles, but he ones we had hid behind since childhood: caretaker, leader, martyr, controller, procrastinator, manipulator, victim. Living in such close quarters and walking side by side every day, things emerged from our unconscious—judgments, expectations, old wounds, and even feelings of loneliness—that were not pretty.

One day in the Midwest, I found myself alone for once, my companions either far ahead or behind. It was hot in the blazing sun: 90°F and 90% humidity. Sweat poured down my face. The pleasant countryside had disappeared and all around me lay nothing but acres and acres of corn, and the pungent smell of hot pig manure singeing my nostrils. *What the hell am I doing here?* I wondered. *I'm supposed to be making a difference! Nobody even knows I'm out here in the middle of nowhere. Who even cares? The pigs?* I stopped walking for a moment and heard a little voice inside answer: *You do.* I looked at my surroundings in a different light. I didn't need anyone else's acknowledgement for being there. I thanked the farmers for all their hard labour. I thanked the sun and water for making the crops grow, and I thanked the pigs and corn for sacrificing their lives. Then I resumed walking.

From this point on, my work was now no longer dependent on—or relevant to—the efforts of others. If I woke up at 4:00 a.m., climbed out of a flooded tent to cook breakfast for 500 people and was the only crew-member who showed up, I could complain about how the others weren't doing their share. Or, I could work alone, even if it meant standing in a foot of mud. I had to laugh, remembering the fancy advertisement that had attracted me to the GPM in the first place, with its promises of solar showers, laundry trucks and other luxuries. None of that seemed to matter now. I didn't work because I was expected to; I didn't do it for anyone else but myself. It just felt good and I saw the same shift in others.

But not everyone cared about us and some people actually went out of their way to make our lives difficult. Occasionally, a car sped by with someone yelling, "Dirty Commies!" out the window. Other folks staged counter-protests when we protested or blockaded at military institutions. Fair enough. Some towns refused us camping permits. But in others, almost everyone offered beds for the night in their homes. They engaged us in conversation, and saw that we represented all colours of the political spectrum. We just wanted what they did—a safer future for our grandchildren. Many confessed feelings of powerlessness and frustration with the government for decreasing budgets on social programs, health, farm subsidies and education. I explained that before I'd joined up, I'd been so stuck I had a breakdown. After talking to us, many ordinary people—farmers, mechanics, waitresses and homemakers—committed to do whatever they could for the cause. Our momentum was gathering.

Along with canvassing towns for billeting hosts, we asked for donations. Occasionally I drove the volunteers who went door to door. A new member joined my crew one day, a huge tough guy dressed in camouflage pants and steel-toed boots. I wouldn't have wanted to meet him in a dark alley. James, his name was. As we chatted, I learned that his attire wasn't just for show. He was a Vietnam veteran. "I've been there, man," he said, in a surprisingly soft but intense voice, as he stared out the window of the van. "It ain't pretty. I never want to see that kind of thing again in my—or anyone else's—lifetime."

As we approached our first house, James began to tremble and looked over at me with terror in his eyes. "Get me out of here!" he begged. James— the man who had taken lives, had lost control of his bowels and was shaking all over. We drove away.

I felt nothing but compassion for James. We returned to camp, and after he cleaned himself up, we talked. He told me about the war, describing first its big picture: an army serving and protecting its country and citizens. I couldn't help but be stirred by the heroic tales, the camaraderie, the honour and pride. But the rest of his story revealed the smaller picture, the dark side: individual soldiers facing their deepest fears of suffering and mortality, then witnessing horrific events and committing acts that no human should ever be asked to undertake. "You wouldn't believe what I saw, brother. It screwed me up," he said, looking me right in the eye. "I can't even drive a car like a normal person. I'm afraid I'll black out at the wheel and kill someone." He had Post Traumatic Stress Disorder. And still he'd been willing to come on this walk, put himself out there in the world, and not hide away in fear.

"I see things that aren't there," he explained. "I get scared for no reason. But that stuff, and what I went through in 'Nam, is nothing compared to the scale of Hiroshima and Nagasaki. And somehow America felt justified in this because of Pearl Harbor. But there is NO justifying nuclear war. It's...." He trailed off, shaking his head and pausing with a sigh. "It's insanity. IN ... FUCKING ... SANITY!" he yelled. "I can't let it happen again."

After another heaving sigh he continued on, calm once more. "You're one of the only people I've been able to say this stuff to," he said, tears welling in his eyes. "I didn't know what I was fighting for in Vietnam. I want to fight for something now. We have to change things. If not, we're screwed."

"Amen, brother," I answered, and we hugged, for what seemed like minutes. Never again did I look at a soldier disparagingly.

By August, the walk had made it to Chicago, Illinois, the largest nuclear-free city in the world. Here, with plenty of billets in the peace community, we knew that housing and sanitation wouldn't be a concern. Now, our issues were traffic and crime. While canvassing in affluent areas, we encountered the usual sprinkling of support, indifference and disdain, but it was different in the ghettos. We ran up against volatile, fragile people, and outright hostility. How dare I even talk of world peace in a place where priorities were so clearly shelter, food, and for some, the next drug or alcohol fix? But some people came out into the street to ask us why we were walking and we found common ground. With government at all levels allowing them to fall through the cracks, they could relate to our anger about the military budget.

November 15, 1986, was the day we had all been waiting for. I felt both elation and trepidation. Thousands of people lined the streets, cheering us on and waving madly as we funnelled into the city through a forest of buildings. As I stood before the White House, I felt like Dorothy at the end of the Yellow Brick Road. I'd even encountered a real tornado in the Midwest, which had miraculously changed course when it neared our camp. Now, entering the Emerald City, I wanted to see the wizard behind the walls. But Ronald—the Wiz—Reagan, was not at home. *How dare he not be here to welcome us, or even to confront us,* I thought. What a disappointment. But I remembered—he didn't hold the power, *we* did, each of us.

We had struggled and scrimped our way across the country, blistered and bandaged, soaked and sunburned. Almost 600 of us by the end. We'd eaten beans and rice for days on end, and had worn our shoes to shreds. We'd had births, marriages, deaths. We'd demonstrated at military sites and been arrested. We had also talked to thousands of people about peace, held conflict resolution workshops, and had amassed enough assets to donate $50,000 to peace groups by the end of our trek.[3]

It was time to celebrate. After 260 days, Peace City had arrived in a dizzying blur of banners, speeches, music, and TV cameras. The inimitable Pete Seeger—icon of American Folk music and tireless worker for peace—looking like a salty sea captain in his blue jeans, cap and sweater, serenaded us with his banjo and ringing voice. I added my own words to his song: "I am not great, I am not small, I am but part of it all."

Problems can seem so huge and all-encompassing that we are rendered powerless by them. But once we acknowledge our fear, we can learn to transform what seems impossible into something possible. None of us on the Great Peace March knew how to walk 6,000 kilometres, but we recognized that the seeds of everything we needed were right inside us. Instead of being overwhelmed by our losses, the magnitude of the task ahead, and a myriad of differences, we came together. We engaged in a chaotic learning process, making peace with ourselves and each other.

We had made history. Before the days of online petitions, the cellphone camera revolution or even YouTube, this is how we spoke out and made change. Had the Great Peace March stopped nuclear weapons? No. But

---

3   The march was also nominated for the Nobel Peace Prize that year, and since 1986, the GPM has been studied and cited by numerous organizations and individuals.

instead of being paralyzed into doing nothing, we did *something*. In our desire to birth change in the world, over the course of nine months we had crossed an entire country and given birth to ourselves, one step at a time.

CHAPTER 6

ON THE MOVE

Back in France, the young women and I sit in the deep grass on the roadside, overlooking the Moselle River. We are sharing their thermos of strong, milky coffee, and a bag of apples from Mary's cart. I've just told some stories and we all feel like old friends.

"*Incroyable*," whispers Charlotte, shaking her head slowly, gazing at me now more in admiration than puzzlement.

"But Derek," says her sister Danielle, holding out her half-eaten apple like a question. "*Comment êtes-vous arrivé ici*? You are born in the war, you march across America, and now here you are still on the road six years later, with a beautiful pony. I still do not understand how you come to be here."

The pony in question nudges my shoulder. I reach back and hand my apple core to Mary's velvety lips, feeling her teeth grasp it firmly. I consider the question.

It could have been a twist of fate, but I blame my unique circumstances on the pure obstinacy of my mother.

Elsie Youngs was known as *Mam* or *Mammy* to me. That's what all the kids called their mothers in our part of England; it had nothing to do with the word *ma'am*. And my Mam? You didn't want to mess with her because if you crossed her just once, she might give you the cold shoulder for good.

My father Frederick, who worked in a munitions factory in London, died of pneumonia in 1943. This left Mam with three-year old me and my eight-year-old brother, Howard, to provide for. It must have taken extraordinary courage for this proud woman to ask her brother in South Africa for support.

My uncle Arthur had emigrated years before and was now a wealthy businessman. He agreed to help, telling Elsie that if she arranged my and Howard's passage to Johannesburg, he would take us under his wing. There was no mention of her coming with us. I can easily imagine Mam, who never held her tongue, blurting out, "Damn you and your plan! I'll take care of my own children!" Outraged and determined to keep her boys, she never spoke to him again.

What if she'd said *yes*, though? I wonder what kind of childhood I'd have had in the days of apartheid. I imagine a grand house in an all-white neighbourhood, with a staff of black servants. Would I have taken my privilege at face value or questioned the prevailing norm? I like to think I'd have recognized racism, but perhaps such an upbringing would have set me on a completely different course. Are we all destined to walk the paths we do, or can a twist of fate change things forever?

Times were tight in wartime Redcar, especially for a widowed mother of two. Determined to make ends meet, she offered room and board to soldiers stationed in the area. That way she kept food on the table, but rationing meant that our family was restricted to one egg a week per person, four rashers of bacon, and eight ounces of sugar. Later on during the war it was one egg per *family*. We ate a lot of dry bread. These were hard times in Britain, and it wasn't until the late 1950s that rations were finally lifted.

What a lonely, hand-to-mouth existence for a young woman. One day, a Scottish soldier named James Millington came to stay and romance blossomed. Jim, as we called him, was kind and generous, and he immediately set out to provide for us all. We survived on whatever morsels he could beg, borrow or steal. One day I caught sight of him crouched in a corner with a saw, his arm moving back and forth roughly. I crept closer to watch, and—my horror—I glimpsed flesh. It was part of a dead horse, and he was tearing every last bit of meat from the bone for Mam to cook up. I never mentioned a word of it to anyone.

One day, the soldier and Mam were married and he whisked us all off to Glasgow. I learned a new word then—AWOL—Absent Without Leave. Once we settled in Scotland, Jim secured work as a truck driver and then got an additional job at night.

As attentive as Jim was to Howard and me, it was my mother who ruled the roost. With a slow, deliberate turn of the head and a searing glare from one eye, she could send us scattering to our rooms like tenpins in a bowling alley. She reigned over her husband too, who was not allowed to discipline us. Consequently, he remained a stepfather to me, not a father. In fact, I was well into adulthood before Mam's evil eye no longer terrified me and I worked up the courage to call him *Dad*.

Mam was strict with us children and we did our best to comply. However, I did my utmost to ignore two iron-clad rules: no playing with girls or Catholics. The latter would earn us the harshest penalty. When I was around eight, a Catholic family with ten kids, at least half of whom were girls, moved in next door. I'd sneak over the little wall that separated our houses and play with them, scooting back home before Mam caught me consorting with the enemy.

In 1953, Mam and Jim had a baby, my little half-brother James, whom we also called Jim. And once more, we picked up and moved.

I heard years later that we tried for South Africa again, but thanks to Jim's aunt who offered to sponsor us, our destination was clear: Canada. We packed our steamer trunks with our warm sweaters, woollen trousers, and a few small treasured items each. We set sail on March 4, 1954, aboard the steamship SS *America*, bound for New York City.

Violent seasickness kept most of my family bedridden for the duration of the journey. This was my first time on a ship, and I didn't much like being on the water, but somehow I remained immune to the nausea that sent everyone else to their quarters. Alone and bored, I ambled up and down the halls, watching passengers stumble, weave, and cling to the handrails. There was a group of Catholic nuns on the ship who'd boarded when we made a brief stop in Ireland. Although we kids called them *penguins* because of their black and white habits, they grew greyer and greyer throughout the trip, and every day I noticed one less bird in the flock. By the end of our voyage, only the Mother Superior remained on deck, tottering about proudly. After our final night's dinner, though, ashen-faced, she rushed outside to the railing and neatly projectile vomited over the side.

I marvelled at how the crew could perform every duty with the utmost professionalism, undeterred by the ship's pitch and roll. One day I was transfixed by the sight of a waiter delivering room service. His eyes were focused forward with the intensity of a tango dancer. The epitome of grace, with his left hand on his hip, right hand held skyward and laden with a tray of precariously piled dishes, he strode down the long corridor and into the dim recesses of the ship. I tried imitating him, balancing a couple of books on my hand. Out my doorway I marched, books toppling. But after a while I was confidently wending my way down the halls in pursuit of more items to balance. Of course Mam cut short my experiment. *Perhaps*, I thought, *I will be a waiter on a ship one day*. I had never thought of life as a grownup and what I might do. But now, temporarily forgetting my aversion to water, I was beginning to see possibilities. There was something about being on the move that spurred my imagination.

A week after departure, the ship steamed into New York Harbour, horn blowing, excited passengers leaning over worn wooden railings to gawk at the Statue of Liberty as we slowly chugged by. I was enchanted by her, as the millions of immigrants before me had been. Stately and majestic, she was a potent symbol of the new world of opportunity that lay beyond.

I looked down into a swirling mass of tiny white blobs. What was this vision? Below me was a sea of white-gloved hands belonging to hundreds of men milling about on a pier. Over the ship's PA system I heard an announcement: the dock workers were on strike and we would have to carry our own baggage. As we dragged our huge trunks down the gangplank in a tangled mash of bodies, the white-gloved dock workers looked on in sympathy, cut couldn't—or wouldn't—lift a finger. From our first steps in North America, we were pulling our own weight.

The next day we were declared official landed immigrants in Canada and we made our way to the city of Hamilton, Ontario. Relatives helped us set up house and find Jim and Howard work in a machine shop, settle me into school. It all seemed to happen quickly, and for me, it was not an easy transition. As I was nearing the age of 14, fitting in was paramount, and with my thick woollen short trousers and equally thick Scottish brogue I stuck out like a tartan thumb. To defend against snide remarks and mockery at school, I turned the tables on my classmates, dropped the accent, and became the class clown, even learning some magic tricks that I practiced at home with my baby brother. It was better to get laughs for being clever than for being weird.

School work didn't interest me, but people's behaviour did. I watched how other kids tried their own ways to fit in, and it made me sad and angry to see children being mistreated by their peers. I was not a fighter, but I tried to stand up to the bullies who made life hard for others.

Mam's stubbornness had launched us on an entirely new life, and the force of her will maintained our home. I admired her strength and knew there was an element of it in me. But my nature was different from my implacable mother's. The little picture in my life at that time was simply about getting along. The big picture, although I wouldn't have articulated it as such at the time, was beginning to reveal itself in small glimpses.

CHAPTER 7

LOST

Looking back at my teenage years, I see a young astronaut lost in a swirling galaxy of hormones. Like most of us at this age I was a clumsy navigator who often went astray. Living with my parents and my little brother, I spent as much time out of the house as possible, usually with my pal Jimmy Ricci. None of Jimmy's friends knew how to pronounce his Italian last name, so we knew him as the boy with two first names: Jimmy Ricky. He was as Italian as spaghetti, but our regular hangout was Fong's, the local Chinese restaurant. And once a week, we'd meet with our friends—an unsavoury dozen teenage boys—to participate in a distinctly 1950s-era ritual.

At 10 o'clock every Friday night, we arrived at the restaurant dressed to conquer. Our clothes were chosen for maximum effect on females: blue jeans, Ivy League herringbone jackets and matching caps to cover our greasy ducktail haircuts. The crowning touch, white buckskin shoes, had been painstakingly whitened and brushed the previous evening until they glowed. I'm sure we'd have made Pat Boone proud.

Living in hope, as young men do, we'd mill around outside Fong's after dropping a stack of coins into the restaurant jukebox. The latest pop songs floated out the door, providing a suave soundtrack for our posturing, as we assumed our positions on the sidewalk and waited. One popular tune of those days was "Standing on the Corner" by the Four Lads. It described our scene to a T:

> Standing on the corner
> Watching all the girls go by
> Standing on the corner
> Giving all the girls the eye....

Each of us had an arsenal of pick-up lines reserved for this occasion, and as soon as an unsuspecting female passed by, we'd launch them:

"Hey doll-face! I lost my phone number. Can I have yours?"

"Say, I just realized you look a lot like my next girlfriend."

"Do a lot of travelling? How about a trip to the drive-in?"

"Do you have any raisins? No? How about a date?"

The next stage of the ritual commenced after inevitable failure with the girls. A carload of thugs from the east end of town would pull up across the street, boys pent up like caged animals in the back, voices spewing insults through the open windows. We'd retaliate with our own volley of profanities and mockery. Then came the challenge, as they burst out of their car waving tire chains and baseball bats. The opposing testosterone-fuelled clans would then decide where to face off. Word spread like wildfire to the rest of the neighbourhood. "Come on, the East Enders wanna rumble at the park!"

We piled into our cars: Chevy low riders with fender skirts wrapped around gleaming whitewall tires, interiors glowing blue from the dashboard lights. Wheels screeching, the troops made for Eastwood Park where we vaulted from our cars to face the enemy, the ritual continuing predictably in a bloody battle. But—I didn't fight. Neither did I actively try to break things up. I couldn't raise my hand to hurt anyone, but watched in resignation as the drama unfolded. It was a strange line to straddle between loyalty to my pals, and my own sense of right and wrong.

At some point during the free-for-all, a handful of clean-cut cops would storm in, round up the misguided warriors, and deposit them overnight in the holding cell of the Hamilton jail, while I walked home. The morning after, I'd find myself sitting on the other side of the jail cell bars. My buddies, their bravado gone, poured out their hearts to me, confiding their anxieties and feelings of alienation. My tough-guy pals were just frightened, confused boys trying to be men, struggling to grasp the consequences of their actions. Rebels without a cause.

Television shows like *Leave it to Beaver* or *Father Knows Best* said nothing about the reality of our lives. On the verge of adulthood, we weren't children or grownups; we were in limbo. Our sense of belonging came from our camaraderie, as we placed our trust in and took our frustrations out on each other.

When we were little, before we were old enough for school, many of our fathers were off at war. Some, like mine, died during that time. Others returned from the horrors of battle withdrawn and volatile. We sons didn't have the chance to form deep connections with our fathers because they were either not physically or emotionally present, and lacked the resources to process their experiences. As a result, we failed to learn to handle our own violent impulses. Imagine a lifeboat adrift with a group of adolescent boys. We had the guts and the willpower to paddle for our lives, but what we needed was a compass.

Sitting in that visitors' area at the jail, questions filled my head: *Why am I friends with these guys? Why do they think they have to be so tough? What the hell am I doing here?*

CHAPTER 8

MY OWN TWO FEET

Behind bars or not, none of us boys knew what the future would hold, but for many it did not look bright. Like many of my pals, I dropped out of high school when I was around 16 and found a job. It didn't strike me until recently that my earliest work involved walking. Was this some kind of destiny?

Like many youngsters, my first job was a morning newspaper route. I enjoyed being up before the rest of the neighbourhood, listening to the birds at dawn. Before long, I took a second job in the afternoon, traipsing around a golf course, caddying for the Hamilton elite. It was exciting to contribute my wages to the family and to think that one day in the future, I'd have enough money to stand on my own two feet.

Still, I wanted something a little more glamorous and what I tried next was anything but. I worked for a company that employed kids and mentally disabled adults to sell magazines door-to-door. Gullibly, I believed I was being given a step up in life. In reality, management knew that kids and "retards" (as they were cruelly referred to) would elicit sympathy, thus selling more subscriptions. Many year later laws were passed against this kind of exploitative marketing.

The first morning, our sales crew of ten climbed into the back of a pickup truck, and we were driven several hours from the city. One by one, each of us was handed a two-page script to memorize and then got dropped off at some remote rural spot. Alone on a back road, I wandered in my too-large suit and tie. I'd find a tree to lean up against and rehearse my lines aloud. Children on their way to school giggled at me. I shrugged them off and kept practising.

From my naïve perspective, the countryside was full of bored homemakers who were eager to read about glamorous urban life, romance, or celebrity gossip. In magazines like *Canadian Home Journal*, *Chatelaine*, and *The New Liberty*, I could provide that to them. All I had to do was follow my script and fill in the blanks, starting with the resident's name, which I'd spy on the mailbox at the entrance of each house.

On my approach up the front walk I continued rehearsing in my head and as soon as the door opened I began reciting at breakneck speed. "Good morning!" I said with a big smile, barely pausing. "Are you Mrs. *So-and-so*? My name is Derek, and I'm selling subscriptions to help raise money for college. Could I show you the list of magazines we're offering?" We'd been told to expect a polite refusal. Quickly, I searched my mental list for *Negative Response #1* and blurted out the appropriate counter-response, looking as convincingly forlorn as possible. Eventually, after enough dialogue, Mrs. So-and-so would sign up, right on cue.

I honed my act quickly. It was all about timing. If I arrived at lunch hour, the mouth-watering aromas of hot soup and freshly baked bread would be wafting out from the kitchen while I plied my trade in the front room. When I'd exhausted my sales pitch, successfully or not, I'd sigh, and remark, "Well, I guess I'd better find a café somewhere."

"My, my," the woman would gasp, on cue, "don't you realize where you are? The nearest town is 30 miles away, and there's only a gas station!"

Next, I'd gaze at the floor, and in pathetic tones, respond, "Oh, I'll be OK."

"Oh, poor boy," she'd reply, as the final lines of this play unfolded. "Come in. There's plenty to go around." I will forever remember the innocent hospitality. I didn't yet see how shameful it was to take advantage of people this way, as we all did.

I was still living with my parents at this time, but during the work week I'd stay with the rest of the crew in a seedy motel. Most evenings we'd wander down the main street, find a café, order greasy food and drop what few coins we had into the jukebox. I've never been a fan of Country & Western music, but some of those songs—by artists like Jimmie Rodgers, Hank Snow and Tennessee Ernie Ford—stuck with me for good. I get a craving for hamburgers whenever I hear Johnny Cash singing, "I Walk the Line".

After a while, I began to realize I wasn't making money. The manager covered all our living expenses in advance, but by week's end when I expected a paycheque, he'd shrug and say, "Sorry son, but I've totalled it up and you actually owe us $15. But don't worry; you can pay it off next week." So I did, week after week after week. When finally I caught on to the scam, I never went back.

I found work next as delivery boy for a bakery. Even in the Toronto of the 1950s, this was still by horse and cart. I had no experience with horses, but I grew fond of the animals and learned how to put them at ease.

Every morning I'd walk the deserted city streets, passing through shadows and into the glow of street lights. Eventually I'd arrive at the back door of a small factory and enter a hive of activity. There was a warmth to the air and a familiar, perversely comforting smell: a fusion of fresh bread and horse manure.

My horse stood silently, already bridled, head down and blinkers on, as I harnessed him up. The strange alchemy of odours was now topped off with the pungent scent of leather tack. Next, the delivery boys would scurry around, loading up our wagons with fresh baked goods, glancing up periodically to acknowledge each other with a nod. Then we started our rounds.

At the first house the horse stopped without prompting and I'd swing my arm through the handle of a big wicker basket, jump down, and make my deliveries to the lady of the house. There was an aspect of subtle sales-manship here, as I strategically placed a pie or two in the basket next to the standing order of bread. More often than not, I made a successful impulse sale. Then I'd hop back in the wagon and the horse would continue on to the next house. It was a predictable day, including the bratty kids on their way to school who ran behind the wagon chanting, "Jackson's bread is as hard as lead. When you eat it you fall down dead!"

I guess I liked change, because I rarely turned down a job offer. Next, I was hired by a printing company, first as a delivery boy, on bicycle, but soon they began training me to set print. I learned how to arrange tiny lead letters with tweezers, but I also learned how to drink whiskey.

One day I noticed that most of my coworkers at the printing company kept a small bottle of booze hidden under their desks, sipping discreetly all day long. Wanting to fit in, I started packing a bottle too. Not being a seasoned drinker I'd have to go sit at Fong's after my shift to sober up before returning home. By morning, somehow we all came through the door ready to do it all over again.

After working in typesetting for a while, I anticipated a promotion to colour reproduction. One day the foreman asked me to fetch some green paper stock, but when I brought it back he looked at me with eyebrows raised. "This is red," he said. "I think you may have a problem." I learned about colour blindness that day. No wonder I never got as excited as other people did about summer leaves or Christmas lights. With my type of colourblindness, both red and green looked greyish to me. I could appreciate yellows and oranges, purples and blues, but that wasn't good enough to earn a promotion. Thus ended a very short career that I'd felt had a long, profitable future. Then again, maybe it's a blessing and I averted liver failure. I rarely drank hard alcohol again after that, quitting as easily as I'd started.

I missed the variety of working on the road. So, back I went, door-to-door, this time for the Singer Sewing Machine Company. I can't say I acted much more honourably than I had selling magazines. "Think of how much money you'll save sewing your own clothes. And there's no downpayment!" It was easy to persuade homemakers they needed to buy a nice shiny new machine that they couldn't necessarily afford. Whenever sales were down for the month I'd canvass the town's poorest neighbourhoods and bring up my quota. I was happy to appease my boss, and when customers defaulted on payment and the machines were repossessed, I'd be selling to someone else.

The best part of the job was meeting the other salesmen at the local pool hall every morning for a quick game. The loser paid for breakfast. I paid for at least the first month and then rarely after that. Now, after almost five decades, I still feel safe in saying, "Would you like to play? Loser pays for two eggs, sunny side up, with bacon and toast!"

With enough experience as a sleazy salesman under my belt, I hit the big time in the insurance business. Now I was driving a respectable new 1959 Studebaker, purchased with money my wife Mary and I had received at our big Hungarian wedding. With a smart leather briefcase in my hand, looking like a proper businessman, I felt important. And instead of merely reciting lines like an actor in a play, I got to know a little bit about each client, asking them about their lives, their interests, their families. I was still expected to *sell*, but gradually my focus shifted. *How much* I was selling seemed less important than *who* was buying. For the first time I began listening instead of talking. I threw away my script and encouraged my clients not to sign up for expensive, complicated insurance plans they couldn't afford. After shaking hands at the end of every client meeting I knew I'd created an atmosphere of trust and had sold them only what they needed. I felt good about this, but my superiors didn't. I was fired. "You'll be sorry!" I felt like saying as I turned to leave the office. Then it hit me—how would I feed my family?

CHAPTER 9

TOEING THE LINE

Trying to fit my chequered work history into a pattern with a clear direction, theme, and lesson, I can report that after a period of slow inner growth, I emerged from a cocoon, a new man who made different choices. But while some choices were made from the inside out, others were from the outside in, as I responded to others' needs and expectations. Clearly it was not yet my time to fly.

I was in my twenties with a family to support and my responsibilities demanded a stable job. So when my stepfather arranged for employment with Stelco, a massive steel company in Hamilton, I sprang at the opportunity. Everyone wanted to work there, as the medical and dental benefits for the whole family were very good. Paycheques were automatically deposited into the Credit Union, and if you needed to buy a car, go on a vacation or buy some hi-fi equipment, no problem—the Credit Union never turned you down for a loan. I was excited to be able to bring nice things home to the family, but I watched co-workers get trapped in a loop of earning, borrowing, and spending, their roads ahead paved with interest payments. Ringing in my head like a warning was, "I owe my soul to the company store." Thanks for the song, Tennessee Ernie Ford.

There was tremendous pressure for husbands to bring home a sizeable paycheque for the family. I was under great stress, and I kept the effects as secret as I could. For years, every morning at work before the rest of the staff came in, I'd have to sit in the bathroom for an hour while my intestines went through horrible contortions. Sometimes the pain was so intense I thought I'd pass out. It boggles my mind now to remember what I endured, but it was so normal that I didn't think to investigate any further. I just put up with it. I am sure I could have had food sensitivities that added to my stress, but nobody knew about such things back then. And then there was Mary. By this time, I'd quit heavy drinking, but I saw that she had her own problem. The word "alcoholic" didn't occur to me; that was for the drunkards you'd see passed out in dark corners of bars at night. Mary wasn't like that. But I realized that I was taking us home from dinner parties early sometimes before things got a little out of hand.

This was the 1960s and it was impossible to ignore the swelling tide of social change. I felt very fortunate to have job security, a house, a beautiful wife and two sweet daughters, but intuitively I knew I needed *more* in my life. I needed to contribute to something bigger. So I volunteered with the Big Brothers organization, which helps underprivileged boys. I met Steve, a teen who became my "little brother" and we'd hang out and talk, and sometimes he'd come for meals with the family. We've kept in touch to this day.

I also started giving my time to the John Howard Society, an organization that helped incarcerated men and their families. Volunteering gave me purpose and some peace of mind. It was as if I led two lives, though. As a volunteer I was esteemed for my dedication, but—because of my growing political beliefs—I was branded a communist at the steel mill. I brought in magazine articles to show my co-workers about equal rights, and tried to engage them in conversation about current events. They looked at me blankly and returned to dissecting the previous night's hockey game.

Eventually I gave up bringing magazine articles to work and even stopped reading them altogether. Unable to reconcile what was going on in the world with life at the steel mill, I was disheartened and confused. Everyone seemed to have blinders on, as securely as the bread-cart horses had. So I kept my mouth shut as I scaled the workplace ladder, rung by rung, all the way from floor-sweeper to metallurgist. I was pleased to have my own office and to bring home more pay, but not happy to be flirting once again with the suit-and-tie thing. It wasn't *me*. So who was I, then?

I noticed that everyone in management positions sported middle initials. Guys on the floor had regular one or two-syllable names like Joe or Pete. I was actually known as "Jerry" to my co-workers, as the guys had misheard my name on my first day of work, and I hadn't bothered to correct them. Upstairs, men had middle initials, names like Phillip T. Jones and Rupert G. Smith. I'd never had an initial, let alone a whole middle name, but it was time to change that. I chose "W" for my father's middle name, William. Sometimes for fun, I changed it to Wexford. This was one of the few things I could change and not cause a stir, although my hair was slowly inching longer.

Now, as a middle-initial man, I was entitled to more perks, including well-earned holiday time. That first summer I took my family camping for a few weeks and Dave, a young college student ,arrived to replace me. "What are you doing in a steel mill?" he asked. "You seem different from the others here."

Of course this went straight to my ego, so I puffed out my chest and replied, "Yes, you're very perceptive. I'm leaving soon. You won't catch me toeing the line, waiting for retirement so I can play golf or buy a hobby farm in the country." We looked at each other, nodding smugly in mutual approval.

The next summer, Dave returned. "You're still here?" he said. "I thought you were leaving."

"Oh yeah, I'm still planning to go," I replied, my chest distinctly less puffed out this time. "But my kids are still in school, and they need stability. Just a litte longer…." Dave seemed to accept this line of reasoning.

The following summer rolled around and Dave appeared again, looking really dismayed to see me this time. "Well," I hedged, "it's just that the right opportunity hasn't presented itself yet. Believe me, when it does I'll jump on it!" Dave rolled his eyes.

Dave came and went, and other students too, just as eager and idealistic. And every year saw more excuses, but of course they didn't seem like excuses to me. There were good reasons to stay put, with my family being the most important. Then one summer, as I repeated my pallid monologue to yet another fresh-faced student, I could tell he wasn't really listening. I looked in his eyes and suddenly saw what he was thinking: *This guy's full of crap*. He was right; I *was*. I had tricked myself into thinking that change was going to happen magically. But I would never get out if I kept waiting for magic. *Ouch*. It was up to me.

At this time, hippie kids were going "back to the land", starting from scratch, building log houses and living communally. This didn't sound entirely appealing and, realistically, it would have been too radical for me and my family. But the idea of having land where we were free to roam—that was exciting. We could have a stream or a fishing pond, and we could watch the stars at night. I went home that night, and called a handful of real estate agents, and arranged to look at large, wooded acreages in northern Ontario. On my days off I toured around with the agents, strutting through the countryside with a pipe in my mouth, trying to look distinguished, nodding my head in approval at beautiful but expensive pieces of property. I was dreaming big.

My good friend Carl at the steel mill had been keeping a watchful eye on me. "What in the heck are you doing, Derek?" he queried one day. "You can't afford to buy land. You've already got a mortgage on your house!"

"Yeah, you're right," I replied hesitantly. "But I do have a good rating at the Credit Union." Of course my line of credit was only good for as long as I stayed at the steel mill. I was trapped and I knew it. "You know what, Carl? For the first time I'm doing something instead of just talking about it. It's a start. I really am on my way out of here."

Carl stared up at the ceiling for a moment. "You know what?" he said, looking at me now. "You need to meet my friend John who works at the newspaper. You have a lot in common. He makes a good living, he's married with two little girls and he's as quixotic as you are!"

"Fantastic!" I replied, not knowing that by *quixotic* he'd meant I was a dreamer. Carl had a real way with words and I thought he was complimenting me.

Later that week, our family got together with John and his wife, Harriet, and their two girls. After a spaghetti dinner, the girls played together while we grownups shared our dreams over a bottle of cheap red wine. It was the first meeting of many and, thanks to a small loan from a relative, six months later we purchased an old general store in the little country village of Princeton. The price was ridiculously low, but it had been on the market for years and the sellers were eager to accept any offer. The store wasn't quite the vision of a hundred acres of pristine land with a stream running through it, but it felt good. We all moved in together: John and Harriet in one bedroom upstairs, all four girls in the other, Mary and me on the main floor in a little room behind the shop.

I'll never forget the morning we moved in. We stood in front of the building, stunned, mouths agape, brows furrowed and eyes glazed. We unlocked the door and entered the shopfront. There were a few dusty, yellowed cans and boxes left sitting on the shelves. Should we try selling the items or ditch the decaying inventory? We turned to the old cash register with its rows and rows of worn buttons. "Let's open it!" I exclaimed, trying to generate some excitement. "Maybe there's money inside!" No one had the faintest idea how to get the cash drawer to open. *What have we gotten ourselves into?* I thought. We had no clue how to run a store.

Later that week, when we had the cash register figured out, the local teens shuffled in to buy potato chips and stare at me. My hair was long now and I sported a scruffy beard. They'd probably heard titillating rumours about hippies from the city, so we set them straight: sorry kids, but no LSD, no love-ins. When we asked what they wanted to see in the store, excited voices piped up for the latest comic books and favourite soda pop flavours. The following day we made a trip to the city, found everything at the supermarket and brought it all in. It was like magic; they made wishes and we granted them. Strangely though, we made no money. Then we learned about wholesale and retail, and sure enough, the pennies started rolling in.

Our tight quarters posed challenges. The kitchen was tiny, and there was only one bathroom for the eight of us. The kids had no qualms about living like sardines, though, and they loved being able to sneak into the candy jars at any opportunity. However, both couples knew we'd have to steal away every so often to the city for some much-needed time alone.

One night, weeks after we'd spruced up the shop and filled the shelves, we all went outside in the dark. One of us started counting down from ten and the rest chimed in, and on the count of zero, the sky lit up. Our new electric sign above the door proclaimed "Village Variety" and we glowed with pride just as bright. In that moment, I knew it was really OK to dream. Had I ever imagined such a thing as this shop? Not exactly, but my dreams of *more* had brought change. And not just nickels and dimes.

CHAPTER 10

RIPPLES

How thrilling it was to transform the mouldering place into a real community asset—and make a profit. But I was wary of growing stale, like an old box of cornflakes. I knew that still *more* was possible, and this time I wouldn't stall for years until following my inner voice.

So eventually we left the Village Variety. Mary found the change difficult, but she was supportive, and for this I am always grateful. By this time, we'd bought our own house with some money she'd inherited, and John and Harriet had taken over the living quarters at the shop. They were sad but gracious when I took a new job and we left.

Though I was wary of working for wages again, I became a commuter. My workplace in Brantford, about 30 kilometres away, was in a quiet residential neighbourhood. On the outside, the place was much like any other nondescript one-storey brick dwelling built for an average middle-class family. But once inside, past the TV and overstuffed couch, you sensed this house was not set up for regular folks. A hodgepodge of chairs surrounded a worn table, where a towering stainless steel urn of coffee bubbled away day and night. This was the heart of the house, where the family—a group of eight ex-convicts—gathered to worship at the Holy Urn. Before I knew it, I became a devotee myself, not as an ex-con, but as a counsellor, helping parolees make their transition from prison to society.

In my early days at the St. Leonard's Society halfway house, I was more of a babysitter than counsellor. Mind you, this wasn't like Wendy tucking in Peter Pan and the Lost Boys at night; I was there to enforce the no-alcohol policy and to break up fights. I knew I'd never overpower these men physically, so I had to gain their trust, and in time we developed a good rapport. I was street-savvy, honest, funny, and I didn't try and cajole them into becoming good little citizens. I had always tried to treat my own children like individuals, giving them control over what they were capable of handling, and I did this with the men, too. I listened to their stories, always finding something unique and praiseworthy, but I could also identify the ring of falsehood. "Yes, but what *really* happened?" I'd ask sometimes, after hearing some boastful tale. "Can you be straight with me?" Sometimes a guy would shout, or break down in tears, but slowly, over time, many of them gained enough confidence—in themselves and me—to be vulnerable and tell the truth. What humility and strength of will it took to change from simply surviving to beginning to thrive on the straight and narrow.

Around this time my teenaged brother Jim, who had been experimenting with drugs, began to get in deeper. I tried my best, armed with all my experience from the halfway house, to help change his path, but he wasn't interested. My brother Howard's efforts had fallen flat, our parents' as well, and now everything I could think of was failing, too. It pained me that I couldn't help him when I was having such success at work. Why could I help strangers and not my own family? And then along came Nancy. A beautiful young woman, she had her act together, perhaps because she was naturally a sensible girl, or maybe because she was a member of the Bahá'í faith. Jim quit drugs almost overnight. A woman and religion saved him. Hallelujah!

Soon after I started at St. Leonard's, I became the assistant director, assigned to a brand new office in a newly constructed wing of the building. Once of the first things I did was get rid of the desk in my office, and replaced it with a picnic table that I built. I knew the residents would feel more comfortable sharing concerns around a picnic table than facing me across a big imposing oak desk. In truth, I was more comfortable too.

The place was run by Peter Willis, a tweedy Englishman with glasses perched on the end of his pointy nose. I had a long beard and wore sandals. One day he brought in the board of directors to see the new wing, and of course, the new A.D. They knocked on my door, shuffled inside, and—with a very audible and unified gasp—they stopped in their tracks. They saw a hippie sitting at a picnic table, smiling and offering them coffee. They turned around and filed out in silence.

Peter told me later that there'd been a heated discussion about me. He explained to the board about the table, which they conceded on, but they strongly suggested that I wear a suit and tie. I wouldn't budge, though, and thanks to Peter's vote of confidence I continued there happily for some time. In fact, he was preparing to open another halfway house and I was slated to become its director.

One evening not long before this new halfway house was to open, I took a detour on the way home from my shift. I stopped the car at a local nature park, got out, and stood looking out over a small pond. I was tired. As much as I found my job emotionally rewarding, I wasn't sure I wanted this new position. It was all too predictable, climbing the long straight career ladder, eyes on the top rung. I'd gone along, gauging my progress against what others achieved and accumulated. I enjoyed my new car, nice house, and the prospect of buying a summer cottage. But when would it stop? Was there ever really a top rung? The ladder metaphor wasn't serving me any more. I was serving the ladder.

I picked up a stone and hurled it in the water. Watching circles spread out on the surface of the pond, I felt clearer and clearer. Life was most definitely not linear. When I immersed myself wholeheartedly in life, possibilities were ever expanding, like ripples.

The next day I told Peter and the residents that I was quitting. They were shocked. I felt some remorse knowing how much we'd all miss each other, and for not having a backup plan, but I knew it was the right thing.

Now I had to screen candidates for my replacement. The job criteria included a master's degree in social work and at least three years of practical experience. I just had to laugh. Me, the long-haired high-school dropout, interviewing guys in suits.

CHAPTER 11

THE CIRCLE

All of life is lived in relationship to everything and everyone else—friends, animals, nature, the whole universe or a stranger on a train. Ultimately, the relationship I have with myself is the most important. But to me, the juiciest relationship is the intimate kind we have with a lover or life partner. It's the most fun, it gives us the most opportunity for growth, but it's also the most difficult.

I met Mary when I was 20 and she was 17. We went steady for several years and I was proud to have this cute, blond girl on my arm. One evening we went to a school dance and she disappeared with another boy. I heard the next day that they'd been seen kissing. Feeling angry and rejected, I refused to talk to her for months, and spent my time conjuring up all the things they might be doing together—talking, dancing, going to the drive-in. That's where boys got to first and second base with a girl—and even farther. Both of us were virgins, and I worried myself sick imagining that the jerk who stole her away might have pressured her into doing more than kiss. And worse, maybe she'd *want* to do more. Jealousy raged inside me. As soon as I got the news of their breakup I swooped in and proposed to her. Mary was still a virgin, to my relief. Our marriage was my triumph. (It was also a strike against my mother's prejudice. She disapproved of Catholics, and my wife came from a big Hungarian Catholic family.)

We wed in 1963, honeymooning at Niagara Falls and New York City. We barely left our hotel room in Manhattan and not just because we were newlyweds. We were so unaccustomed to the hustle and bustle of the big city that we were too scared to leave the hotel to see the sights. Looking back now I can hardly recognize that young man.

Mary and I separated around the time I quit working at the halfway house, in the early 1970s. We married young—too young to know anything but what society dictated—but I can't say it was a bad marriage. We loved each other, and we created two beautiful daughters. But we didn't even know ourselves, and how deep can a relationship be when you don't even know yourself?

Eventually I realized my wife and I were very different. Communication was never something I was willing to compromise on, but it was difficult for her. I shared my dreams for the future, but they didn't excite her. On top of that, she had trouble articulating her own. Though she'd supported me and my unconventional ways, I'd sensed a current of unvoiced resentment. She had anticipated a straight path in life, and I kept taking turns. So despite our attempts, we just kept growing apart. Then I fell in love with another woman.

Lani was unconventional. She practiced yoga, did pottery, smoked French cigarettes and lived in a house full of artists. She opened up a whole new world for me and in her presence I felt more myself than I ever had with my wife. Lani switched on a light, but it wasn't something that she possessed and could give me. It was right inside me. This was the *more* I had been yearning for all these years.

At first, and for a long while, Lani was just a friend; our connection unfolded slowly. Mary invited her to share the pottery studio we'd built in our backyard, and she became a part of our lives long before we were involved romantically. Over time, feelings began to change, but I was committed to Mary and was not interested in an affair. How I ended up alone at home one evening while Mary and Lani were off together I do not remember, but I poured myself a drink and scribbled out a ten-page letter, trying to work through all the conflicting emotions that were balled up inside of me.

Part of that note read:

*Kids and I came back from supper at 7:30. Everything
cool. Kids changed, cookies and apple juice, and watching
TV.... I've put them to bed.... Kids make me feel good. The
only love that I can define. God, do I love them. No matter
what happens they will come first.... Now I'm finishing
my first glass of Southern Comfort. Funny, I never thought
about the comfort part of it until tonight.... I am afraid
to write what's really on my mind. Mary, Lani, Mary,
Lani.... How can I love you both? It's obvious I can't walk
away from this. Why can't the three of us work it out? None
of us want to hurt each other.... All I want is PEACE.
Why is that so hard? I think I am drunk but I feel love in
my heart. Mary, Lani, Mary, Lani, help me!... All of us,
gradually, we need time if there is going to be a change. Why
can't we help each other?... I love! I live! That's all I ask
for my brothers and sisters. Why do I cause hurt, anxiety,
pain, longing? For me and the ones I love, forgive me!*

It had been years since I'd touched hard liquor, and I don't remember falling asleep that night or waking up the next morning. But it was clear I had to do something.

By then I'd been working with ex-cons, dealing with difficult issues co-operatively, diffusing anger and building trust. Coffee was always a part of the process, so I gathered Mary and Lani around the kitchen table one evening, and we talked into the night, coffee mugs in hand. We spent months of evenings like this, sharing our feelings, worries, hopes and values. It was a long haul, but we didn't stop talking until we came to a mutual understanding. Eventually the three of us agreed that Mary and I separate, Lani and I would rent a house together, and we would all share in parenting the children.

This process of coming together in honest communication was reflected many times in my life, the biggest example being the Great Peace March when hundreds of us formed a giant circle in the desert to find a solution. I suspect that the circle is the most organic way of coming together as humans, as our ancient cave ancestors did. Our survival depended on it, and still does.

Reflecting on the dissolution of my marriage and on coming together with Lani, I began to see relationship itself as an entity in its own right. Later, I would call it *The Circle*. Everything that is said, thought, felt, and done by either partner goes into the Circle: love, caring, understanding, resentment, anger, pain, and so on. If you are conscious of this, it can support you.

Mary and I didn't understand any of this when we got married, but now I had a chance to create an intentional relationship with Lani. We had no idea where it would lead. Neither of us wanted a legal marriage, and we needed to honour our own changing feelings and circumstances. But we wanted deep and honest partnership and this is what we created. It would expand, be tested, and our commitment would lead to a deep and lifelong friendship. Its uniqueness defies description. We were in *The Circle*.

CHAPTER 12

SKETCHING THE CIRCLE

Derek and I created our own Circle—many years later, of course. It was central to the way he viewed relationship, and we talked about it a lot when we came together. Initially he called it by another name that didn't resonate with me. One day as we were chatting about the concept I began to doodle on a notepad and came up with a sketch.

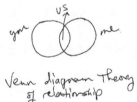

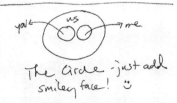

"Aha!" Derek said. "That's it exactly." It became much more concrete for both of us then—and I got to take credit for something!

The two dots inside the large circle are *you* and *me*, floating freely inside the relationship. A more conventional relationship might be shown as two overlapping circles, with the crossover area showing where the individuals hold shared values, interests, and attraction for one another. The remaining portions of the two circles are the autonomous part of the individuals. Derek didn't see relationship this way. You don't get to hold anything back from your partner. It's all or nothing.

The Circle, as Derek said, is a place for emotional, psychological and spiritual growth. It's an energy field, a container, where we can dance together, learn together, reveal our true selves, question, fight, and resolve, all within a safe space.

The Circle's energy also radiates outward, like those ripples in the pond that Derek talked about. Don't underestimate the effects that a truly loving relationship can have on the world. As well, The Circle is a microcosm of humanity's relationship to this planet. As Derek would say, the *little picture* and the *big picture.* What we do as humans affects not only our own evolution but everything else.

Relationship is dynamic. Our emotions are in flux, our bodies are in motion, our ideas change, our communication varies in frequency and strength. Not only affects us as individuals, but it affects the quality of the relationship itself. If we become too fixed in our thinking, too withdrawn emotionally, or if we don't extend ourselves enough, then relationships can become tenuous, brittle, or rigid. Everything is consequential. The thing is, many couples don't even know about their Circle and therefore are not conscious of their responsibility to it. If you starve or poison it, you will be depleted and the Circle will wither away. But feed it well and it thrives, nurturing you in return.

The Circle is not a bond of obligation; it is entered into freely. When we became intimate with one another, Derek said to me, "I love you, but I must be able to let you go. And I ask the same of you." This frightened me. But then he told me that we didn't get to jump out of the circle. If you want out you step out carefully, but only after looking at the uncomfortable stuff together. This allayed my fears but it was one thing to agree with this in theory and another to practise it. Talking about the difficult things often created more discomfort. It also shifted energy and created trust. And it meant that every day we spent together was out of choice. I couldn't imagine a better or more rewarding choice.

CHAPTER 13

CHANGE

I think I'm generally a cup-half-full kind of person. Or maybe even *all* full. Sometimes I wonder why. What inclines certain people towards happiness and others to sadness, some to flexibility and others to stability? Is my disposition the luck of the genetic draw or due to whatever mix of neurochemicals is whizzing through my brain? Or is my experience perhaps the result of past lives? Is it karma or chemistry? Or both? And how much choice and power do we each possess to change ourselves and our lives? I don't have the answers, but as far as change goes, I do know that it has been important for me to notice the signs—like the ripples in the pond that led me to quit my job. And I like to joke that on this following occasion, *Monty Python* showed me the way.

For a while after leaving my job at the halfway house, I was a stay-at-home dad, and I loved it. In the winter, I made an ice rink in the backyard and we'd all go skating. Before bedtime, I braided the girls' long blond hair. Other times, we'd dress up in outrageous costumes or spend hours cutting up family snapshots and rearranging them in amusing ways. I think I was inspired by the surreal animated montages on the TV show *Monty Python's Flying Circus*. A two-dimensional pastiche of cutout characters from Renaissance paintings hopped across a cartoon background of rolling hills or castles in the sky. And then suddenly, a big animated foot came out from nowhere and stepped on everyone, or the big finger of God (expropriated from Michelangelo's *Creation of Adam*) descended from the sky and tickled someone. Or sometimes, in the middle of a live-action comedy sketch, a voiceover would announce, "And now for something completely different!" and the scene abruptly changed.

I was with Lani on the streetcar in Toronto one day and looked up suddenly to see a sign flash by through the window: **Massage Therapist, 2ⁿᵈ floor**. I felt my hands tingle, and could almost hear the Monty Python voiceover and feel the big cartoon finger prodding me. I'd never even had a massage in my life, but somehow I knew this is what I wanted to do next.

Lani and I did some research and found a program in Toronto where I could get certified. This meant I had to go to school and I was terrified. *How will I get in?* I worried. They required a high school diploma and I didn't have one. *And what if I do get in? What then?* The course was not just practical, but involved a lot of book learning. *I don't know if I have the brains! Do I have the discipline to study every day?* I didn't know. But I followed my instincts.

Lani had faith in me, and helped me gain the courage to apply. I had long been flouting rules, but what I did next didn't make me entirely comfortable. I told the admissions committee that I was expecting my educational records from England. (Try doing that now in this internet culture with easy and instant access to information.) To my outright shock, I was accepted without question. Of course the records never did show up.

Every day I'd drive 40 kilometres to the railway station. From there I'd sit on the train for an hour, then hop the subway for a ten-minute ride, and finally walk another kilometre to school. I worked hard preparing for exams. Memorization was a challenge, with all the intricate details about muscles and nerves, bones and fascia, but I had to prove to myself that I could excel. When I aced my first exam, I was both surprised and relieved. It was a huge boost to my self-esteem but also a clear sign that I was on the right track. I continued to earn good marks and got my diploma. Around the same time, Lani completed her training as a yoga teacher. Now it was time for a huge change.

On Hallowe'en 1977, our new lives began in Vancouver. We rented an apartment and Mary had already found a place with a friend. We tried various living arrangements, and eventually Lani and I found a large house where the girls had plenty of room.

Change

The city had so much to offer. Every chance we got, Lani and I roved the streets, exploring Vancouver's hidden corners, discovering its funkiest coffee shops, prettiest parks and longest beaches. But we were soon busy working full time. Lani started teaching yoga, and after I jumped through a few hoops getting my licence to practise in British Columbia, I began working.

Massage enabled me to get close to people, which I treasured. I listened—with my ears and my hands—but often what I learned nonverbally would be the most revealing. I could feel tension and other issues that lay deep below the skin, and I could sense what was happening in their energetic field. I got to the point where I could often tell what was happening with my clients without even touching their body. Sometimes all we did was end up talking, and that was healing in itself.

It wasn't just important for my clients to cope with sore and stiff muscles. Occasionally that's all there was, but often there were underlying issues that manifested in unhealthy behaviour and thoughts, which in turn caused—or at least exacerbated—physical problems. Without addressing these things, relief was only temporary and people returned with the same complaints, eager to pay me to make it all go away.

"I'm in such pain," they'd say. "What can I do?" I'd respond by asking what they were up to in life, and often long stories would tumble out: long-standing career dissatisfaction, disappointments in relationship, and even childhood trauma. Some people were profoundly unhappy. Their surface might show no traces of this, but there was no mistaking the far-reaching effects that were playing out in their health.

Eventually, together, we would conclude that changes were in order and would work eagerly to define the first steps in a plan of action. Some folks plunged ahead, and it was beautiful to watch their progress towards self-empowerment and better health. Even if recovery wasn't total, kindling a positive attitude did wonders. One of my favourite clients, an elderly woman named Marlis who eventually became a good friend, suffered from a slew of chronic and acute conditions. I was always inspired by her relentless optimism, her joy, and her creative drive. Every time I saw her she'd bring me a gift, some new creation she'd whipped up in the kitchen or on her craft table.

Others, despite their often desperate wishes to live pain-free, didn't have the willingness, patience, or ability to take a step in the right direction. Why was this? Some blamed their troubles on a lack of resources and of course there's truth in this. I believed that resistance was the larger issue though, and that the ways and means would come once it was dealt with. But the prospect of change just seemed too overwhelming. These clients agreed that more exercise and fresh food were in order, and perhaps a change in job or relationship, but there was "no time" for all that. They couldn't take even a small step *because, because, because*…. It was one excuse after another. Sometimes my patience and compassion wore thin, listening to folks who were interested in talking about their problems but not so keen on doing anything about them. They'd boxed themselves in. But then, of course, I'd flash back to myself at the steel mill. I'd been there.

Sometimes years might go by for a client, and then—facing a serious health condition like arthritis, digestive distress, chronic fatigue, or cancer— they were finally willing to confront things head-on. The fear of dying surpassed the fear of change itself. But I was amazed that, on rare occasions, even this wasn't enough.

It seems like human nature to get stuck. But why? Until the stakes get high enough, the comfort of routine can trump pain. And some of us wait in fear for a sign from heaven: the big Monty Python finger. I could credit God for the finger, but I believe it was really my own intuition, which had begun to flow once I tuned into my feelings and knew to trust them. I could have dismissed the flashing sign in the window and the voiceover in my head. But I paid attention, and with some willingness and hard work, my life transformed completely.

In helping others, I always have to look at myself. Fear held back my clients and it held me back. It's why I took so long to leave the steel mill. I was afraid I would leave my family destitute, that I'd lose the respect of my friends and family, that I wasn't smart enough to do a different job. But I changed.

Change is simple, if far from easy. But you start by tuning in to yourself. Open your mind. Notice the signs. Take action. And soon change starts rippling through your life, affecting your health, relationships, everything. In the big picture, this is how we change the world.

CHAPTER 14

BIRTH

Life is a circle, from birth to death, and—some say—on to rebirth. It's the ultimate circle, and, strangely, one we are terrified to embrace. Instead of experiencing love and intimacy in birth and death, we can be gripped by our fear of the unknown. I was 23 when my first child was born, and like most men were at the time, I was relegated to a hospital waiting room to squirm and fret away the hours until my baby arrived.

This was standard procedure in the early 1960s. My wife Mary lay alone in a sterile room, which was off-limits to the expectant father. Husbands sat together in a waiting area on threadbare chairs, complicit in this abandonment of our wives, but knowing no better. We smoked, stared at aged magazines, and exchanged nervous smiles, rising in turn to pace the floor like caged animals in a tiny holding pen. The four walls of the room were a putrid colour and nothing adorned them except for a conspicuous telephone near the door. This was how a father learned of his baby's birth. I wanted to smash that phone, desperately wanting it to ring, and equally afraid that it wouldn't. Then, it did ring. All three husbands looked at each other, gesturing for the others to answer. As I was closest, I picked it up and heard the words, "Mr. Youngs, please."

My stomach flip-flopped. "Yes," I answered weakly, composing myself. "This is Mr. Youngs."

"Your wife gave birth to a six-pound, five-ounce girl." The voice rattled on in a practiced manner. "Everything is fine. You can come up to the viewing room in an hour."

I hung up the phone, stunned, and then elated. The other fidgeting fathers-to-be stared at me until I gave them the thumbs-up sign, and all at once they rose to shake my hand and slap me on the back.

The hour's wait felt like a year. But then I pressed my face against the window of the nursery and gazed at the rows of cribs. And then I saw her—beautiful Pauline. It was love at first sight. It would be another while before I could hold her, though. Families were routinely separated like this. Imagine the loneliness a mother would feel, her baby whisked away to be cleaned up and dressed. And how confusing for the baby to denied a warm nurturing bosom after the shock of birth. Nevertheless, that's how it was done and nearly four years later, the procedure was repeated with my second daughter, Christine. I was no less anxious, nor enchanted when she arrived. Obstetrics have changed a lot since then and fathers can be an integral part of the delivery process. I am thankful to those who worked hard to change the system. The circle of those efforts rippled into my life, with the opportunity to witness the miracle of birth several times, decades later.

After starting my massage therapy practice in Vancouver, I soon built up a reputation as THE practitioner for pregnant women. This specialty wasn't something I trained for; it's just that there weren't many people in the field at that time. Clients said it was my gentleness and rapport that allowed them to feel safe with me.

One afternoon, I received a phone call from my friend and client Laurie, an expectant single mother. "Derek," she said, "My water has broken! Can you come?" I hastily scratched down her address on a scrap of paper, ran out the door and hopped on a bus.

Strangers in the seats next to me must have wondered about this bearded fellow with a huge grin on his face, clutching a wrinkled piece of paper in his sweaty hand. After what seemed like hours I got off the bus and ran to Laurie's house. Timidly, I knocked and was let in by one of her friends. Then I was led to the bedroom where she lay, surrounded by women, who left the room one by one upon my arrival. I felt honoured but uneasy being the only man. I pretended I was one of the three wise men visiting the Virgin

Mary. My friend smiled radiantly and my nervousness dissipated. I sat on the edge of her bed, massaging her belly gently.

For months I had been massaging Laurie, and feeling the other body inside hers. Now at long last I was going to be able to see the being who had been growing under my very hands. Soon, her contractions became more frequent and intense, and I pressed down on her lower back to ease the pain. Friends rotated in and out of the bedroom for hours, swapping duties, re-energizing one another. Once, during a bathroom break, I found myself going *huff, huff, huff*. As I came out of the room, someone else went in, doing the same thing. No longer was the idea of being "all one" just a concept.

This was truly a labour of love. Between contractions, Laurie's eyes would sparkle, a gentle smile crossing her face. Then some time around five in the morning, there was a change. I could somehow feel the baby's consciousness shifting. This marked the beginning of a long period of pushing and resting. I knew that my friend was tolerating a huge amount of pain, but somehow her love, willpower, and trust in the process won out.

At long last, the top of the baby's head appeared, a sight that is etched in my mind forever. Can you imagine—another, complete, whole, tiny human being, coming out of another, larger, human being? Surely it isn't possible! But—slowly at first, and then with a knowing deliberation, my friend gave what seemed to be her last reserve of energy and pushed one final time, letting go of everything. A little boy slipped out quickly, turning with arms outstretched to greet the world, and a tiny cry poured from his lips. I wept too, seeing the look on Laurie's face. It was pure love.

Gently, the baby was laid on his mother's belly, and he rested there calmly while the rest of us exchanged glances full of admiration, relief and joy. The umbilical cord was cut and tied, and the boy—Benjamin—was brought to his mother's breast. I laughed quietly to myself as I saw the surprised look on his face when a huge nipple was gently placed between his lips. I swear it filled his whole mouth. He seemed to lie there confused and bewildered by it all, but then, astonishingly, he started to suck. I felt a flash of pride and I looked at everyone for confirmation that he was indeed the first baby in the whole world to perform this miracle.

As mother and child got lost in each other, in their own beautiful world, the rest of us gradually became aware of the world outside. We could not remain forever in that warm, soft bubble of light and peace. As I stood up to leave, I reached out and took Laurie's hand. No words were necessary. Nor can my meagre words now describe how profound it is to witness life entering the physical plane. How can this process we all go through, so natural and common, be so entrancing and seem so unique?

I helped catch several babies over the years, each one a miracle, but the last was my very own granddaughter Chamille. How amazing it was to be with my daughter Pauline as she prepared to bring her baby into this world. She was so strong, embodying the essence of Woman. As her labour pains increased, she leaned on me for support and looked into my eyes, crying, "Oh, Dad!" I could do nothing to help but just continue to hold her—her body and her spirit—in that sacred and mysterious place, as the universe prepared to open the gate for a new being to set foot on Earth.

CHAPTER 15

TRIPPY

By 1980, Lani and I had opened up one of the first interdisciplinary alternative health clinics in Western Canada, the Integrated Health Centre. Amongst our ranks were a herbalist, an iridologist, and several massage therapists. Lani acted as coordinator, taught yoga and later began to focus on the Japanese healing art of Reiki, giving sessions and training new practitioners. The clinic hadn't been open too long before we were invited to caretake a waterfront home on Galiano Island, one of the Gulf Islands not too far from Vancouver. The laid-back pace of Galiano would be the perfect balance to our busy city life, and we reasoned that since Pauline had moved into her own place, and Christine was spending more time with her mother, this would be a good time to move. So we took the opportunity.

The Gulf Islands have always been known for their "alternative" subculture: hippies in the 1960s and '70s, and "New Agers" in the '80s. Although our lifestyle reflected alternative values—we had long hair and grew alfalfa sprouts in a jar under the kitchen sink—we were still professionals and worked long hours. We commuted from island to city, sleeping during the week on foam mattresses on one of the treatment room floors. On weekends at home, we fancied ourselves country folk more than anything, but our collection of crystals and regular chanting practice fit the "New Age" paradigm. *Yeah, I guess some people think I'm pretty trippy,* I'd say to myself.

If the trade-off to embracing all of myself and the world around me was a few raised eyebrows, so be it.

Lani and I had been introduced to kirtan, or Hindu chanting, in Vancouver, and had even held weekly sessions at our home. This chanting was an aspect of *bhakti* yoga. Many adherents of this spiritual tradition also connect to the divine through a guru. I didn't have one, but even just looking at a photograph of any of the Indian gurus would make me instantly joyful. And the repetitive chanting made me feel both calm and energized at the same time. It was *bliss*. Bhakti yoga was all about love and that worked for me!

We weren't hosting kirtan on Galiano, but we did begin to offer Reiki workshops. Participants stayed overnight on our floor; I'd tuck them in at night and read them a story, and Lani would make a huge batch of muffins and scrambled eggs for breakfast in the morning. This was our own form of bhakti, caring for our students in such a loving way.

At this time, Lani was also giving "soul readings" and I was leading men's groups. I would take a group of guys on a quest, guiding them barefoot and blindfolded up the island's mountain. I would tell stories and we would make masks, build a fire, and chant. I had come a long way from the steel mill.

As much as I valued the men's group, I actually preferred gatherings with both sexes. This felt more balanced to me, as we all possess both masculine and feminine energy—*yin* and *yang*. At one workshop on mythical spirituality, men and women were separated for most of the time. The culmination of this weekend featured the men's group performing a ritual in front of the women, and vice versa. After three days of learning about the spirit of the bear and the lion, after grunting, whittling spears, and making rattles out of stones and animal bones, we men felt rather proud in our danced display of savagery. Little did we know what was awaiting us.

Now it was the women's turn to show us their stuff and they rose to the challenge. From the midst of their circle, out strode one of the most corpulent bodies I'd ever seen. She was huge, dressed in a just a skirt, with long beaded necklaces draped over her huge pendulous breasts, her face painted with charcoal. She looked like a warrior. She walked towards us, slowly swaying and gyrating her ample hips while the other women, faces painted as well, singing fiercely, stood guard.

I'd seen this kind of ferocity when witnessing women give birth, but it was really something to experience it along with other men, while feeling so vulnerable. In a way that was immediate and visceral, this ritual forced us to look at our own prejudices and assumptions. Back in the normal world, this woman may have endured mean-spirited criticism and jokes about her size. But out here in the wilderness we were at her mercy. As she danced, she approached each of us men in turn, looking us straight in the eye. Then, taking each of her breasts in her hands, she slowly and enticingly thrust them in our faces. I was spellbound—frightened and aroused at the same time. It was a strange feeling.

She was the embodiment of Kali, the fierce Hindu goddess, essence of *female*, destroyer of evil, and source of all life. Also known as Shakti, she is inseparable from the male god of all, Shiva. Yin and yang. This god and goddess are of equal strength, but at that moment I felt anything but strong. I sure knew I was alive, though.

When I had time alone, I spent as much time as I could outdoors. I watched the eagles and listened for killer whales spouting as they swam through the ocean channel in front of our house. As soon as I heard their unmistakable, *Pffff … pffff …* I would run to see if I could spot them.

Animals had long been a part of my life. My stepdad had bred dogs, and when I married my family kept dogs, cats, and birds. Now, Lani and I had chickens and goats. Pepper, the billy goat, was rough and feisty. Pearl, the female, was smaller and demure, but she wouldn't be outdone by Pepper. She could hold her own. Every morning I'd take my mug of coffee and saunter into goat pasture, where they'd come to meet me. Then, together we would gambol down the hill, and at the end of their run they'd leap onto the cedar shake roof of their shelter. At least Pepper would. Pearl would falter and slip, but eventually she would scramble her way up, and the two of them would stand there proudly stamping their hoofs in a great clatter. I'd look up at them from below, stamping my feet with them. Then I'd feed the chickens, watching Renaldo the Rooster, ferocious guardian of the hens, patiently waiting his turn.

I had always been able to talk to animals. Something of a Doctor Dolittle, I guess. We didn't communicate in words, but when I paid attention and moved slowly with clear intentions, animals seemed to trust and understand me. I once rescued a hummingbird that flew into my house. As it darted about, I spoke in gentle tones, and when it stopped its frantic swooping I approached it slowly and picked it up. I could barely sense the weight of its tiny body resting in my curled hand. Once outside, it sat for a moment, looking me right in the eye as if to thank me, before zooming off.

In shamanic traditions, animals impart great wisdom, which I learned how to hear. I was initiated by a Native American elder in the ways of the owl spirit. Generally, while Owl is often feared, it is considered a messenger of change, death, and rebirth. It is also a healer, and can see the hidden truth in any situation. This all resonated with me.

After my initiation, I had a powerful experience with a different animal. One evening, in my back garden, a young buck stumbled out of the woods, approached me tentatively and then collapsed. Though I saw no blood, clearly the deer was wounded. Cradling him in my arms, I held him as he took his last breath. In that moment, I felt its innocence, and knew somehow that this magnificent creature signified *peace*. I confirmed this later with a shaman.

I buried the deer myself, and did a ritual in his honour, thanking him for trusting me with his life. I took the name Deer Dancer after that, and for many years this is how many friends knew me. I learned more about Deer: not only is it a symbol of peace, but it is considered the gentle healer, possessing keen intuition and moving swiftly from place to place, touching those it meets with unconditional love. For people born between May 21 and June 21, the deer is said to be their totem animal in the Native American zodiac. My birthday was June 16, and this description fit me to a T, though I did not yet know it.

As I continued to explore shamanism, I saw and felt amazing things. The material world, though I didn't want to be too heavily identified with it, was still very real to me. It troubled me to see friends get seriously diverted by the metaphysical realm, using it to escape the pain and suffering of a physical existence. We humans, in our insecurity, personify our hopes and fears in larger-than-life archetypes and stories, manufacturing alien conspiracy theories, looking for signs in tea leaves. So I was skeptical, yet I knew there was *more*. Although I don't go searching, I feel privileged by the glimpses I've had into other realms.

There are a two glimpses I can share with you. First, I was hiking alone down a quiet road— more of a wide trail, really—not all that far from civilization. Suddenly I heard rustling in the bushes and noticed movement in my peripheral vision. Then, to my surprise, a group of little people emerged through the leaves, each about the size of a toddler. They laughed and pointed at me, and then scuttled across the trail and back into the undergrowth. I could hear their singsong voices trailing off into the distance. *Fairies? Leprechauns?* I stood there for a moment in disbelief and then thought, *Well, why not*?

On the other occasion, a friend and I were camping one evening, sitting by the fire in a meadow surrounded by forest. It was just after sunset but the sky was still light, and a mist descended, blanketing the campsite. With no warning, something crashed through the trees. We heard the thunder of hoofs hitting the ground, and swivelled around to see a huge snowy white horse emerging from the mist, running in our direction. We froze. Time slowed down. As it approached, I noticed the animal's muscular flanks, its flowing mane, and, protruding from its forehead—a long spiralled horn! The beast galloped past, missing us by no more than a few metres, and then disappeared into the woods. After a few moments of stunned silence, my friend and I looked at each other, eyes wide in disbelief, and then both exclaimed, "Did you just see that?"

Other experiences from my past are so sacred that to share them with the world would be to diminish or even extinguish something very precious in my core. And if, after hearing the few I can share, people judge me and think I'm a little trippy or even crazy, well, that's OK by me.

Derek didn't tell many friends this story and he waited a long time to tell me, knowing I'd react to it and have judgments. It's true. As a child I had my own mystical experiences, but growing up created a kind of amnesia and I found it hard to resist the certainty of rational materialism. Since Derek's death, I am opening up again to the mystical. I've had visions, received messages, felt shifts of energy. I have no reason not to believe in fairies if my very sane husband saw them. So I am beginning to admit this to friends. To some this revelation is no shock; to others it's puzzling, even disturbing. I worry that the reader will be turned off now and will dismiss Derek or me because of what's been revealed. But Derek bolsters my confidence. If I can't be myself, then who am I being? Even if occasionally Derek gave short shrift to things like astrology, he never dismissed anything wholesale. He was very careful about what he focussed on, though, and this came from his trippy days reaching into the extremes of life. He needed to do this so that he could eventually find his centre. *Go for it!* Derek encourages me. So I will. I am.

GREEN RETURNING

Golden plums send branches to the earth
where a deer's apple banquet is lavishly prepared.
Something different scents the air.
I touch the changing texture
of my skin. And I know.

CHAPTER 16

LETTING GO

As much as I have always felt it important to find my own way in life and learn lessons through experience, I also must give credit to the teachers in my life, two in particular. Let me tell you first about Bethal Phaigh, my beloved crone. As an elder, after a successful career as a Gestalt psychotherapist (training with its originator, Fritz Perls), she decided to learn Reiki, and eventually became a Master at the age of 65. She trained Lani and me in this healing art.

These vastly different modalities—born in Japan and Germany—lived very compatibly in Bethal and informed her whole way of being. She was gentle, yet incisive, radical approach to teaching. Once she led a Gestalt workshop dressed in only her underwear. She was completely at ease with herself, a provocateur in the name of personal growth. In another session she fell asleep, conspicuously, which was disconcerting to some of the participants. Perhaps they even felt disrespected. She continued to snooze until someone nudged her, whereupon she opened her eyes and said calmly, with a smile, "Aha … and now we really begin." In this way, I think she was revealing to everyone their own judgments and expectations. She was telling everyone to wake up.

Lani got more into Gestalt than I did at first. Sometimes the emotional delving seemed indulgent, even though I'm into feelings. "Now don't you go *Gestalting* me!" I'd snap at her sometimes. But at its core is the value of being true to yourself—however that individuality is expressed—especially in relationship to others. The idea of being one's real self, not in an egocentric way but in a considerate and wholesome way appealed to me. For how can you have a fulfilling life and intimate relationships if you are hiding or repressing aspects of yourself?

One day, Bethal found a tumour on her breast. For a number of years she underwent intensive Reiki and other alternative treatments, and her cancer went into remission. Later, though, it returned and doctors didn't give her long to live. A practical woman to the core, she didn't let it faze her. She took out a two-month rental agreement for an apartment in Vancouver, and gave away her possessions. Those of us in her circle—Lani and I, our friend Zachariah, and others—flitted in and out like butterflies, tending to her, and relieving her main caregiver, Shari, by helping with daily tasks.

We were there because we loved her and to do service was a reflection of that love. But we were also there to keep learning. We talked long into the night, all seated around her, and we recorded those conversations. The entire experience was something beyond the ordinary and we all knew it. The process of entering and leaving this world are almost the same thing. They are the transformation of life energy from one form into another. It is a great privilege to witness someone's dying process, especially someone who was such a conscious participant in her own life.

After several weeks, the pain became severe enough for Bethal to want painkillers. She saw no reason to tough it out in agony. However, she didn't want to completely blunt her awareness, so she asked for just enough morphine to make the pain bearable. That way she could still feel the pain to a degree but not be rendered too woozy to be alert, and she could continue teaching us.

Bethal's health continued to decline but never her mood. At times she would lapse into an altered state, but every day there were moments of lucidity where she was her loving, direct self. She made us laugh, and she tested us, as always. Every day, one of us came to Bethal's bedside to attend to her, brush her teeth and hair, and help with other personal matters. The dressing on her wound was supposed to be changed, but this didn't happen as often as it should have. We tried cajoling and encouraging Bethal to let us do it, but she just kept saying *no*, gently yet forcefully.

Every day that passed, we knew the wound was continuing to fester. This was not good for Bethal, or for us. It put us in a tough position. How could we let her go on like this? We were committed to complete honesty, so we spoke up, knowing Bethal did not want to be treated any differently now that she was dying.

"Bethal, we know you're in pain, but you need a clean dressing and your resistance is making it hard on us."

"Aha," she said. "I see. This isn't about me, it's for you. Yes, of course." She relaxed and graciously allowed us to change the bandage. This was her gift to us.

Everyone felt certain that Bethal was going to die on December 25, so we enacted a big "cutting the cord" ritual to send her off, but she rallied that day and ended up enjoying a delicious Christmas dinner with us. By the new year, though, we all felt like we were holding her back. In those last few weeks, the energy in the room had really changed. There was a quickening. This was the same thing I'd experienced when waiting for a birth—that life was suspended in the balance. So we did another ritual, more for *us*, to let go and say goodbye. In the end, there was only one friend with her and I think it was meant to be that way.

Bethal died on January 3, 1986, hours after we had said goodbye. Sitting in a cafe together having breakfast, we all felt her passing. It was clear to me that connection exists no matter where you are.

We grieved our teacher, but she left a rich legacy. Bethal had given us permission to be outrageous and outspoken. When I'd been a teen and young man, searching for purpose, it had taken courage to be myself. Now, having witnessed Bethal's own integrity, I knew that being myself was not just important for me, but it was good for those around me, too.

Dhiravamsa was a Buddhist monk from Thailand. One day Lani noticed a poster advertising a three-day meditation workshop he offered—seren- dipity: right place, right time—so she attended. She came home bubbling with enthusiasm, which wore off on me. As a spiritual practice, Buddhism didn't swell my heart like bhakti yoga did, but its practicality appealed to my rational side. Bhakti for the heart, Buddhism for the head.

A scholar and monk since the age of 13, Dhiravamsa later moved to the US and gave up his robes. Although he continued to live a very simple life, he began writing and teaching from his own unique perspective. He didn't just promote "spiritual" practices; he also believed that *body* was integral to the human experience.

Dhiravamsa delivered lessons in a soft voice, his warm eyes shining, his Mona Lisa smile sometimes spreading into a huge grin. Then, we'd meditate for an hour, sitting in silence, eyes closed. This is not as easy as it sounds. At first, it's OK. It's peaceful and relaxing, but in no time, it's anything but. Your bum goes numb. You want to shift your weight around. Your leg begins to spasm, or you feel the agonizing sting of an itch just crying out to be scratched. And you're supposed to just sit there and not flinch. It's uncomfortable and frustrating.

The first time I sat, my mind felt like a puppy straining on its leash, eagerly sniffing at anything in its path. *Why can't I control my thoughts?* I would think about specific things, and then any old random thing, and then I was just thinking about thinking about thinking….

The next time I sat, my thoughts were like cars lined up on a race course, gunning their engines. When the bell rang, off they zoomed. I tried mentally easing up on the gas, but it seemed the more effort I exerted, the faster they'd fly, crossing tracks and veering off wildly. With more practice I could make them idle, but before I knew it, one would tear off again. *Damn!* I just wanted to park my brain for a while. Eventually, the cars seemed to run out of gas on their own accord, as I remembered to simply let thoughts and sensations pass in and out of my attention. This is how I developed the Witness: the part of your consciousness that doesn't react or respond to what you do or say, but just quietly watches and listens. After much practice, I was able to sink into a peaceful place more quickly. There was nothing else I wanted to do for the rest of my life.

Dhiravamsa's workshops were not always about sitting, though. After an hour—GONG!—came the signal to stop. The ringing pierced my dreamy state. *Hey, I'm meditating here!* I thought. *DO NOT DISTURB!* Next, Dhiravamsa directed us in a session of gentle movement. *Hmmmff*, I pouted, stumbling to my feet. *But I was so comfortable!* I felt clumsy and cranky, but eventually my body began to enjoy the flow of energy, and I really got into it, inhabiting my body totally. I was free!

GONG! Time to change again. *Oh, not now!* I resented letting go of that beautiful energized feeling. It took time and effort to mentally slow down and direct my attention away from the body to the breath, from the external to the internal. But once again I became submersed in blissful stillness. And the whole process repeated when the gong sounded again. This made for an exhausting day.

After some time, I understood how valid—and valuable—both activities were, and that it was my own resistance that wore me out. Once I released it, the gear shift became progressively easier, smoother, then seamless. This did not happen overnight. But change is inevitable, and you cannot hold on to experiences, things, and people that pass in and out of your life. Life is a constant flow.

Non-attachment is one of the key principles Dhiravamsa taught. We all have natural loving connections to one another, and with things that make us feel good, but there is a clinging, grasping kind of attachment that Buddhism highlights as a key stumbling block to health and happiness. It is one of humankind's greatest and most common foibles.

I learned that if I let go, I could experience more. One of my favourite scenes from the movies (aside from any Monty Python film) is from *The Jerk*, with Steve Martin. Steve Martin's character, Navin, didn't fit in with his family. As a young man, he struck out on his own and transformed from poor sharecropper to millionaire, alienating his girlfriend in the process. In a bitter rage, he tells her he's leaving her, saying (I am paraphrasing here), "Alright then, I'm outta here! I don't need you. I don't need anything! Well, except this ashtray and that's it," he whines. As he exits the room he continues, picking up random objects in his way. "That's all I need, the ashtray and this ping pong paddle. The ashtray, the ping pong paddle and the remote control, that's all I need…. The ashtray, the ping pong paddle, the remote control and these matches … and this lamp … and that's all I need!" He slowly made his way out the door, in his bathrobe, crying, his arms full. As he shuffles down the sidewalk away from his house, the last thing he tries to take is his dog, who growls at him. I love to reenact this scene with my friends to show the futility of attachment. When I leave this world, I do not want to be held back by attachments. I want to be free—in love with life, in love with my friends—but free.

Dhiravamsa and Lani developed a special relationship as teacher and protégée. Once he asked her to sit with him on stage, throughout an entire workshop weekend. It was uncomfortable for Lani to endure the envy of other students, and he knew that. It was his way of preparing her to become a teacher. He spent time with us both at our house, but after a while I started feeling a little like chopped liver, like Dhiravamsa wasn't really seeing me for who I was or acknowledging me as Lani's partner. Though he'd been a monk, he was still a man. Yet, I had to admit he wasn't doing anything improper. He was gracious, yet impersonal, as a spiritual teacher should be. Still, I felt just a twinge of jealousy, the kind that had roiled inside me when Mary left the dance with another boy. I said nothing, and the niggling feeling never left me.

Years later, Dhiravamsa was giving a three-day meditation workshop in Vancouver and I'd been dithering about attending. Lani was with Bethal in Hawaii at this time. Though my urge to go was strong, by Sunday morning I still hadn't left home and the workshop finished that evening. I realized that if I didn't go, I'd regret it. I needed to see Dhiravamsa. I raced off to catch the one and only morning ferry, getting there just before departure. I made a beeline for the venue and by the time I arrived there were only a few hours left in the workshop. I opened the door quietly to witness at least 100 people seated cross-legged on the floor, eyes closed, in calm, blissful contemplation.

Dhiravamsa was sitting on a low stage by himself. I removed my shoes, quietly crossed the room in my bare feet and stepped up onto the platform. The master's eyes remained closed. I sat down at his right and closed my eyes. Inside me tumbled mixed emotions. *What if Dhiravamsa opens his eyes and sees me here?* I wondered. *What am I hoping he will say? What business is it of his, the mental contortions I have gone through? What am I even doing here?* After a while I stopped thinking and just sat. It was a relief.

After perhaps an hour, the gong sounded. I opened my eyes to a sea of surprised faces. Dhiravamsa did not look at me, however, but remained calm and focussed through the remainder of his teaching. I felt conspicuous and anonymous at the same time.

Letting Go

When the students got up to leave, Dhiravamsa finally looked at me. He didn't act shocked or upset but nodded and acknowledged me with his gentle loving smile. "Ahh, Derek," he said. "How good to see you."

"Dhira," I said. "I just had to come and tell you that I've been angry at you for the past few years. I felt like you ignored me when you came to visit Lani and me, and this bruised my ego. I've held it against you this whole time."

"And how do you feel, now that you've revealed this?" he asked.

I thought for a moment, and then answered, "Better." And that was that.

CHAPTER 17

LEARNING TO FLY

The girls laugh at my punchline. I enjoyed acting out my stories, playing the goofy, flustered Steve Martin character, and then the implacable Dhiravamsa. My delightful new French companions and I recline in a patch of shade as my pony does the same. Not one of us seems keen to get up and on our way.

"Would you like to hear another one?" I ask.

"*Bien sûr!*" says Danielle, as her sister nods eagerly in agreement.

"Well, how about the time I learned how to fly?" I asked, flapping my arms. They laugh and look at me in mock disbelief.

This was the time of my spiritual crisis leading up to the Great Peace March. Lani was away. Being in the cabin was like living in an eagle's nest in the trees, with the ocean below, but I couldn't see the beauty around me. Or within me. I was losing touch with that *self* I was supposed to be true to. I felt that the roles I had taken on in my life were constricting me. Who was I, if I let go of *healer, teacher, father, partner*? Who was I without the meaning—and rewarding ego strokes—all those roles gave me?

I consulted rune stones and performed shamanic rituals in hopes I'd hear a message of guidance from—God? The universe? My higher self? But I heard nothing. This was a situation I couldn't meditate my way through. I searched for direction, but after a while I was doing less searching and more sleeping.

One afternoon I was napping soundly in the cabin and awoke to loud, rapid knocking at the front door. I almost jumped out of my skin. Island living meant my door was always open and friends would just walk in. No one ever knocked, let alone pounded.

"Yes?" I called, hesitantly, pushing aside the crocheted throw and hastily smoothing my hair. The door burst open and in strode a tall, muscular young man in a black leather jacket and boots, with several strands of beads around his neck. His arm flew up like gunslinger's, and I stumbled up off the sofa to shake hands. His grip was pulverizing.

The man's dark eyes flashed, as did his teeth, which were blindingly white. "*Hola, Señor* Deer Dancer," he said in a heavily accented voice.

"Do I know you?" I mumbled, still dazed.

"No, my friend, but I know you. I have come to find you." He referred to a mutual acquaintance, a person I barely recalled.

"Oh, OK…. Well, let's put the coffee on and chat," I replied, intrigued and slightly unnerved. He nodded, smiled, and sat down when I motioned towards the kitchen table.

"Deer Dancer, I feel I have been called to meet you," he continued, looking me right in the eyes. "There is something important we must learn from each other." This wasn't such an unusual greeting in my New-Agey crowd, but he didn't quite fit the mould. I sensed a darker energy that I couldn't quite get a read on. He sat quietly, smiling and watching me prepare the coffee as I shook off sleep.

I filled our mugs and sat down across from him. "I'm flattered you've searched me out," I said, "But why are you really here?" I asked. For the first time, he looked away and as he spoke, the confidence seemed to drain from his voice.

A story came trickling out. As a teenager, he had left his home in South America. When recounted his farewell with his older sister, it was obvious that he missed her deeply. His eyes dimmed momentarily as he talked about his little brother who'd been just a baby at the time. He didn't mention his parents. I guessed that they'd died or that there had been some trauma that he didn't want to elaborate on. He went on to describe an intense, personal quest.

Perhaps I'm meant to help him, I thought. "So where is your path taking you now?" I asked.

"I think I need to go home and spend some time with Hector," he replied.

"Is he a friend?"

"Oh yes. But much more than that. He's a shaman."

I controlled my urge to scream in excitement like a teenage girl, and I sat for a moment to gather my flurry of thoughts. Suddenly I grasped that it was not I who was meant to help him but the other way around. I had spent the last year or more involved in shamanism but knew I still had much to learn. I had been paying attention to signs and opportunities, and this felt like one. Finally, someone who might steer me down the next part of my path.

"Can I come with you?" I blurted out. "You've shown up at the perfect time in my life. You see…" I went on, excitedly explaining my story, and how it must be fate that he had come to my door.

"Yes," he said, smiling, once again embodying that self-possessed persona he'd walked in with. "You will come with me and meet him. Do you ride?"

"Yeah, sure!" I cried. And then I realized he wasn't talking horses or bicycles. "Oh, you mean—"

"A motorcycle, yes. That is how I travel. Do you have one?"

"Yes! I mean no. Um … it's a moped." This was how I tootled around to visit friends or pick up groceries. It was so tame even Lani's mother could drive it. I envisioned riding side by side down the highway, *putt-putt-putt*, trying to catch up with this strapping fellow on his motorbike. Ridiculous.

His head fell back and his huge chest began heaving with laughter. Then, still chucking, he turned to the door and without looking back said, "I'll be back next month. *Hasta luego*, Señor Deer Dancer."

"Wait, wait!" I cried. "How will I find you?"

"Oh don't worry. I'll come to you," he replied, closing the door behind him. I heard another laugh as he called, "Ditch the moped, man!" I didn't move for some time, thinking maybe this was a dream and I would soon wake up from my nap. I took a sip of coffee and replayed the strange encounter in my mind, realizing I couldn't remember the fellow's name. Had he even told me?

The idea of taking an epic road trip like Jack Kerouac or Robert Pirsig was thrilling. I imagined myself and my new young friend in our cool riding gear, roaring down the highway. What colourful characters would we meet along the way? And then at the pinnacle of our trip, I'd be introduced to the shaman. What wisdom would he share with me? Would he recognize the shamanic potential in me? Perhaps he'd teach me to access the astral plane. Perhaps I'd learn to temporarily leave my body in shamanic flight. I wasn't going to get anywhere without taking some action. And first I'd have to get up to speed and learn how to ride a proper motorcycle. So I signed up for a training course and asked my dear friend Ashala, who lived on the island, to come with me.

The two-week intensive program was held in Vancouver. The training was excellent, and after the first day of wobbling I felt confident. I was a quick learner and a safe driver. *Lookin' good!* I said to myself, under the helmet. For my road test, I was accompanied by an instructor on another bike who took notes on my performance. I rode through the city streets, navigating turns, showing proper use of signals and procedures. It was going smoothly and the test was almost complete when my front tire slipped, the bike skidded, and suddenly I was flying over the handlebars. Time slowed down as I sailed through the air. I found myself thinking, *When I finally leave this travel-worn body of mine, will I continue to fly? Is this the sensation people talk about when they have a near-death experience?*

After the impact, I got up and walked. "I'm fine," I told the instructors, asking them not to call an ambulance. "I'll just go home with my friend and schedule another test for later." Everything seemed fine, but once I was on the ferry home, the pain started. I went to the restroom and saw blood in my urine. Stubborn man that I am, I insisted I wouldn't go to the hospital. Hospitals were creepy to me, and I didn't trust the medical system. I trusted Ashala, though, who was not only a nurse, but did Reiki. I think she saved my life. She took me home and sat with me for days at a time as I sweated through a terrible fever. Eventually I was passing no more blood and the fever went down. Then, I just had the embarrassingly huge bruises to my body and pride to contend with.

While I was healing, I waited for the young South American to appear. Week after week he failed to show up. Had he returned home? Had he connected with Hector, his shaman friend? Or had he just been a product of my imagination? With no solid leads and no internet back then, I had no way of tracing him. But the shaman still sparked my interest. I decided to book a flight and trusted that everything would work out once I got there.

Eventually I was on my way. Or so I thought. The flight was cancelled— not once, but twice—due to bad weather. And then, on my way to the airport the third time, the ferry from Galiano Island was called back to port for some kind of emergency and I missed the plane.

Clearly the universe was telling me NO. So, what was I meant to do? And where, when, how, and with whom? These were the days when I hiked up the mountain to clear my head, but now I'd come back down the trail just as confused as when I'd left the house. I lit a fire and with each log I added, I stoked my fears and negativity. *You're lost, Derek. Who's going to help you now?* The little voice in my head, which had many times been helpful, turned nasty, like a little gremlin on my shoulder.

That evening a storm came to the island. The cabin, though attractive and functional, was largely cobbled together from bits of driftwood, and with every gust of wind that swept across the ocean, I could feel the floorboards lifting. The area rugs almost became flying carpets.

Outside, trees twisted and turned, snapping in the fierce blasts of wind. The commotion echoed the turmoil I felt within. I had learned to navigate my life by following my heart and signs in nature if I needed them. So what was I now being told with all those dead ends (including mine, almost) and now with Mother Nature roiling? I prayed to the universe for peace—outside and in.

The electricity failed and the house went black. I sat by the hearth, gazing into the fire. The blaze roared and crackled, seeming to suck air from every draft in the house. As the flames were fanned, so were my fearful thoughts. *Ha ha,* the gremlin cackled, *you think you're so smart? You think that everything's supposed to be easy? Well, it's not! You're powerless!*

I listened to the trees swaying furiously, and rain pelting the side of the house. It seemed that nature was trying to catch my attention. She was telling me I was small. Simply a part of it all. She was right. I was not in control. I wondered, almost casually, if it was my time to die. I sat still amidst the fury, and fell into a meditation. I submitted myself to nature and fell into a deep sleep despite the din.

When I awoke, daylight was streaming through the windows. The fire had long gone out, but I welcomed the chill. It meant I was alive. I went outside and surveyed the damage. The house was intact, but outside was a mess of fallen branches, some of them enormous. Yet the old heavy trees stood firm with their deep roots, and saplings seemed to bear no obvious scars. They were saved by their flexibility. I inhaled the sharp new smell of wet forest. My eyes drifted closed, then slammed open again. *Wait.* There was a message here. It was all very well—perhaps essential—to be strong and clear in myself and my dreams, but I also needed to be flexible about how my dreams manifested.

I didn't need South America or a motorcycle journey, and perhaps I was not meant to further my education as a shaman. There had been something so attractive in these ideas, but that had been my ego's need. I had to admit that this aspect of me didn't always know what was best. In trying to control my dream of *more*, I had imagined the exhilaration of shamanic flight. But instead, I had fallen.

CHAPTER 18

PERSPECTIVE

It's the summer of 2015. The manuscript has been scoured for typos, grammar gaffes and errant punctuation. It's almost ready to go. But, yesterday I heard back from one of my readers who comments that the structure seems flawed to her. *This far into the process? No, it can't be!*

I want so badly to do a good job with *Walking to Japan*. I want people to see the man I loved, through my eyes. I want them to understand how the little Yorkshire boy became the man who ran a five-and-dime store, and then the millworker, and then the peace walker. I want all those parts of him to come together.

I stay up late making tweaks that I think work to address my reader's concerns. I send the changes to another reader. She's in total disagreement. "Scrap them," she says.

At this point I feel ready to give up. It's not just the book that's getting to me. These past few weeks have been difficult ones, with a friend who is seriously ill, and forest fires ravaging British Columbia. Smoke from three of these fires has blanketed the city for days, and every morning I wake to a thick orange sky. *Apocalyptic apricot*, I call the hue, trying to lighten my mood. It doesn't work. There's a serious drought in the region, in fact down the whole Pacific Coast.

I am worried about what this means for the crops, trees, animals, and of course people. This brings climate change close to home. *Now will you get serious about doing something?* I ask myself.

I attend a neighbourhood meeting. Before it starts, there's chit-chat. I am annoyed by the little conversations about vacations and golf games. And I'm annoyed at myself for being judgmental. I bring up the topic of voluntary watering restrictions. I stammer and stutter, trying to remember the statistic's I'd just read, but I am locked into my own incredulity that these people—ethical, intelligent people, or so I thought—seem totally blind to what's going on around them.

I am not blind to the parallels between this and Derek's experience. Before going on the Great Peace March he was in crisis, feeling powerless about the state of the world. He wanted to *do something*. He knew there was *more*. His remedy was to hike up Mount Galiano. I hike up Mount Douglas.

I go up there almost every morning. It's a hill really, but it's steep and rocky enough that I get a good workout. Up in half an hour, a little breather at the top where I look out at the trees below, the city and ocean beyond, and a horizon of mountains. Even if just for a moment, I think about how fortunate I am to be surrounded by this beauty. But for the past week, I've reached the top only to confront a thick bank of smoky fog. I can't see the ocean. I can't see the mountains. I feel trapped.

This morning, I hike up again, with a fervour, yet almost reluctant to reach the top, knowing that once again I'll be denied my precious view. But this time something's different. The wind has come. The air smells fresh once more and I can see the mountains. I find a rock to sit on, not thinking about where I have to be or what I have to do next, and look out at the world. I remember that Derek watched the eagles from his Mount Galiano perch. Here, I watch vultures circling in the draft. I have learned that some native cultures call this bird the "peace eagle". They're the benevolent cleaner-uppers of the land.

I focus now on the farmland fanning out across the valley. I turn and see sailboats skimming across the strait. Though it has been just a week since I last saw this view, it looks totally new to me. I soak it in. My muscles relax. I stretch my feet out in front of me, open my

Perspective

arms out and let a long full breath in and out of my whole body. How reassuring it is to be able to see the lay of the land again. *Perspective*, I hear Derek whisper in my ear.

He reminds me that I can get hyper-focussed on the "little picture" details and overwhelmed by the big picture sometimes. But if I can just sit and look, without judging, without needing to problem-solve, I will see that everything has its place.

CHAPTER 19

LEARNING TO SIT

After the flying lesson, my body healed long before my poor ego did. And then, the Great Peace March gave my dreams feet, and even wings. I was earthbound, but flying after all.

Once the GPM came to an end, I'd like to believe I possessed the foresight and common sense to have planned my next steps, but in truth I was just trying to stoke my addiction. I had grown accustomed to my peripatetic lifestyle. I'd also forged a deep connection to my fellow walkers, and developed trust in the process of talking and working together. This had grown into a type of faith for me. This faith was leading me somewhere. And my first stop was a little town in New England.

Most GPM participants returned home after the march. They were keen to share their experiences from Peace City: the epiphanies and sorrows, the challenges and thrills, the simple values of working together and respecting each other. But it was hard to explain what it meant to be a peace walker. Their attempts at explaining were met with polite nods, as friends tried not to wrinkle noses or raise eyebrows in puzzlement or suspicion. Reintegrating into the routine activities of daily life was a challenge. Shopping for groceries was now fraught with the awareness of excess. Preparing huge meals for only a handful of people seemed wasteful. Many things seemed unnecessarily complicated. There was a harshness to the world of concrete, of honking cars and chemical smells. Gone were the grinning, grubby peace-walking pixies, busily pitching tents every night. Now there were locked doors, alarm clocks, and the evening news. It was a harsh dichotomy.

I didn't share this re-entry crash, but I had the difficult task of calling Lani. I told her I needed to keep walking. She understood my passion of course, but she was not happy. Our separations had been challenging in the past, but now—an ongoing one? Over several long, difficult conversations on the phone, we hashed it out, yelling and crying. Could we let go of each other and still be committed to our relationship? Yes. It's just that the form of our relationship would be different, requiring adjustments on both our parts. The Circle was open, yet unbroken. And I would keep on walking.

So here I was in New England, signing up for a ten-day retreat at a medita-tion centre. *What have I done?* I thought after paying my fee. *I don't want to sit on my ass for ten days!* But perhaps, I reasoned, I could calm my itchy feet, recharge my spiritual battery, and find a new direction.

Before the retreat started in late November, my buddy Zachariah drove all the way from Vancouver—clear across the continent—to visit me in New England. Throughout the GPM, he had stood by in the background, mailing out bulletins to keep other friends apprised of my progress. We shared a sense of humour, so his letters always included a quotation from *Monty Python.* This reminded me to laugh even when knee-deep in mud, mosquito-bitten or nursing a swollen ankle. We spent our reunion reciting the "Cheese Shop" sketch and others until we were rolling on the floor in stitches. At the end of his visit, Zachariah flew home, leaving me with my trusty, rusty Volkswagen camper.

A week of goofing off made my transition back into "normal" life easy. But now I faced another transition into the retreat, and it was bumpy. I had started the GPM walking, talking and camping with strangers, but waking up with friends. It was like a large, nurturing Circle on the move. Now, at the beginning of the retreat, I was informed it was forbidden to speak to or even look at the other participants in the small group. Any physical contact was out of the question. Men and women didn't even eat meals in the same area. *Aw, you're kidding!* I whined to myself. *I guess Mr. Touchy-feely's going to have to buck up.*

Going without a daily hug was like going without coffee, which I'd also have to give up now. I began to sweat just thinking of the ten days of caffeine deprivation that lay ahead. This retreat was no longer feeling like such a great opportunity. *I have to get out of here!* I suddenly thought. *I know how to meditate. I've taught other people how to meditate! Why should I have to behave myself like some kid?*

Oh, stop it, you big baby, I told myself. *This is resistance, and you're justifying it because you're afraid! If you can walk across a country, you can do this! Just try it on.* This was not a lifetime commitment, it was merely like trying on a new shirt or coat! I could wear it around for a while, see how it felt, and if I didn't like it, I would never have to wear it again.

So I tried on the new coat. Each morning at the retreat, we rose at 4:00 a.m. to the sonorous tones of a huge gong. Sitting lasted for ten hours including several short breaks, and we retired to bed at 9:00 pm. It was painful. During the Great Peace March I had tried to meditate a few times but had simply fallen asleep from exhaustion. My practice was very rusty.

This particular meditation centred on the breath. We were instructed to observe the in-breath and then the out-breath; the left nostril and then the right; sensations in the nose, lips, and diaphragm; the depth or shallowness of each breath. Focussing on the breath that intently felt anything but natural. It seemed complicated. And this was no easy 15-minute session, but hours, and sometimes I yearned to just jump up and scream. But I didn't. I managed to witness the impulse, allowing it to rise and fall, rise and fall. And then, the meditation master would say, "Start again."

That phrase was repeated daily, many times. If I was bored or distracted by noises, or felt an overwhelming desire to squirm, "Start again" would trigger me to let go of whatever had caught my attention, and get me back on track. If my mind wandered to the GPM or raced ahead to imagine what I'd be doing after the retreat, "Start Again" brought me into the present. It reminded me that every moment was a new opportunity to just *be.*

Eventually I came to stillness. And in the stillness, I began to hear the *monkey mind,* the runaway train of thought, the endless stream of chatter we all have running in the background of our consciousness. I saw myself revert to old patterns of thinking: trying to fight the monkey mind, push it away, or divert. Thoughts whirled around at breakneck pace and it was dizzying.

After hours and hours, though, there was no fighting the meditation, no freaking out, only witnessing. I even witnessed my own excruciating caffeine withdrawal. The headaches were terrible, but I breathed through them. I realized, *there's no bad or good, no right or wrong: it just IS*. After some days, my headaches subsided. And now I wasn't consciously watching my breath anymore, I was just breathing. Inhale, exhale; inhale, exhale. Nothing else mattered. I felt a deep connection to my body. But as soon as I grasped, it would slip away. And I would have to *start again*.

When not sitting for hours on end, I was walking again. But now it was a meditative walk, at a snail's pace, around the room slowly, in line with the rest of the students. Heel, toe; heel, toe. I could have walked a kilometre in the time it took to walk across the austere, cavernous meditation hall, and my body was longing for that kind of exercise. But no; there was nowhere else to be, nowhere else to go. Heel, toe; heel, toe. Paradoxically, this simple movement at first felt like a very elaborate martial arts move. I had never been so aware of all the subtle shifts in balance and muscles that go into taking a step. But after some time my awkwardness settled naturally into fluid rhythm.

During the retreat, we were served two small meals a day. My instinct was to wolf down the beans and rice and rush back into line with my tin plate for a second helping. But we had strict orders to take tiny bites, chew slowly and then hold the food on the tongue before swallowing. To my amazement this opened up a world of nuanced flavours. Then I witnessed an incredible eight-second journey from mouth to esophagus to stomach. After a while I found I didn't need huge meals to satisfy me. The impact of this experience remains in me to this day. I cannot eat without first acknowledging my appreciation. Food is an incredible gift, delighting us, nourishing and sustaining us down to the smallest cell in the body.

I can't say I enjoyed following all the rules, but I reminded myself that I had choice. I had tried this coat on willingly. And playing by the rules didn't mean I was a conformist. Perhaps one of those rules might even be useful to me if I could adapt it to my own circumstances. I decided to experiment. How long could my ego withstand being lectured to? How many rules could I follow and not feel I was losing myself completely?

The experiment went well after my initial resistance and within a few days my petty resentments wore away. I learned to savour the abundance of what at first had seemed so meagre. I felt regard for everyone's personal space and at the same time an energetic unity that was very nurturing. I felt a deep respect for my teacher and the practice itself even though I knew that such discipline was not for me in the long run. Perhaps found the retreat easier than some of the other students did. A few of them left early. Some had emotional breakdowns.

It's so easy to fall asleep in life, seduced by an infinity of things: career, relationships, entertainment, etc. After ten days of sitting, those things did not pull my attention. I was free, at one with my surroundings and awake to my own existence. It had tried on that new coat, and it fit perfectly. It was comfortable, and its fibres were woven loosely, with room for air to flow between the threads. At the end of the retreat, I slowly took the coat off, and—

—Lo and behold, I had *become* the coat. Now this was either an utterly meaningless revelation or a brilliantly simple and powerful one. I prefer to think the latter. It describes how I felt at the time, anyway. I sensed the unity of it all: of me, the other students, the building, and the world outside.

I emerged from the meditation retreat a changed man. I'd even freed myself from my addiction to coffee. Victory! I left the monastery feeling on top of the world. I got in my Volkswagen van, turned the ignition and started to drive away, not knowing where I was headed next. But my body knew. I sped downtown, hopped out at the first coffee shop I saw and ordered a huge double café latte, and a huge slice of lemon cake and ice cream. I gorged myself—and it was worth it! After that pure and virtuous week I needed to be bad. Still, from somewhere beyond the hedonistic indulgence, I heard the small stern voice of the meditation master saying calmly, "Start again."

CHAPTER 20

START AGAIN

So I would *start again*, walking, but where and how? Suddenly, an image from the GPM popped into my head. I laughed, remembering the moment I'd first met Sawada.

It was when we were snaking long the road up to Loveland Pass, the highest point in the Rocky Mountains at over 3 ½ kilometres in elevation. I had seen him first as a flash of golden orange in the distance, the Japanese Buddhist monk in his long brightly coloured robes. I was so fascinated that I ran for several hundred metres to catch up with him. I puffed along in his wake, the two of us switching back and forth up the long road, hour upon hour as we ascended the tortuous route.

Not once did I spot any sign of distress or complaint from him. I admired his seemingly effortless ability to focus on his task. Head held high, chest out, eyes pointed straight ahead, he chanted and beat a drum in time with his footsteps. Although I didn't understand the words he kept repeating so stoically and hypnotically, I mumbled along as best I could. But it became more and more difficult for me to breathe because of the increase in altitude, so I stopped chanting and fell behind.

Later that day we talked. Sawada belonged to the Nipponzan-Myōhōji sect of Buddhists, who were not seeking enlightenment but the eradication of nuclear weapons. After atomic bombs were dropped on Japan in 1945, their leader, Nichidatsu Fuji, declared that they would leave the temples and take to the streets. Since then they had been walking around the world, bringing change through spiritual activism. A number of their monks took part in the Great Peace March.

What an impressive sight they were, with their orange robes and shaven heads, solemnly drumming and chanting, *Namu Myōhō Renge Kyō*, their peace prayer. (A precise translation is difficult, for there is a world of meaning and intention beyond the words.) Each monk beat his drum, which looked like a large ping-pong paddle inscribed with vivid Japanese calligraphy, with a hollow stick, sending a resonant clap through the air. It was easy to believe the sound was a message to, or even from, God.

After my meditation retreat, I remembered that Sawada, who had returned to his temple in L.A., told me about a Nipponzan-Myōhōji temple in Massachusetts. But how would I find it? These days they have a website, of course. But I had to drive around until I found a phone booth. I called the operator, doubtful she'd come up with anything, but within a minute she had the listing. The temple was located in a town called Leverett, several hours away. I hopped in my van and off I drove.

As I arrived at the monastery gates that evening, the sky was turning a deep indigo. A small, discreet, handmade sign on the edge of the property requested: **No Visitors After Sunset.** I looked up at the dark, winding gravel road and continued on, in spite of the sign, hoping they hadn't gone to bed already. I parked and approached the front door of the building. The ground-floor windows were dark, but I noticed a few lights in the front top-floor windows. I stood there for a moment and then I heard drumming. I was in the right place!

I rapped gently at the door, but no one came. I knocked louder, expecting an irate monk. But shortly, the door opened and a man in orange stood in the doorway, bowing, unsurprised. He ushered me quickly into the kitchen, as though I had just returned from the neighbour's house with a cup of sugar. There, three more Japanese monks bowed in succession and steered me towards a dark stairway.

Up the rough-hewn wooden steps I climbed, coming to an abrupt halt at the top. Before me was a psychedelic vision: bright lights, lavish decorations and huge bouquets of flowers in all colours of the rainbow. In front of a towering gold statue of the Buddha sat at least 20 monks dressed in flame-coloured robes, drumming and chanting in unison, united in a tight ball of prayer amidst their ornate surroundings. As I lowered my body onto a cushion, I felt myself melt into the room.

Later, a monk named Utsumi laid out a sleeping mat for me, and the same fellow came to wake me up. Before breakfast, he explained that monks from the U.S. and Japan had converged to take part in a four-day ritual of continuous chanting, and he invited me to stay for the rest of the gathering.

So I took my seat on a cushion in the hall and mumbled along as best I could with the chant, which was much more complicated now than just *Namu Myōhō Renge Kyō*. After a while, I noticed from behind that the head monk, who sat up on a little podium, had his head down through most of the drumming and chanting. Was he performing a silent ritual? Or taking a nap perhaps?

Impatient to satisfy my curiosity, I stood up and peered over his shoulder indiscreetly. He was reading the newspaper! *How crafty*, I thought. Sure, why not bring in some reading material to relieve the monotony? The following morning I brought some magazines for myself and they really did help with the tedium.

That night after supper, the head monk stood up. "Someone reading during prayers. This is NOT permitted!" he barked. "Only two exceptions: works of Nichidatsu Fuji, and *Boston Globe*." I snickered, thinking that he was kidding. But the monk didn't smile. Suddenly I was overcome with shame, but thankful he hadn't singled me out. I was embarrassed and confused by what seemed so hypocritical and arbitrary, though, and it was only later that I asked for an explanation.

"We are politically active Buddhists," one of the monks told me. "It is important that we keep abreast of current world events." So it was true; they considered that particular newspaper a reputable and objective source for news.

I had listened to Buddhists from various sects speak in philosophical terms about enlightenment, dharma, karma, etc, and it all sounded so esoteric and ethereal. This order stressed involvement in the physical world. They talked about politics—Reagan, Gorbachev and missile systems. I remembered that the Buddha himself is pictured as seated in meditation with his eyes half open, in a state of calm awareness. He is not asleep to the world's suffering and neither were these monks. From then on, I engaged in the chanting more actively.

After the four-day gathering ended, several monks walked me down the driveway to say farewell. Seeing my van, Utsumi remarked, "Oh—you will join walk to Cape Canaveral? I will meet you, Christmas Day, at White House. Yes? We will do vigil and then go."

Realizing there was no way to refuse, I took a deep breath and said, "Sure." *Christmas vigil? Cape Canaveral? What have I gotten myself into this time?* I wondered, spinning possibilities in my mind.

"Ahh, Derek," Utsumi said, "You will need this!" He reached into his satchel and pulled out a drum, pointing to the bold black calligraphy inscribed on the back. "*Patience—Earth—Action.* This is *you*," he said, presenting it to me. "Each Japanese character represents a sound in your name." Feeling overwhelmed and unworthy, I hoped my eyes would express more gratitude than my voice could.

I got into my van, and, until a bend in the drive hid my friends from view, I kept glancing in the rearview mirror. Each time, the monks were still there—receding, bowing incessantly. I drove away grinning.

CHAPTER 21

US AND THEM

I must admit I love having an audience. I was in my element with two beautiful French girls hanging on every word as I confessed to the literal ups and downs of my flying lesson. And now they were intrigued by the story of my drum. I paused dramatically, and then reached into my satchel. I pulled the drum out by its long handle, along with the drumstick, and started to play and chant. Immediately my ego's delight at impressing the girls melted away as they listened, eyes closed. I closed mine too. The whole ritual was like a refreshing dip in a stream. It always refocussed my energy. A few minutes later I was done.

Silence lingered and then Charlotte said, "Oh, what a strong sound, Derek. So spiritual."

"You *are* a shaman," said Danielle. "A magician. A guru!"

I chuckled, and looked down at my white t-shirt and white baggy cotton pants. "Yes, I suppose I look like a guru—and some people have called me that. But I'm not. I guess I am a teacher, though. This is not something I chose to be, but sometimes seekers come into my life looking for answers, and I simply share what I have learned from my own life. In fact, I met one such person soon after I got my drum."

"Was this at the White House?" asked Charlotte.

"The president, maybe?" Danielle said, laughing.

I laughed too.

"But Derek," said Danielle, brow furrowed. "You have told us some incredible stories, but I still don't understand what any of this has to do with Japan."

"Now don't get too far ahead," I said with a wink. And then I resumed my tale.

Christmas at the White House—well, that was a new one for me. No decked halls, no turkey dinner or gifts, not that I cared much for that stuff. I'd never been too excited about Christmas, except for my kids. Monks and supporters circled the building, slowly walking, drumming, chanting, praying and protesting the upcoming test launch of the Trident II missile system. It seemed to me I was closer to the real meaning of Christmas than ever before.

For some reason, Utsumi wasn't amongst our group at the White House. We knew he'd left Leverett, but where was he? We continued chanting and drumming for two days, and then got ready to leave. We packed up the van, thinking that we'd start driving around to search for him. Just then, we heard distant thumping. Sure enough, we spied orange robes in the distance: it was Utsumi, with his shaven head, backpack, and drum echoing through the deserted D.C. streets.

We drove to the Kings Bay Naval Submarine Base in Georgia, near the wide mouth of the St. Mary's River. A group of 200-odd people milled about, waiting for the walk to begin. *Odd* was the operative word for this motley bunch of activists, with their varied attire and placards. But the monks stood out even in this crowd. *Hmm*, I thought, standing there with my drum. *I almost feel like a monk already. I even have an orange T-shirt.*

Once everyone had assembled, there were speeches. This would be the first major peace march in the very conservative state of Florida and we weren't sure what we would encounter. Protesters were already congregating at Cape Canaveral and the scene sounded tense. The Trident II missile, in wartime, would be armed with 12 nuclear warheads that had the explosive power of 35 Hiroshimas. The cost in dollars (aside from the many other costs) was projected at 69 billion. *How obscene*, I thought.

With a mixture of dread and zeal, we set out along the river's edge, to walk inland for a day along the banks until we could cross the bridge into Florida. After a short time, though, a noisy speedboat sped up alongside us. At first we were alarmed, but then, noticing the familiar Greenpeace logo, we were relieved to meet comrades and not detractors. They had arrived to give us a quick ride across the river's mouth into the Orange State. Everyone agreed we should accept their offer, and one by one we climbed aboard enthusiastically, the monks and I drumming and chanting as we got in.

Sitting cross-legged on the flat-decked boat as it flew across the river, we continued to drum and chant over the roar of the engines. The scene was almost absurd, and I was engulfed in a sensation of drunkenness. It was a kind of spiritual delirium; at that moment I couldn't imagine life being any better. Then suddenly from out of the waves rose a pod of nine or ten dolphins, diving and leaping joyfully through the air like shooting stars. I was on a magic carpet to heaven, now escorted on each side by these sleek protectors from the sea.

The ecstatic vision cratered when we reached the day's destination. Putting up tents that evening on the grounds of a local church, we were startled by the shrill blast of a police siren, and then a patrol car skidded to a stop beside us. A figure jumped out and gesticulated against the backdrop of whirling red and blue lights. It was the sheriff, complete with intimidating mirrored sunglasses. "Listen up," he hollered. "Anyone camping in my county will go to jail, you bunch of hippies and Negros!" In utter shock, we appealed to the church authorities, but all they could do was shrug and turn away. Clearly, they were under his thumb.

As daylight faded, so did hope. After trying other churches and community centres, we encountered the same response: "Sorry, but we just can't help you." Apparently everyone knew the sheriff. We were preparing ourselves to start trudging on through the night, when a young man arrived announcing that he'd found us a place to stay: a tiny church we'd overlooked earlier. We managed to cram all our bodies into the tiny building, bedding down in the vestry, the aisles, around the altar and in the pews. Instead of psalms that night, you could hear a symphony of snores.

We woke up to creaking bones, but we were fairly well rested and, mercifully, not in jail. Once on the road again, however, our unease returned. As we walked, people came out of houses and taverns, not to greet and encourage us but to fire guns at the sky and yell profanities. There were no smiles, but snarls. "Commies!" they'd yell. There was no flashing the familiar two-finger peace sign, but one middle finger, waved aggressively.

Communism was a dirty word in America's Reagan years. Many locals were employed on defence projects and were angry at us for threatening their livelihood. I could understand this, but the hostility was shocking. I'd never encountered this level of aggression in my life and it was upsetting to many of the walkers.

Nathan, a lad just out of high school, had been hanging around me, asking about the Great Peace March. His desire to change the world was fervent. I listened to him, quietly nodding and acknowledging his anger. I don't normally like to offer my thoughts unless I am asked.

"What a jerk that cop was the other day," he said, shaking his head, fists clenched. "I mean, shouldn't we have reported him to his superiors or something?"

I sat for a while, not quite sure what direction to take the conversation. But Nathan seemed to genuinely want guidance. "Yes," I ventured, "the officer should be held accountable, but in this case, it was better for us to walk on. Otherwise we'd have been caught up in the blame game, just like him. *Us and them.* We could choose to see these last few days as *us* against some very ignorant Americans. In fact this entire protest could be seen as *us versus the government.*"

"But isn't it? Aren't we against the government?"

"We're against this specific project, most definitely, in the little picture. But take a look at the big picture. *Us and them* seems to be who we are as humans. Us versus: Germans, Jews, Muslims, whoever. Just fill in the blank. Collectively and individually we seem to need someone to blame, so we don't have to look at our own faults. Healing this divide means acknowledging the potential villain within. Only then, when I can take responsibility for my own anger, my own destructive nature, will I truly know that harming others is the same as harming myself. As Pogo said, 'We have met the enemy and he is us.'"

"Hey, that's cool." said Nathan, thoughtfully. "Who's Pogo, though?"

"Well," I said, "imagine a smarter, funnier, more political Snoopy, but he's an opossum."

"Um, OK," he said, looking puzzled.

Maybe this serious kid doesn't even read comics, I thought.

"Then, if it all comes down to our own stuff," Nathan continued earnestly, "why do we protest? Doesn't that still imply us and them?"

"For me," I replied, "it's really important for my voice to be heard. Not because I'm wanting to blame, but because I want to call more attention to the big problems we've helped create. If there is a nuclear war, we'll be wiped out and so will the Russians. If one of us strikes, the other will retaliate. And when it's over, the ashes of the capitalists and the communists will look the same. I know that a lot of ordinary Americans understand this, and I'm pretty sure that ordinary Russians would too."

"So," Nathan went on, fingers absentmindedly stroking his sparse beard as he looked at me intently, "if we are all responsible for peace in the world, you should look inside at your faults, and try to be a better person. But is that enough?"

"I've learned a lot about responsibility," I replied, "and this is how I explain it now. Imagine a dinner party, with good friends sitting around a lavish table. There's sparkling conversation, wine and candles, the whole deal. Or maybe it's you and your buddies sitting around with a case of beer. But suddenly, you hear a screech of tires from outside, and then a loud crash. It sounds like a car accident. What do you do? There's a whole range of choices. You can go on talking, acting like nothing happened. You can run and hide in your bathroom, frozen in fear. You can sit around and speculate about what might be going on out there. You can say, 'Well, I'm sure someone has already called 9-1-1,' or, 'It's OK, it's all in God's hands.' You can freak out and scream. Or, you can rush outside. And if you do that, there's no telling what you'll find—maybe it's just a fender-bender and there's nothing to worry about. Fine. But maybe there's an injured child. Now what to do? You can pick that child up and try to help. Then again, what if there's a spinal cord injury? Aren't you supposed to just cover a person up in that case, and wait for paramedics?

"There is no right answer. And every choice leads to more hard questions. What's clear to me is that talking isn't enough and reacting isn't enough. If we all reacted naturally to the situation our world is in, with the proliferation of nuclear weapons, and greenhouse gases, and famine, we'd all be out on the street, screaming or crying. We would do that if we weren't so conditioned, so desensitized. Reacting this way would at least be genuine but it probably wouldn't help. We need to feel these things, but then we need to respond from a place of clarity and compassion. This is our ability to respond. Response-ability."

"Derek," asked Nathan, "is it OK if I use that story?"

"Sure," I replied. "It's your story to tell, any time. And now—for something completely different! Let's take off our shoes and walk backwards on the sand!" We did just that, and finally Nathan laughed.

The group continued our slow southward trek and one day yet another commanding figure stopped us in our tracks. This time it was no sheriff. Our chatter trickled quickly to a hush as each one of us laid eyes on the towering dark-skinned woman in the road, who was wrapped elegantly from head to toe in brightly patterned scarves. She looked like an African queen. "You can all stay with me tonight," she said, her eyes flashing.

I wasn't sure what was more outrageous, inviting 200 people to sleep over, or—her appearance. My eyes wandered to the satchel that was slung over her shoulder and hung low on her hip. Covered with peace buttons and slogans, it was bursting at the seams. As I looked closer, I saw that it was full of nothing other than—her hair! Her dreadlocks trailed down her back and then snaked into the bag at waist level. The dreads were so long that the bag prevented them from dragging along the ground. I estimated at least seven feet of thick tresses, just about the dimensions of a small python.

As she spoke, she gestured constantly with her right hand, her wrist encircled in bracelets made of shells and coloured beads. Suddenly, as she raised her left hand for emphasis, I saw that the fingers of this hand sported curled nails, like claws, each of which must have been at least ten inches long. Dazed, my friends and I tagged along behind.

Our host's home was nothing more than a shack on the sand. But she spoke with pride and authority, directing us to set up our tents above the tide zone. The next minute she was giggling coyly like a girl. "Maybe later I'll sing to you," she said. Nodding obediently, we agreed. Later that evening around an open fire, we sat, whispering amongst ourselves as we waited for our eccentric host, wondering what we'd hear.

All at once, our group fell quiet. She entered our midst, this great black diva, standing straight-backed, looking around slowly at each one of us in turn. Fixing her eyes on the distant horizon, she drew a long, slow breath. Her lips opened and out poured one clear, luminous note. The sound crescendoed to an unrestrained roar and subsided to a delicate ring, like pure crystal, punctuated by the most sensuous consonants. I can't remember the words, but the feeling is still in my heart. I soared on that song, over the campfire, shack and tents, into the vast black night and the river of stars. When she stopped singing, there was a long hush.

We sat for a while in the silence, as the music rang in our bones. And then, she shared her story. Known as the Beach Lady, her real name was MaVynee Betsch. Her great-grandfather, a millionaire, had founded this beach community—American Beach—in the days of racial segregation, as a safe holiday haven for African-American families. Born in the US, MaVynee had been educated in Europe, and had sung opera professionally there for years. She came home to spend the rest of her life and money on environmental causes, and on promoting the black history of American Beach.

MaVynee spoke passionately about a rare butterfly that lived in the area. Soon she would be going to court to prevent any development of its natural habitat. Before she died in 2005 at the age of 70, American Beach was preserved and awarded status as a national historic site, thanks to the unstoppable Beach Lady.

The next day, our bodies still full of music, we resumed our walk down the beach in the warmth of the morning sun. To the left, the rolling surf kept us company. Every so often, we'd be captivated by the aerial acrobatics of a flock of pelicans skimming the waves. On our right lay rows of people on towels and folding chairs. What a bizarre sight we must have been to them, like an orange-fringed cloud sweeping across the sands, our drums like approaching thunder. The lotioned sunbathers leapt up, mouths agape, to watch our colourful parade.

As strange as we must have looked marching down the beach, we did attract some positive attention. Suddenly, I recalled a term I'd heard used in the environmental community: *critical mass.*

I found my young protégé Nathan and gave him a nudge. "We don't all have to be as gutsy and outrageous as MaVynee to make an impression, or to make change," I said, the thoughts forming as I spoke. "But if enough people decided to, for instance, wear their hair in a seven-foot dreadlock, it would probably catch on. This is what fads are all about."

"Yeah, but we're doing something a lot more serious," countered Nathan.

"Yes, that's true. But it's the same principle. It's a natural phenomenon that things change exponentially."

"Which means," he continued, "if enough people talk about peace and act peacefully, they'll make it popular, and eventually peace will be the norm!"

"Exactly!"

Cape Canaveral Air Force Base is where our walk ended and where our work began. Protesters and activists had been gathering for days to bring attention to the Trident II nuclear missile system. Numbers had swelled to almost 5,000, in what was now the largest-ever peace demonstration in the southeast United States. Most of us suspected that the best we could do was delay, but we hoped against hope that we could abort this $30 million weapons test. Civil disobedience seemed the only way.

For days on end people attempted to infiltrate the testing grounds in order to occupy the launch pad. Those who succeeded in making it past the barbed wire and vast alligator-infested swamps were met by military or local police and immediately arrested.

The front entrance to the base was chaos, with people yelling, waving signs, crying, and shaking the fence. There was a significant crowd of counter-protestors too, who were just as angry and afraid as we were. I glanced off to the side and witnessed a tender moment amidst all the pandemonium. Standing at the fence were 84-year-old Dr. Benjamin Spock, the famous author and pediatrician, and his wife, holding and kissing each other tenderly. They smiled at each other, and then the doctor reached up and hoisted himself over the massive ten-foot barbed-wire gate to be arrested along with other protesters.

My camper van had come in handy during the walk; we'd all taken turns driving it as a support vehicle lugging supplies. Now it was on a stealthier mission. After dusk, demonstrators piled into the van and I'd cruise by the base with my side door open, slowing down just enough so the protesters could slide out into the swamp. Hiding until morning, they would then wade through the mucky water to the launch area. One evening I had just dropped off a handful of people and was driving back to join the rest of the action when out of the sky swerved a huge military helicopter. It was so close I could have sworn it was going to land on my roof. Looking up, I saw three soldiers aiming rifles at me. I smiled weakly and waved at them. They didn't wave back. For the next five kilometres, careering down the road, I was like a robot, hands frozen to the steering wheel as the helicopter tailed me.

Then, just as suddenly as it had swept in, the helicopter veered off and disappeared into the night sky. Perhaps they knew I was no security threat but just wanted to scare me. Well, they didn't just scare me—they terrified me.

One morning shortly after my near miss with the helicopter, I awoke to loud rapping at my van door: it was bad news. After numerous delays, the missile launch was back on. I headed for the test site. Suddenly I heard a rumbling and I looked up to witness the huge, dark cylinder lifting straight up over the trees, belching orange flames. It moved as if in slow motion, and the roar filled my ears. The blaze turned bright white, smearing across the sky, and the missile vanished into the high clouds.

Overtaken by despair and disbelief, I pulled over to the side of the road, opened the van door, and fell to the ground. Seconds later, a cop drove up beside me and rolled down his window. "You have two minutes to get the hell out of here or you're under arrest," he said. What I wanted to do was scream, but what I heard was my inner voice, saying, *I shall not preoccupy myself with an enemy.* I looked him in the eye and returned to my van, furious, but holding my tongue. I'd had enough.

I had been almost run off the road, shouted at by townspeople, provoked by the media and even spat on. I'd walked myself to near exhaustion. And now it all seemed fruitless. However, unlike many of my friends, I'd not had my phone tapped, or been beaten by cops, or arrested. I could still do something.

I promised myself that I would pray and drum outside of the jail and courthouse until every protester was released. I stood outside, giving high fives when they were let out. Nathan was there and I was relieved to see him.

"I really liked walking with you," he said.

"Same here," I said. "You're really smart, and really brave. I look forward to seeing what you're up to in a few years."

"You really inspired me. I want to do another walk some time. A longer one maybe, like the Great Peace March."

"You'll do it," I replied, "when the time is right." We hugged for several minutes, and then he left to catch his bus back home to Vermont.

Everyone was out of jail, and I should have been glad. But I was only worn out and angry, at no one in particular. Much of this had to do with the energy it took to be around peace activists. Like anyone, they had their shadow side, and theirs—ours—was desperation and zealotry. I couldn't let my light be eclipsed.

I made another promise to myself—to rest. *This civil disobedience thing is pretty tiring. How about some civil disobedience to protest the personal cost of civil disobedience?* I laughed at myself, imagining lying in dappled sunlight, under swaying palm trees, daiquiri in hand, not even thinking the word *peace.* No one would dare approach me until all my frustration had melted away in the hot sun. Then, in as clear a demonstration of the principle *ask and you shall receive* as possible, a friend made an offer I couldn't refuse. A housesitting job—on the grounds of a millionaire's estate.

CHAPTER 22

REST

The wealthy homeowner was off to Jamaica and graciously entrusted me with her home. The grounds were ample, full of exotic flowers and palm trees. I had to laugh at the nearly literal incarnation of my daiquiri fantasy. I was in a pristine, private garden of Eden, surrounded by a 12-foot wall with an electric gate, and I had the remote control.

The immaculately appointed mansion could have easily slept several dozen, and though it had all the amenities I could have asked for, I preferred sleeping outside. I rigged my hammock up between two palms and awoke every morning to watch two regal swans gliding on the mirror-smooth pond. For breakfast, I climbed trees and picked fresh bananas, softball-sized avocados, mangoes, oranges and grapefruit. What a decadent menu, after beans and rice, and what luxurious solitude after the last year of communal living.

My sanity and energy returned in the luxurious solitude, balancing out the last year's relative intensity and deprivation. *For every action*—remembered this high school dropout—*there is an equal and opposite reaction.* It was a predictable pendulum swing. Thus, like eating cake after my meditation retreat, I allowed myself to indulge within reason because somehow it centred me.

Maybe it's all just physics. Everything, I reasoned, is constantly seeking balance. Politics had always swung back and forth. And then there was the science/religion pendulum, with religious fundamentalism now on the rise. On a more personal level, I thought of one of my massage clients, an obsessive marathon runner. Her hamstring muscles were so overworked that her lower back muscles had shortened in compensation, causing abnormal and painful spinal curvature. Next, I recalled the number of well-intentioned peace activists I'd recently met, who had swung themselves to extremes: anxiety, depression, divorce and bankruptcy. By focussing too much on the goal, they neglected their relationships and house payments. *Dedication, but at what cost?*

Is it ever possible to achieve permanent balance? I wondered. *Maybe gurus, and maybe the Buddha did, after a lot of work, but they didn't start off that way.* What about the natural world, then? On a large scale, the changing seasons, predator/prey relationships, volcanoes and even ice ages are the planet's way of finding balance. In the microcosm, nature adjusts through tiny actions and reactions at cellular, molecular and chemical levels. But humans were tampering with this natural fine-tuning. *The pendulum swing may be natural, but our extremism could very well push us past the balance point for good.*

I saw that we as humans require acute awareness of our effects on the environment and each other. We need to constantly make efforts to change our habits of action and thought, and our technology, in order to live in harmony with ourselves and the rest of the universe. *This is peace-making,* I realized. *We strive for it, but may never quite get there. It's a never-ending process.* I wasn't quite willing to admit that peace might not ever come, though. I had to hang on to that dream.

Eventually, a voice inside began to whisper, *It's time to get back to work!* I began drafting letters to the editor and wrote to friends at home, telling them that I vowed to keep walking until all nuclear weapons were eradicated. Perhaps I was naïve to think that with enough passion and commitment and work, this could happen. But I kept my words to Nathan in mind. I just needed to do my part, not fix the whole world. *And besides*, I thought, *wouldn't you rather be naïve than numb?*

As soon as I declared my readiness, my attention was drawn to a solidarity walk in the Soviet Union. *Wow, isn't that timely?* I thought, after just having seen the missile launch. And Russian leader Gorbachev's new political reform, *Perestroika*, meant that for the first time in years, Westerners were allowed into the country. *What an opportunity.* When I professed my interest, friends formed a fundraising committee for me. It concerned me a little to think that I'd be walking with a big group again, and one that was highly publicized. But I got swept up in the excitement and before I knew it, there was even a benefit concert for me on Miami Beach, and I was interviewed on TV. The media interest was flattering, but it bothered me. They made a big deal out of the political stuff but missed the spirit, which to me meant individual Westerners and Soviets connecting as humans. Not only that, but it annoyed me that the announcers declared I was an American.

I set the record straight: I was a Canadian and just a humble peace walker with no political agenda. But then it hit me. I didn't want to walk for a *cause* this time. I didn't want to carry a banner. *Is this walk really for me?* I asked myself. *No. You need to walk alone.*

I wasn't yet sure where I would go, or when, but I knew I had to approach my supporters about my change of heart. "Look, I'm really sorry," I told them, sheepishly. "I really appreciate all your hard work, but—I just can't do this. If you're still into the solidarity walk, I know someone to take my place. But if you still want to support me, and my own journey for peace, then I'll accept enough money for an airline ticket, and the rest of the funds can be given to my young friend."

"We're with you 100 percent," they enthused. "Are you sure all you want is the plane ticket? We can give you enough money for months of walking."

Calling to mind the monks, I bowed three times, and answered, "Thank you. The ticket is all I need."

CHAPTER 23

WAR GAMES

I was now on a plane to London. My first international flight ever. I was thrilled by takeoff and the strange yet exhilarating sensation when the ground suddenly drops away, your body is pushed back into the seat, and pressure builds inside your head. Soon we levelled out and I felt normal again. Out the window, massive banks of fluffy white and silver clouds dominated the sky and I could barely grasp how big they really were; they seemed motionless despite our hurtling speed. I laughed to myself, thinking how odd the scene would look if the plane were invisible: rows of seated passengers, casually eating pretzels and reading magazines, dwarfed by clouds, sailing through space at unnatural speed. We just sat there, acting as if this feat were entirely normal. *Things are not what they appear,* I mused.

It was all relative, I realized. To my friends, it might have seemed that the scale of my life was somehow beyond comprehension. I had walked across the US, drummed and chanted with a group of orange-clad Japanese monks, watched a missile launch, house-sat a mansion. But each hop, from one thing to another, had been my way of finding balance. Now, I had only a vague idea of what would unfold after we touched down, but it was all feeling very normal to me.

We landed at Heathrow Airport and I got through customs quickly. Isabelle, my dear friend from the GPM, met me at the gate. Soon, we made plans. I wouldn't be walking alone as I'd hoped, but I could let go of that for now.

First we took the train to the Greenham Common Airforce Base, in Berkshire, about two hours west of London. For six years a group of women had been camped to protest nuclear weapons on the site. We sat in the rain with them under a huge tarp, drinking tea congenially by the fire and listening to their concerns. These women were no mere worriers, they were *warriors*. Not only did they patrol the perimeter of the site and take down wire-mesh fences with bolt cutters, but they held events where up to 70,000 protesters would come together. They once even formed a continuous human chain from the camp to an ordnance factory 23 kilometres away. They constantly rebuilt and reoccupied the camp after countless arrests and evictions. They also *glooped*.

Convoys of missile-laden vehicles exited the military compound regularly. People who lived and worked along neighbouring roads were not always aware of what the trucks carried, and it was possible that a mishap could one day prove tragic. Women climbed trees to conduct surveillance and when a convoy-load of missiles was spotted, they'd rally a glooping crew. Gloop was concocted out of water, flour and pink food colouring. This was no biscuit dough but a tool for subversion when scooped into plastic baggies and lobbed at the convoys, to alert citizens to vehicles carrying dangerous cargo. I wasn't sure I agreed with these tactics, but these women were *doing* something. My commitment to peace was strengthened in their presence.

(The camp would continue another 13 years. Nuclear missiles were finally removed from the base in 1991, but protestors remained, in opposition to the British Trident initiative. Some of the women had been at the camp for 19 years. The airforce base at Greenham Common is now a park, and the campsite a national historic site for peace.)

After our meetings in and around London (and eating more than our share of fish and chips, scones and slices of Victoria sponge cake), Isabelle and I travelled to West Germany. The Cold War was still in full swing and the country was full of nuclear weapons.

After the Second World War, the eastern part of Germany was taken over by the U.S.S.R., the western side became a democratic republic, and a guarded border was created between them. At this time, in 1987, East Germany was still very much controlled by the U.S.S.R. Against the threat of warfare, almost a million NATO personnel, including 250,000 American troops, were stationed in West Germany. They patrolled over 1,000 kilometres of the East-West border with nuclear weapons, rockets, and landmines on both sides.

The Fulda Gap is a forested mountain pass about 100 kilometres northeast of Frankfurt, straddling East and West Germany. For many years it was considered a strategic route for Soviet invasion if World War III were to break out. Every summer about 25 grassroots protesters entered the area and walked along the wooded, fenced border. Isabelle and I now joined them.

As we approached the Fulda Gap, Isabelle noticed something nestled amongst the trees: tanks painted in mottled green camouflage. Next we spied jeeps and even a two-storey camouflage-painted building. Suddenly, helicopters and small jets planes began to swoop overhead, and we heard men yelling, "Halt!" A long line of soldiers with semi-automatic rifles drawn, advanced towards us on foot, and stopped in front of us. It was like some kind of futuristic Wild West scenario.

Beneath all the armour though, I saw the faces of children. Although they were young adults, they looked like kids playing a very deadly adult game. They lowered their weapons when they realized who we were and the tension dissolved. The higher-ups and our organizers exchanged words as we milled about, waiting to walk on.

I was curious how the young Americans felt, living in this potential war zone. They were missing out on whatever their pals would be doing back in the States: studying, playing sports, going on dates. So I approached a soldier who looked almost eager to talk. "What are you doing here, so far from home? I asked.

"I'm a medic," he said. "Here for a little life experience, I guess."

"And how's that experience treating you? I asked.

"Not bad, I guess," he said. "I haven't seen much action, really. I feel good about defending the world from the Russians, and so far, so good." I listened, not reacting but nodding for him to continue. "Occasionally we get East Germans trying to cross illegally," he went on. "They're just ordinary people, hoping for a better life. If they're caught on the eastern side, they can be shot dead. On one hand, I'm glad they escaped, but then we're supposed to send them back. It's tough."

"I can imagine." I said. "What a responsibility."

"Yeah, they call it peacekeeping, but I dunno. Sometimes I feel like I could be doing something more. You know, to make the world a better place."

The word *more* resonated with me, but I wasn't sure I should jump into that kettle of fish. "So, what kind of training do you receive in nuclear warfare?" I asked.

"Not much. We're trained for conventional war. If there's a nuclear attack, we're told not to touch other survivors, but I'm here to help, so how could I not?"

Survivors? I thought. I didn't say anything.

The boy started looking nervous, perhaps that his superiors might be watching him.

"I'd better let you go," I said. "But, you mentioned doing more. You could request some literature from the Physicians for Social Responsibility. It might be somewhere to start. Just an idea."

We shook hands, and I left with the other walkers. I remembered Nathan, the young man I'd met on my walk to Florida. These two had different paths, but a similar dream.

Next, Isabelle and I headed south, eventually parting ways with the German walkers. Once in Greece, we met up with the Nipponzan-Myōhōji monks and a small group of their supporters who were walking to Athens. Sharing bows and smiles with Kijima, our friend from the Great Peace March, we joined them trekking silently through the rolling hills. I was stunned by the beauty of the countryside and the clear blue ocean. We passed through tiny villages of gleaming whitewashed houses, which seemed sleepy until heads popped out of windows shouting, "*Eeereenee … eereenee!*" I was baffled until I learned what they were yelling. *Eiréné*—peace. My first word in Greek. This country's long history was war after war.

Temperatures soared that summer in Europe and we heard reports of hundreds of people dying from heat exhaustion. As we walked, the horizon was a splash of brilliant red and ochre, forest fires blazing beyond the hills, with my orange-robed friends in the foreground, their bald heads shining in the sun. Every day we'd start off before dawn to catch cool breezes off the ocean, but we'd be drenched in sweat within the hour. I felt like I was suffocating. My tired legs turned as soft as gelatin and there were times I just wanted to sit down and cry.

The monks showed no sign of exhaustion. They immersed themselves in the moment and carried on walking, drumming, eating, sleeping, and then doing the same again the next day. They were not attached to outcomes; they were just doing what they do. Nothing seemed to faze or frighten them, either—not heat, not unfamiliar languages, not even the lack of anything, like money, beds, or food.

Walking across the United States, I had seen how basic requirements like food and shelter were huge priorities that took time and energy to arrange. But now these needs, as important as they were, diminished. When we were sleepy, we slept—on the ground if there was nowhere else. When hungry, we ate—if there was food. Full meals were scarce, as we had little money to survive on. The monks even gave their money away to people in need. I had first experienced dumpster-diving with the monks in Florida, scrounging for leftovers in restaurant and supermarket trash bins, but there were no such offerings in Greece. I knew we'd be OK though. I trusted the monks, and myself, and had faith that what we needed would always show up. I began to lose weight, but I consciously decided to think of it as *fasting* instead of starving. It's amazing how my outlook changed when I framed it differently. Living in this way, everything was a gift.

When we did eat, it was often *karpoúzi*—watermelon. It doesn't take long to tire of watermelon when that's all you ever have. As we took a short break one morning, I was relieved to stop walking, but when a monk named Nagase brought out his Swiss Army knife and carved small slices from yet another *karpoúzi*, I became nauseated. Too weary even to groan, I turned away and hunted for a patch of precious shade. I found a spot away from the group and sat in silence, my head dropping little by little as I succumbed to mid-day fatigue in the cloying heat. I nodded off until my head gave a slight jerk, and then I sensed somebody's presence. I squinted up at a shadowy figure and gasped in amazement at a haloed figure. For a moment I thought I was seeing the Buddha. It was Nagase, standing quietly, silhouetted between me and the sun. With a tender smile he bowed three times and offered me a piece of watermelon.

How could I refuse? I bowed, accepting the melon, and tried not to wince as he looked deeply into my eyes. Words were unnecessary, as it seemed at that moment that Nagase understood everything that I felt, and there was no judgment or pity, just a knowing. As he walked away quietly to serve the others, I wondered if I'd just experienced a Star Trek mind-meld from a Japanese Spock.

The watermelon was now like rain on my parched throat, and gradually my energy and gratitude returned. I looked around at the monks who were still holding their heads high. Dusting off their robes, they hugged their drums to their chests, ready to walk on. I picked up my drum and joined them. I felt like the caboose in a long orange train, but instead of the whine of the diesel engine and clickety-clack of wheels, we'd travel to the rhythmic drone of chanting and the steady beat of drums.

As dedicated as the monks were, they understood balance. Walking was work and sometimes we needed play. So at the end of a long day we would go swimming in the ocean. Once in the water, the monks were like children, delighting in the refreshing cool water, laughing, shouting, and splashing each other mercilessly. Gone was their solemn demeanour. When they finished bathing, they calmly gathered up their robes, bowed three times to the ocean, and we all continued silently down the road.

One evening we had a meeting with a peace committee in a town, which took place in a small office building. The lobby had only had one small elevator, so we let the monks in first, and up it went. Suddenly, an alarm went off. The elevator was stuck. Isabelle and I ran up the stairs and tried prying the door open to no avail. The blaring continued for almost half an hour as we scurried about, until a whole battalion of frenzied firefighters arrived with pick axes and hoses. After ongoing discussions and assessments, one of the crew ran off, leaving the rest of us to wait and worry. He returned soon enough with a metal grinder in hand, and began cutting into the doors, sparks flying. Finally out tumbled seven monks, like clowns from a phone booth. One of them was cradling a huge watermelon. They picked themselves up, bowed, and marched purposefully and quietly down the hall with their watermelon. I peered inside the elevator and saw a tiny notice inside. I am sure it read, "Limit: two persons," in Greek.

On another occasion we were all invited to a banquet with a town mayor. We sat at a long table and watched a parade of waiters bring huge platter after platter of hot steaming seafood of every description: octopus, anchovies, smelt, mackerel, scampi and sea cabbage. It was mouthwatering. The monks ate everything. And when they were done, out came more: savoury meat pies, golden potatoes, and stuffed grape leaves.

The monks hadn't eaten this variety or volume of food ever. Buddhists always finish their meals, but the Greek custom is to leave some tidbits at the end of a meal; cleaning the plate meant you were still hungry and expected more. So as soon as the monks finished, out came more food: cheeses, honey-drenched pastries and sculpted towers of fruit. By now I had stopped eating, and I sat back to watch this incredible comic drama unfold. Out of the corner of my eye I saw one of the monks nudging another and gesturing under the table. He was shovelling food into his satchel. The other monk joined in, and before long all the monks were stuffing baklava into their satchels and under the folds of their robes. The mayor returned from the kitchen, and, seeing still more empty plates, shook his head and yelled, "*Kialo fagytó—grígora!*" More food—quick! That was my breaking point.

Jumping up, I bowed to the mayor. "Thank you, sir," I said, "for your generous hospitality. Now we need to go!" In synchrony and without hesitation, the monks stood, bowed three times to our host, and filed quickly out of the room. I followed, glancing back to see a flummoxed mayor slump into his chair.

Each morning we rose before dawn to a chorus of zippers and snapping tent poles. Peering out of my tent, I would see our little village being dismantled in the dark by shadowy robed figures floating silently to and fro. I dragged myself out of my sleeping bag and followed the monks dutifully, as I had done for months, not knowing where we'd end up next or what we'd be doing.

At the end of one very long hot day, after trudging up a steep incline for hours, I was fantasizing about a shady open-air tavern at the top of the hill. The fantasy included a beautiful view, a huge table piled high with rich greasy snacks and pitchers of wine, and a comfy bed upstairs waiting just for me. Instead, we found a long barbed wire fence along the ridge and armed sentries flanking a massive steel gate. The monks, one after another, spread out in a smooth line in front of it. Then they bowed in unison, sat down, and continued drumming and chanting. I followed. Lifting my eyes from the ground, I noticed a large sign:

WARNING!
NO TRESPASSING
U.S. MILITARY BASE

Oh hell. We had just formed a blockade. Nobody in; nobody out. *Namu Myōhō Renge Kyō....* I felt like I was chanting for my life. The drumming took on new intensity, evoking something ancient and tribal. A call to arms—or more accurately—a call to disarm. *No more war,* the drums rang out.

Before long, truckloads of soldiers jumped out and lined up in front of us with rifles aimed. Next came the ominous wail of sirens, louder and louder, heralding the police. Greeks are generally known as excitable people, so this was not going to get any calmer very soon. The cops jumped out and ran back and forth down the line of us, waving handguns in our faces, yelling frantically. *How absurd this is,* I thought. Their words were meaningless to us, but their actions spoke volumes.

As the barrage of threats continued we kept going, but I began to feel a kernel of fear swelling inside. *Oh, please let us be safe,* I pleaded to myself. *I'm just a guy who wants a better future for his grandchildren!* Before too long, I was shaking in terror, hardly able to hold up my drum. I knew that this chaotic scene could turn violent if just one person panicked, so I took a deep breath and closed my eyes.

The next moment is very difficult for me to find words for. It was as if a warm cloak of complete calm, serenity, and oneness had been draped around me. My fear had transformed into love.

Hours later, our confrontation came to an end when we stopped drumming and chanting, bowed towards the military base, and quietly walked away. I will never forget that moment of calm in the centre of chaos, and I wonder if this is what people talk of when they say they are with God. I suppose it's not always necessary to climb to the top of a mountain to experience God. It seems s/he can also be at the base, and in this instance a military base.

Was it God who kept us safe that day? Was it our collective good intention? Was it that the soldiers themselves raised their own consciousness while we were there? I cannot say. But we were doing what we knew in our hearts was right. It was our willingness to be vulnerable that was actually our strength.

I may not always be kept out of trouble when I follow my heart, but if I don't think ahead, don't think back, and stay in the moment—in that blockade, or walking on fire, or speaking publicly in front of a group—I will most definitely be on the right path.

CHAPTER 24

CRANES

Thousands of bodies circled the Acropolis, hand in hand, as we joined with folks who had assembled for a yearly peace vigil there. I felt elated but a little strange, almost jarred out of time, amongst the imposing ruins. What a way to end our long, hot walk.

Later, Isabelle and I joined a crowd of people sitting in the grass, folding origami birds. I had seen the paper cranes on the GPM and knew they were symbols of peace, although I didn't know why. A friend had demonstrated how to take a coloured square of paper, fold it about two dozen times, and end up with a three-dimensional bird. It was magic, but I had no confidence that I could repeat the feat. Although my friend had insisted I was capable, I am quite adept at retreating when I feel shy, so I gave it one embarrassing try and gave up.

Kijima approached me now with a sheaf of multicoloured paper, telling me to start folding. Forgetting how gracefully I had squared off with the soldiers earlier, I pulled out my best avoidance tactics, protesting, "I can't do this. I've tried before, and I just don't get it. I just … can't …." I trailed off, mumbling how sorry I was, my fragile ego flailing.

Unfazed, the monk glared at me sternly. "Make," he ordered. Technically, there is no word for "no" in Japanese, and perhaps he did not care for the concept either. I countered with my most vigorous whining, but he shoved the papers in my hand. "Do," he said, turning on his heel, and leaving.

My ego didn't stand a chance now. I began folding a piece of paper, worrying that my fumbling hands would draw unwanted attention to myself. *People will think I'm stupid,* I imagined, berating myself silently. *Children in Japan probably have this skill as they come out of the womb, so what's your problem?* I suddenly felt eight years old, trying to follow arts & crafts instruction in school, and failing miserably. I needed to turn my thoughts around and encourage myself. *Hey, you were the A student in massage therapy!* I reminded myself. *And you used to do magic tricks!*

Shuffling off to a quiet spot with Isabelle, I worked away diligently, with her help, until I learned to make a peace crane. It wasn't perfect, but my whole heart was in it. When I finally swallowed my pride and let go of my fear, I forgot to care about what others might think and enjoyed something new. It became a meditation. And it was almost as if with every fold, something in me was actually unfolded and set free. Reverse origami!

That night I retired to bed with a sea of images and feelings swirling in my head. The day had gone from one extreme to another: from a rifle in my face, to the experience of pure love, to the satisfaction of mastering a new skill. I felt admiration for the monks, and sadness that we were parting ways. Now it was time to find balance again. So, Isabelle and I found a remote beach, plunked ourselves down, and didn't move for days.

CHAPTER 25

PRIDE AND PATIENCE

While typing out the last chapter, a flash of memory hits me. It's a few years ago, and I sit at a table, fumbling with a small square of paper, annoyed with myself. I am not as quick a learner as I thought, nor as dextrous. I watch Derek as he calmly and methodically demonstrates how to make an origami bird, slowly pressing each crease between two fingers before starting the next fold. He doesn't even use the table to flatten the folds against; he holds the bird aloft in front of him. How come it's so easy for him? I wonder, my pride bruised. Watching this white-haired fellow with his large muscular hands making such delicate birds, I feel defeated.

We're sitting in a café. It's cool and dark inside the room; the stone walls are almost two feet thick. Light streams through a window onto the table littered with coloured paper. I pick up another sheet of paper and try again. "It takes a lot of practise," says Derek. "Believe me, it might take a dozen more tries but you'll get it. I promise. Just be patient with yourself." Patience isn't my strong suit.

After several attempts, watching him intently, I finally get it right. "Very good," says Derek. "Now try again on your own." I miss a step, mistaking the bird's tail and head for wings. I grumble, rolling my eyes in frustration. Derek generously gives me the hint that sets me back on course and after another few birds I've got the sequence of folds memorized. At least for today.

"Dos más cafés con leche por favor!" pipes Derek to the smiling woman behind the worn wooden countertop. "This calls for celebration. Oh—and a piece of Tarta de Santiago with two forks," he adds, with a twinkle in his eye, gesturing with both hands. She brings us the cake. I take a bite and roll my eyes again, this time in delight.

CHAPTER 26

FATHER

The whole thing felt like fiction. In my hand lay a creased and faded black and white snapshot of a tall man posed stiffly beside a small baby in a carriage. The baby was supposed to be me, and the man my father.

Scant memories of my him were all I had. After my mother remarried, she stopped talking to my dad's relatives, and to this day I don't know why. I wondered if her volatile temper had anything to do with it. When my wife and I started having kids, it dawned on me that they didn't have a paternal grandpa or great-grandparents. And aside from my mother and Jim, there was no family on her side. I goaded her to reveal something—anything—about my relations, but she was tight-lipped. "That's in the past," she said. "We don't talk about it."

"But it's partly *my* past, too. Don't you think I should know?" I replied. She turned and left the room. I never asked again and resigned myself to the complicity of silence.

There was so much I didn't know. Now, with some free time in London, England, after walking in Greece, I couldn't pass up the opportunity to dig at my roots. I looked at the photo again. *Are you really my Dad?* I asked the man in the picture, before tucking it carefully back into my jacket pocket. I put on my backpack and hopped onto the District Line of the Underground. I got off at Kew Gardens, a short walk to my destination.

The Registry of Births and Deaths was a huge room filled with books and papers from floor to ceiling. It smelled musty and slightly perfumed, like an old lady's parlour. The desk clerk required that I fill out a written request, which I did, and then he disappeared off into the stacks. Some time later, he returned with an enormous ledger, which must have weighed 30 pounds. He eased it onto the desk in front of him, and gingerly, even reverently, began turning pages. Then, he stopped, swivelled the massive book toward me, and pointed to my name. Somehow I was shocked to see it in print. A shiver crept up my neck. There I was, Derek Youngs, born in Redcar, Yorkshire, to Frederick William Youngs and Elsie Nimmo Youngs, both also born in Redcar. I nodded politely in confirmation, but inside I was shrieking, *Yes!* My name in black and white made my existence official, and seeing my father's name caused some old, half-buried feeling of uncertainty to settle. But now I had to learn more. I bought a bus ticket to Redcar.

I awoke from half-slumber as the coach navigated a series of roundabouts. Through the streaky window I saw lush green Yorkshire farmland abruptly giving way to row houses, businesses, and shoulder-to-shoulder shops. The bus dropped me off at a corner downtown and I stumbled off with my pack, straining to get my bearings. The hours in transit had left my head fuzzy. Ahead I could spy smokestacks on the horizon, where I realized the steel refinery must be. To my right I glimpsed blue through the cracks between buildings. *That*, I reasoned, *must be the ocean!* In a few short minutes I was at the water's edge with shoes off, waves lapping at my toes and fresh salt air renewing my lungs. I walked barefoot in the sand until I felt completely grounded. *I'm home!* I thought. And then, before too long—*I'm famished!*

Luckily there was a fish and chip shop nearby. The huge battered chunks of cod and golden crispy sticks of potato were greasy, salty and satisfying— food for the soul. It was time to find my dad. *Where do I go now?* I wondered, as I got up and hoisted my backpack on. I left the shop and began walking down the street, imagining my dad doing the very same thing all those decades ago when he lived here. I tried to see traces of him on the pavement, or hear his voice whispering in my ear. And then I did. Or at least I thought so. *The graveyard ....*

Of course! I wasn't absolutely sure that my father was buried at all, or even if Redcar had its own cemetery, but I ran back to the fish and chip shop and burst through the door.

"Is there a cemetery in town?" I blurted to the man behind the counter.

"Yes," he answered, hesitantly, eyebrow raised.

"Great!" I exclaimed. "Is it far?"

"No, it's not, but you'd better telephone first to see if the gates are open." He dialed the number for me and passed me the receiver.

"How may I help you sir?" queried the man at the end of the line.

"Could you look up Frederick William Youngs?"

"Certainly," he replied politely, and the line went quiet. I glanced over at the fish and chip man, who didn't appear too bothered. Minutes later, the man on the phone returned. "I am terribly sorry, sir, but there is no such person listed."

My heart sank. "Are you sure? Is there another cemetery here?"

"No, sir, there is not. And again, there is no Frederick William Young listed."

"But there's an 's'—it's Youngs," I replied emphatically.

"Oh, *Youngs*, you say. Allow me to take another look." Before long he returned to the line. "Please excuse my error, sir; we do have a Frederick Youngs buried here, most certainly."

"Great! I'm on my way over!" I whooped. The fish and chip man looked most amused.

The short walk felt like a lifetime's journey coming to completion. When I arrived, two or three employees greeted me solicitously at door of the cemetery office, as if I were a visiting dignitary. "Does your father have a tombstone?" one of them asked.

"I have no idea," I answered.

Leaning over a huge book together, they found the number of his plot: P5-19. But they could only give me a rough idea of its location. "If there's no proper headstone, you may have great difficulty," said one of the clerks, shaking her head. "It should have a small marker stone, but many of these have eroded over the years or been grown over by vegetation. We'd better come with you to help look."

They conferred energetically amongst themselves for several minutes, their voices rising in volume and pitch. Finally, I interrupted. "Excuse me … excuse me! I think I'll just go find it myself."

"Oh, but sir, truly, you'll find it much too difficult," they said.

We argued back and forth for several minutes in a very polite, very English, tug-of-war. Eventually I put my foot down. "Thank you so much, but I really need to do this alone. If I have too much trouble, I will definitely come back and ask you for help. Thank you!" They nodded cordially and off I went.

After about half an hour of searching the long narrow rows and hunting through the grass, I found enough markers in the vicinity to extrapolate the location of my father's grave. By pacing the ground between other plots, I knew I'd found it, though there was no sign of a marker at all. I touched the earth where my father had been put in the ground, my eyes watering. My body began to vibrate as excitement crept through me.

Who were you, Dad? I wondered. *What did you like to do? And during the war, what was it like for you and the family here? What happened during air raids? How did people cope with such fearful conditions? How could they live normal lives?* I left the cemetery on a mission to get these questions answered, promising my dad I'd be back to visit.

A bed and breakfast down the street offered comfy sleeping quarters, and the next morning I descended on the library. There were enough old clippings, photographs, and microfilm to pore over for several days, and I must have driven the librarians crazy with my demands. One of the few details my mother had divulged was the address of our old house: 68 Sandringham Road. The librarian unearthed some photos taken before anyone lived on that street, and I was surprised to find a big wooden Ferris wheel in the spot where the row houses would be built decades later. The neighbourhood had been a fairground. It was odd to envision that the conditions of strife I arrived into overlaid a ghostly backdrop of whirling carousels, donkey rides, riotous fairground music and laughter.

The photos and documents revealed much about the conditions of life in wartime. Townspeople and dignitaries had been killed by a bomb that had fallen not far from my home. As I skimmed the newspaper clippings, old memories began to surface and come into sharper focus. At one point there had been an influx of POWs—Prisoners of War. First there were Italians, who were allowed to walk around freely. You could recognize them from their brown uniforms, which had some kind of symbol on the back. But then the German POWs came and there was a lot of animosity between the two groups.

My mother had billeted Allied soldiers at our house, and one of them was in charge of picking up POWs and transporting them to work in surrounding farmers' fields. My older brother Howard and I were allowed to ride along in the back of his army lorry, sitting with the German soldiers. They sang unfamiliar songs, but we mouthed the words right along with them. They gave us gifts of handmade wooden toys. I am sure many of them had children at home, whom they missed terribly. We understood, vaguely, that these men were our enemies, but they seemed so kind and friendly to us. It was impossible at that young age to reconcile our emotions with what we were told.

Each evening I'd walk back to the cemetery and sit by my father's grave, talking to him in my head, but he still felt far away. Enclosed by the rock wall of the cemetery, I looked around at all the headstones. *Stone.* Instantly I recalled a time back home on Galiano when Lani had done a "soul reading" where it emerged that the element of *stone* would be a symbolic and energetic connection to my father. At first I'd found this disappointingly mundane. Why just regular old rock and not amethyst or diamond? But then I realized that stone was everywhere; Galiano Island was one big rock itself. I amused myself by talking to boulders, but they never talked back.

Now, in the graveyard, I imagined my father saying, *Other people here have a headstone. So why don't I?*

"No problem Dad, I'll build you one." I said aloud.

The cemetery, though full of stones, did not offer any *available* stones. So the next afternoon I scrounged up an empty potato sack from a grocery store, waited until nightfall, and took it down to the beach. I filled the bag with rocks, slowly hauled it back to the cemetery, climbed over the wall with the load, and dumped it out beside my father's grave. Then I began to build the headstone—a cairn really—fitting each rock carefully against the next, like a mason would, but without mortar. I repeated this night after night, labouring alone in the dark, until the job was finished. *Thank you, son*, I thought I heard him say. I felt his pride in me. And our connection, which had seemed so weak only days ago, was now palpable.

The headstone was complete, but *I* wasn't. There was still Sandringham Road. I wasn't sure what or whom I'd find there, but I had to find out.

The next day I made my way past rows and rows of brick houses, with their tiny yards and washing lines, to number 68. I knocked on the door, noticing my darkened hand. After walking through Greece, my skin was sun-blackened, and I hadn't trimmed my long hair or shaggy beard in ages. My clothes were clean but almost threadbare. I felt a little self-conscious.

A middle-aged woman answered the door. "Sorry to bother you, Ma'am," I said, tentatively, "but I was born in this house—" To my utter surprise, she grabbed my arm and hauled me inside.

"Come in, dear!" she exclaimed, and then turned away to call, "We have a visitor!" A teenage girl bounded down the stairs and was now looking at me intently.

"This is my daughter, Molly," said the woman, "And I'm Patricia."

"Pleased to meet you," I replied, shaking hands with them both.

"Do take off your pack; it must be heavy," said Patricia. I eased it off and propped it against the wall.

"Thank you so much for inviting me in," I said. "I must look so bedraggled. Anyway, I really appreciate this—it's quite a big deal for me."

"Where are you from, then?" Molly asked. "You don't sound British."

"My family left for Canada in the '50s," I said, and shared a bit of my story, and they followed along, eyes wide. I enjoyed telling my well-honed story to an appreciative audience, but what I really wanted was to see more of the house. "I hope I'm not pushing my luck," I said, changing tack, "but is there any way I could go upstairs? To see the bedroom I was born in?"

"Oh, of course," replied Patricia.

"And would you mind if I go up alone?" Neither mother nor daughter batted an eye. I still admire their willingness to let this total stranger—and one who looked as bizarre as I did—wander around their home, unaccompanied.

When I reached the top of the stairs, I turned by instinct and faced the main bedroom. It almost felt too much to absorb, knowing that I'd entered the world in this very spot. But I wandered in, went straight to the window, and was stunned by an almost instantaneous flashback. I saw myself at that same window as a young child. It was the end of the war, VE Day, and the whole town was celebrating. Music filled the air, chairs and long tables lined the street, laden with party food, and balloons and streamers hung everywhere. I could almost hear the din of cheering. My day had been a free-for-all, as the neighbourhood kids ran and chased each other through the street, hiding under tables and stuffing ourselves with cake. I was exhausted by nightfall, so Mam wrangled me into pyjamas and off to bed.

I looked at my weathered features in a mirror on the wall and remembered seeing my mother's face reflected, all those years ago, in her own dresser mirror. I had crawled out of my bed and into her room after she had kissed me goodnight. I watched her posing, preening, taking out her curlers, putting up her hair and then applying a deep shade of lipstick. Then she took an eyebrow pencil and began to draw a line down the back of each leg. During the war, stockings were an unaffordable luxury.

"Why are you getting dressed up?" I asked.

"I'm getting ready to go out, love," she replied.

"But Mam," I whimpered, "I don't want you to go out."

"Darling, you've had your day and now it's time for grown-ups to celebrate. You'll be fine. I'll be right outside and I'll come back to check on you."

Whining, (for what I still like to believe was the first and only time in my life) I implored, "No! Please, Mam, don't go!" My begging eventually wore her down and she promised to stay home. Tucking me into her own bed—every kid's special treat—she sat with me until I fell asleep. But hours later I awoke, and she was gone. Panicked, I called out but there was no reply. I climbed out of bed, peeked through the curtains, and saw her in the street below, dancing—with a man—and smiling in a way I had never seen before. I called to her, "Mam...Mammy!" and still she danced. For the first time in my life, I experienced the terrible sting of betrayal.

Trust and unconditional love had been all I knew until then. Forty-odd years later, as I looked out the window again, I felt the pain and disbelief of that moment, and I reached inside to touch that little boy's broken heart. The ache flared and then subsided. My mother Elsie had been lonely and overworked, and deserved some enjoyment and affection, so I couldn't blame her. But our relationship became strained as I grew up and I found her difficult to get along with. Perhaps we would reconcile eventually, starting with my forgiveness here and now.

I rejoined the home's current residents. "Thank you so much for allowing me that time," I said. "It was very special for me."

"Oh, I'm so glad," said Patricia. "It was no trouble. Would you like to sit down and have some tea now?

"Well, certainly, but I don't want to impose."

"Not at all," she replied. She and Molly fussed about in the kitchen, and then we gathered around the dining room table. They leaned in as I shared my new remembrances. They were eager to hear more, but suddenly something occurred to me.

"How long have you lived here, Patricia?" I asked.

"About 20 years, I'd say."

"Not long enough. Hmm. Then would you know any neighbours who might have lived here during the war?"

"Let me see," said the woman. "Only two, I think, both elderly widows. There's Edna 'round the corner and Mrs. Brunskill two doors down. She's lived there a frightfully long time. Since the houses were built, if I recall."

Then, Mrs B. it is, I said to myself. After expressing my gratitude once more, I said goodbye to Patricia and Molly, and walked two houses down the street. I knocked but nobody answered.

Oh well, I thought, *it's not meant to be.*

I returned to the library to learn more about life during wartime. I also continued to spend time at my dad's grave in the evenings, silently telling him of my loves and losses, hopes and dreams. After these visits, I would roam the quiet streets under moonlight.

I reflected on my own role as a father. I had two beautiful, smart daughters who were growing into responsible independent young women, and I was proud of them. Their upbringing had not been conventional, though. Christine, who was like her mother, craved security and normality as a child. She hadn't wanted purple shag carpeting or a cabin on the beach; she wanted a nice house in the suburbs. When we walked together, she'd always stayed a few steps behind me, as if I embarrassed her. Pauline was more like me, an explorer. Both of them had left home relatively early and had gotten involved in things I believed they were much too young to experience. They coped well, however, and were now enjoying their distance from me. I understood this and trusted that in time it would change.

Was I a good parent? I wondered. I'd wanted my kids to experience freedom, but perhaps I hadn't given them clear boundaries. They had often complained, though, that I was *too* strict. Granted, I had not always been the easiest person to get along with. Although I'd always seen myself as a sensitive and caring guy, I didn't always express my love verbally. Not long ago, Christine had gathered the courage to bring this to my attention. *Why should I have to tell her,* was my thought, *when the fact is so obvious?* But she begged me, explaining how my lack of words had affected our closeness and her trust in me. I was stunned and ashamed. "From now on," I promised her and myself, "I will try to remember to tell you I love you every time we speak." I hoped I had not scarred her as my mother had me.

After a few more days in Redcar, I got ready to leave. On my last evening, I returned to the cemetery and said goodbye to Dad as the sun set. I felt satisfied and complete. As I strolled back to the B&B, it suddenly occurred to me that I hadn't returned to see old Mrs. Brunskill. It was getting dark and I wanted only to retire to my cozy, warm room, but a little voice crept into my head. *Just go,* it whispered. I stood on the street corner, torn between comfort and curiosity. And then, without much decision in the matter, my feet obeyed.

As evening's chill set in, I made my way briskly to Sandringham Road, cursing the little voice. I strode up the dark path to the front door, my hand reaching up to knock before I could think twice. I waited, but no one answered. Listening carefully, I heard muffled conversation from inside. *Oh good, I thought, she's home!* I knocked again, louder, but to no avail. I put my ear to the door. The conversation continued, but it was one-sided. *She must be on the phone,* I thought. *I shouldn't bother her.* Turning to leave, the little voice piped up once more. *Try again,* it said very clearly. So I did.

I went to the side of the house. Standing under a window, I could hear the woman more clearly now. I rapped on the pane, but she didn't come. It was time to give up. Again I headed for the street, but now, almost yelling, the voice said, *Derek, you are NOT finished!* The whole thing was reaching ridiculous proportions. *What more can I do?* I asked the voice. *Go around back,* it said. There was no point arguing.

I walked down the side of the house, unlatched the gate, and entered the moonlit garden. In a picture window stood the woman, silhouetted behind thin curtains. *What now?* I asked the voice. Looking like I did, I was likely to scare the wits out of her if I suddenly popped out of the dark. *What if she has a heart attack?* I thought. *Or calls the police, thinking I'm a Peeping Tom?*

Knock on the window, the voice said. I rapped gently on the glass and stepped back, not wanting to shock the woman. I watched as a short, white-haired old lady drew back the curtains with one hand, and jumped at the sight of me, the phone still in her other hand. "What do you want?" she asked in a measured voice, squinting at me from between the draperies, eyebrows furrowed. I started to explain, but she cut me off. "Can't hear you—come to the front door." She put the phone down and I jogged around to the front door. She opened it a crack and peered out from behind the chain latch, repeating, "What do you want?"

"I'm sorry," I said. "Are you Mrs. Brunskill? I hate to bother you, but your neighbour told me you might be able to give me some information."

"I don't invite strangers into my house and I don't talk to people this late at night," she asserted.

"I'm awfully sorry. You're right, I really should go. I am not here to scare you or hurt you. I just thought that because I was born a few doors down, you might remember my father or someone in my family."

"Well, what was his name, then?"

"Frederick William Youngs."

Her jaw dropped, and her eyes went glassy. "Oh my goodness," she said. Her hands were shaking as she undid the latch. She let me in and rushed back to the phone. "Our Derek is here!" she cried into the mouthpiece. "You'd better come straight away."

Our Derek? I thought, puzzled. Hanging up the phone, she turned to me and said, "Your Aunt Annie is on her way over." Still nothing made sense to me. "I'm your Aunt Mary. Your father's sister," she continued. My chest filled with a swift intake of air.

"What?" I stammered. "I've never had an aunt before and suddenly now I have two?" I exclaimed. Time slowed, as the last year or more unravelled in my memory. My feet had walked me across the United States, Europe, and now to my own family.

We sat staring at each other in disbelief and soon Mary's sister Annie arrived, aflutter. After eyeing me up and down and shaking her head with a laugh, she began doling out kisses on the cheek until my face was raw. Then, out came the tea cakes and on went the kettle. The women told me they'd heard my family had gone to Scotland, with plans to emigrate to South Africa, but that was all they knew beyond rumour and speculation. I told them I'd been equally in the dark about them and that I'd had no explanation about the rift between my mother and my father's family. "All I have is this one photograph," I said, pulling out the photo of the man and the baby carriage.

"Just wait a minute," said Aunt Mary, tottering off to a back room, returning shortly with a big biscuit tin. "I think this is for you." The worn image of Buckingham Palace on its lid showed signs of frequent opening. Inside, amongst yellowed envelopes and ticket stubs were faded photographs of my mother and father dressed in wedding finery, and pictures of my brother and me as babies. As I lifted items out of the tin, my hand suddenly froze. I held an identical photo print to the one from my pocket, of the man and the pram. There was no doubt now it was me and my dad—for real!

I continued sifting through the heap of photos and memorabilia. And then I found something else: a photo of my father with hat and walking cane, rambling over the misty Yorkshire moors. "Walking," said Aunt Mary, "was his most treasured pastime."

It was a long while before I could speak. "It looks like my father and I had something in common."

Annie and Mary chimed in and we continued talking until we could barely keep our heads up. They asked me to stay longer in Redcar. My heart was torn, but I knew that in the morning I'd be leaving. I promised to return one day.

At sunrise, I hoisted on my backpack and headed to the beach. I picked up a smooth white stone, turning it in my palm. Now, my father was walking with me. We continued on our way.

CHAPTER 27

MOTHER

Walking for peace seems like a lofty goal to some, a waste of time to others. My mother was one of the latter. She believed life was tough and you just had to get on with it. She had lived through the war in that no-nonsense kind of way the English did, which is admirable. But this included an aversion to *feeling*. She called me a dreamer, which meant I was self-indulgent and unproductive. In reaction to this, I suppressed the dreamer for many years, nearly forgetting he was there.

Initially, after the trauma of our separation after my birth, my mother lavished me with attention. That changed when my dad died. We could have been a comfort to each other, but instead, our connection became discordant. She became a petty tyrant, picking on me for small infractions, and then acting the martyr for putting up with me and other annoyances. Even after she met my stepdad Jim, who certainly gave her the love and support she'd been missing, she could be cold with me, and even cruel. Was it because I reminded her of my father? And if I did, was it his less admirable qualities, or most, that triggered her? Or both?

I had struggled for years to find peace between us. I'm sure my insistence at speaking the truth hurt sometimes more than helped. My mother, despite being diagnosed as 60 percent deaf, somehow possessed the uncanny ability to hear all the things that didn't fit in with her view of the world.

She ignored what I was passionate about, who I loved, and the milestones I'd reached at work. But I kept sharing who I was with her, hoping that one day she would care, or seem to care.

On the phone one Mothers' Day, she launched right into a tirade after answering the phone. "Why can't you just settle down and be normal?" She went on at length, criticizing my unconventional job and lifestyle, my long hair, my move to the West Coast, and even my divorce from Mary, which struck me as blatantly hypocritical, as she'd disproved of the marriage in the first place. I should have known she'd pick on me as usual, but I'd wanted to wish her a happy day.

So this time, recalling what I'd learned in meditation, I breathed deeply while I listened, proud of myself for not reacting angrily. She went on with her rant. Fifteen minutes later, I interrupted, asserting firmly but gently, "Mam, I'm calling to wish you a happy Mothers' Day and to tell you I love you." She continued on without the slightest acknowledgement and I could feel my body tightening. "Mam," I barked. "Did you hear me?" No response.

She continued her monologue until I finally lost control and screamed, "I'm calling to say I love you, for heaven's sake!" She was silent. "Mam," I choked, throat raw, "are you still there? I love you. Please tell me that you've heard me!"

"Oh," she mumbled. "You said something about loving me." My hands unclenched, my jaw relaxed, my shoulders dropped, and my heart opened.

"Thanks for paying attention," I said, "and I'm sorry for yelling." These struggles in communication created so much more distance between us than our geographical separation.

In 1988, my mother was on her deathbed, so I flew to Ontario. Through the hallways of the Hamilton hospital I padded quietly towards the door of her room. Standing there alone for a minute, I felt the weight of accumulated misunderstandings, disappointments and judgments. I needed to be cautious, or old emotional wounds could be torn open for either one of us. But as I entered the space, I knew something had changed.

I felt no separation. Gone was the petty tyrant who had learned to manipulate through drama. Gone were the resentments and the inadequate words. She was letting go. We sat, hushed, holding each other's hands. "Oh, Derek," she said, after some time. "I am so sorry I haven't been who you wanted me to be. And I am sorry for wanting you to be different. I've always been so hard on you." We both began to cry.

Over the next week, she shared intimate details of her life, stories she'd not even told Jim. I felt my love for her expanding with each story she entrusted to me. She told me about my dad romancing her. But she also revealed to me that she'd caught him kissing another woman when I was little. It's likely that she would have left him, but then he deserted her by dying. Her anger had never dissipated. But now she forgave him, releasing resentment's lifelong grip on her.

One day she asked, knowing I would tell her the truth, "Derek, why is everyone crying when they come to visit me?"

"I guess they're feeling sad because they know that you're dying," I replied.

Her face looked like sun breaking through the clouds. "If they know I am dying, and I know I'm dying, then why isn't anyone talking about it?" How ironic, from the woman who had kept so much from me.

"Mam, sometimes sadness runs so deep that it's hard for words to make it to the surface." She nodded and squeezed my hand.

Later she asked why Jim left the room so often. "He tells me he's going outside to smoke," she said, "but he doesn't smoke that much."

"It's his way of handling the sadness," I answered. I was sure he'd never allowed himself to cry in public.

"You're right Derek, but I don't want him to leave me. I want him by my side," my mother said, her eyes welling with tears. "Can't you tell him to stay?" That evening I tried to talk to Jim, but the pain of losing his wife, his best friend, was too much for him to articulate. I wished I could comfort him, but the gap between us seemed far too wide. He was a man's man and right now he needed to be strong. So every day he'd arrive at the hospital room, fluff up his wife's pillow, straighten the sheets, make her "a nice *cuppa* tea" and go for a smoke, leaving her alone and bereft.

One day I couldn't take it any longer. As I watched their tightly scripted routine, I saw the fear in my stepfather's eyes: the fear of her dying, the fear of her *not* dying but living on in terrible pain. My mother could sense this. All their unacknowledged emotions were building a wall between them.

"I'm just going out for a smoke—back later," said Jim.

My heart cried out for them both. "Please Dad, don't leave," I begged. "Can't you see she needs you? Please, just go and hold her." The words were like magic, for without hesitation he walked over to her bed and threw his arms around her. And for the first time in my life I heard my stepfather cry. The sound of their sobbing and their words of love were too much for me. With tears now streaming down my own face I closed the hospital curtain around the two beautiful lovers and quietly left the room.

CHAPTER 28

SADAKO

One day, after the death of my mother, I was thumbing through a book and came across a true story about a young Japanese girl named Sadako Sasaki. When the atomic bomb was dropped on Hiroshima on August 6, 1945, Sadako was only two years old. About 140,000 people died as a result of that blast, but Sadako survived. At the age of 11, despite being an athlete at school, she showed signs of illness. She was hospitalized, and diagnosed with leukemia—at that time called the "atom bomb disease".

Sadako's hospital roommate shared an old Japanese legend that anyone who folded a thousand origami cranes would be granted a wish. Sadako made her wish—to get well, go home, and run races again. Despite crippling pain, she began making birds out of medicine bottle wrappers and any other paper she could find. Each day found her weaker, but she kept folding cranes. Some versions of the story say she did manage to fold a thousand and some say she didn't. It doesn't matter. She persevered. But she never went home, and died before the year was over.

With a deep sigh, I shook my head, and sat with my fists clenched and glued against my belly. My body began to heave with sobs of despair. *How can we commit such atrocities?* I cried. I had known about Hiroshima and Nagasaki of course, but Sadako's story brought it home. I thought of the mindless destruction that was ravaging the planet, the willful violence, the needless suffering. It was hard to have hope. But I also knew that in all our struggles for a saner world, we were surely doomed without it.

I went on reading. Touched by her courage, school friends of Sadako rallied to raise funds for a memorial to honour her and all the children who died from the effects of the atomic bomb. Students from schools all over Japan and across the world contributed to the construction of a statue of Sadako holding a golden crane. Its inscription reads: "This is our cry, this is our prayer: Peace in the world." People were still folding cranes all over the world and sending them to this monument at the Hiroshima Peace Park. This is how the origami crane became a symbol of peace. This is why the monks were so adamant about me learning to make them. Everything now made sense.

As I watched my hands slowly uncurl, a dream was born. I would fold a thousand cranes, and into each I would infuse my love and belief in humanity. I would share Sadako's story wherever I went. I would walk to Japan and place a bird on Sadako's monument.

Because it wasn't a literal goal but a symbol of my commitment and motivation, I didn't have to run off and buy an airplane ticket. I thought back to my thwarted plan to go to South America. That had been a dead end. But this was open. It wouldn't matter when or how I got there. I knew how crazy it sounded, but I didn't care. I was walking to Japan.

CHAPTER 29

JUST DO IT

CRRRRACK! Thunder filled my ears, so loud it seemed to echo off the distant mountains. In a blinding flash, I collapsed to the ground, hitting my head. I lay there stunned for a minute, then touched my head, feeling for blood. It was dry, to my relief. I opened my eyes and blue sky filled my vision. *Huh?* I thought, fuzzily, *no storm clouds?* I pushed myself into a sitting position and then stood up. *Ouch!* Pain shot through my body. Wincing, I fell back on something hard. I looked around. Firewood was scattered everywhere. Then I realized, what my brain had registered as thunder was the clatter of tumbling logs. *I must have dropped them as I was on my way to the house.* And what I'd imagined as the stun of lightning was my back giving out.

I lay in the pile of rough lumber for another hour, unable to move. When I heard Lani coming up the driveway, I hollered and she came running. Together, we got me up to the house and into bed.

By morning, there was no improvement. I was paralysed. Not from nerve damage, but by fear. Any slight movement sent another spasm shooting through my back. It was very likely a herniated disc. I didn't know which was worse: the pain or the deep humiliation I felt, needing Lani's help to pee into a jug. I tried not to think about the implications of all this on my next walk, a trek across Canada.

It was to be my first solo expedition and my longest walk to date; two months longer than the nine it had taken to cross the U.S. I would fly to Halifax, on the East Coast, and head home. I would return with a new appreciation for my own country.

While walking through Europe, people's eyes had lit up when they heard I was from Canada. There is an image about this country that they needed to believe, perhaps to fuel their own hopes for a better future. Canada, the snow-capped, pristine land of peacemakers. God's country. I had found myself breaking it to them that their fantasy was not completely true.

National pride wasn't something I felt often. Partly this was to do with walking, which made borders seem irrelevant. But also, Canada's self-identity was wishy-washy to begin with. We liked to be thought of as *nice* people and found satisfaction in not being American, but even those points of pride were eroding. Although we put on a good show, we were deforesting our wilderness, polluting rivers, and, like our neighbours to the south, our national budget for social programs was decreasing as military spending was rising. I was ashamed.

Lying in bed, NOT thinking about all this, I realized that if I couldn't leave soon, I'd have to wait until next year to walk. What if my back was permanently injured? Suddenly, the little voice in my head had something to say. This wasn't intuition though; it was a gremlin of doom and gloom, roused from sleep. *Get real, Derek—you're stuck here and you know it*, he whispered snidely in my ear. *You might never walk again!*

Riding out that first week of pain, the gremlin's whispers gave way to catcalls. It seemed he took every opportunity to sabotage me. *Ha ha!* he shrieked. *You're an invalid!*

"Shut up!" I yelled out loud. This was not the kind of little voice I wanted in my head right now. "Where's the nice helpful voice?" I whined. For days I lay in bed, Lani bringing meals to me and attempting to cheer me up. I tried to enjoy myself, pretending I was getting the best room service ever. But every time I moved, my back would cry out in anguish. *You're just a lazy bum!* hissed the voice.

How could I silence this gremlin? It seemed pointless to fight back. *Oh, wait a sec . . .* a thought dawned on me. *Have I been I fighting my back?* This sounds kind of flaky to me now, but at the time it was very clear. I just needed to surrender to the pain, and let go of my anger and disappointment, and even my plan to walk—for now. *Damn*. Did it always have to be about letting go?

How about keeping the dream and letting go of the form? I reminded myself. My helpful little voice had returned! *This means you can still cross Canada. You don't have to know how. Just trust.* Alright then. If I had to hobble across the country on crutches, I would.

Living with near-constant pain was tiring, but it taught me. Not only did I gain more empathy for my clients, but I got to witness how I was reacting and responding under stressful conditions.

Snarling one morning, "I'm fine, I can do it myself!" at Lani when she tried to help me out of bed, I realized I was being a jerk. I hated feeling weak and out of control, and that put me into denial. I didn't want to behave like that. I wanted to accept my limitations, accept help, express gratitude. A step up from denial was *diversion*, which in itself was not bad, but there's a slippery slope from the distraction of TV to losing an entire week to reruns. I had to learn the difference between accepting limitations and dwelling on them. Then I could move forward.

It was a relief when I was able to get to my feet and gradually rebuild my walking muscles. I determinedly scaled the hilly roads of Galiano, working out the kinks in my back and fending off the gremlin, mouthy fiend that he was.

One day on my walk, a smiling pixie of a young woman approached me. "Hi, I'm Teoni," she said, inspecting me with her deep dark eyes. "Don't I recognize you from the newspaper or something?"

"Maybe," I said, shrugging. "I'm the guy who walks for peace."

"Cool! Can I ask you some questions? I do a radio show on the local station."

"Of course," I answered, "as long as you don't mind walking." She joined me, and I told her about my plans and my injury. "If it's meant to be, it will all unfold. As long as I keep moving forward, it will come clear. I trust the process," I said.

"That's great!" she said, and then took off in a hurry, leaving me puzzled.

A couple of days later I was lying on the living room floor, my legs up on a chair, when I heard a knock at the door. I shuffled across the room in my housecoat, as the knocking continued. When I finally opened the door, there was Teoni. "My husband Keith and my two girls and I want to be your support team across Canada," she blurted. "We'll drive, you walk. What do you think?"

Either she's crazy or an angel in disguise, I thought.

I reminded her about my back. "I do think that my situation is temporary, but I don't know for sure," I said. She nodded politely, smiling. I was telling her about all the complications and logistics of a long trip like this, when it dawned on me that she didn't really want to know what I thought. Her mind was made up.

"Derek," she said, "you told me you didn't know about the *how.* This is how!" She chattered on about her husband, a photographer, who could document the whole trip. They could camperize their truck. Keith would drive and she would cook, and they could take turns walking with me and caring for the baby.

Baby? I thought. *Is she nuts? Am I nuts to even consider this?*

Teoni's ideas kept rolling, and I had to admit she had good ones. She barely paused for a breath, though, and soon the conversation was too much to cope with. My back was starting to ache and I suddenly felt exhausted. "I have to lie down now," I broke in.

"OK then, rest up. I'll talk to Keith and let's meet next Friday to brainstorm. See you then!" She was on a mission. I was familiar enough with that kind of fervour to know that it could easily wear off when the stakes got real. I couldn't afford to put any faith into this woman's words just yet. My backup plan, if all else failed, was to spend the rest of my life walking the shopping malls of Canada. Ha ha.

A few days later, I went to visit Teoni and her husband. Keith struck me as solid and reliable. Eight-year-old Desiree engaged with me easily and asked smart questions. The baby, Orielle, was delightful and everyone doted on her. I could see they all loved each other. But how practical were they?

"I really appreciate your willingness and enthusiasm," I said. "It's great. But I'm still in a lot of pain and may not be able to walk very far, even with a support vehicle. I'd love to be able to count on you, but I need you to know that you can't even count on *me* at this point. And then, say we do make it happen; I need you to think about contingency plans, especially since your kids are involved. What about authorization from the school district for Desiree, and accident insurance? And we'll have expenses—gas, camping fees, food. We can't just be free and easy about this. Plans will have to be made."

"Oh, but we have it all planned," she replied. "We've looked into all that, and it won't be an issue. We're even going to sell our furniture to finance some of this."

"We really want to support you, Derek," added Keith. "We'll all be in it together, working for peace."

Maybe this can work after all, I thought. *Maybe they're all angels.* The gremlin of doom went back to sleep for what I hoped would be a good long time. But I noticed a twinge of regret, or perhaps longing, realizing that yet again I would not be walking alone. Maybe this is what the universe was trying to tell me. If I was going to make this journey, I would need all the help I could get.

Lani continued to shower me with unconditional love and encouragement. Her healing energy worked miracles on my back and she generously paid the balance of my airplane ticket to Halifax. I had everything I needed.

In no time, Keith and Teoni had made their arrangements, packed up their worldly possessions, fitted their old truck with sleeping and cooking amenities, and were ready to roll off to Halifax. I was amazed that it happened so quickly and that they were so willing to give up their security to be with *me*. What a gift.

For some time I had continued to shuffle very gingerly around the house, trying not to aggravate my back problem. Maybe because of this, or maybe because the floorboards in our cabin were uneven, or maybe because I was lost in thought, or maybe because of fate, one morning I walked out of the kitchen and stubbed my left big toe something fierce. This caused me to trip, and like some kind of superhero with my arms stretched out before me, I sailed across the living room. It was an incredible three-point landing: first my chin, then my chest followed by sprawling legs. I came to rest in a very undignified heap in the corner, my toe pointing east to my foot's north.

Once again it was Lani to the rescue, and she ran towards me, but stopped short. Looking down, she opened her mouth as if to say, *Oh sweetheart*, but instead a tiny giggle popped out. I frowned in deep disapproval. The giggle became a chuckle. Now I was really upset. This elicited neither sympathy nor an apology but a guffaw, as she doubled over and dropped to the floor on top of me, tears cascading down her face. I'm not sure I ever forgave her.

It's amazing how painful a stubbed toe can be. That night I had a feverish dream, vivid and strange, as if I'd fallen down the rabbit hole in *Alice in Wonderland*. I dreamed I was at a ceremony with dignitaries, and was bestowed with a magic superhero cape that had "Save the World" printed on the back in bright purple letters. Strangers gathered around, fondling my new cape with approval. Then a fierce, beautiful woman flew in, banking her wings to stand before me. I knew I was in the presence of Nike, the Greek goddess of victory. She prophesied journeys through mysterious places—the lands of Procrastination, Bellicose, and Thatcherland—and warned of encounters with the fierce dragon Apathy. And then (I'm sorry—I groaned too when I awoke) this is what she said: "Just do it!"

CHAPTER 30

PURPOSE

Several days later I donned my imaginary cape, boarded a plane and followed my newly lopsided toe east to Halifax. Keith, Teoni, Desiree and Orielle would arrive soon to meet me in their newly camperized truck. I had energy to burn, but my back was still sensitive, so I took gentle strolls around the city, talking to the friendly locals and making some contacts in the peace community. With every new person I met, questions arose. "Are you raising money for something? What's your message?" I didn't know how to answer. I wasn't walking *against* anything—nuclear arms, the government, corporations, pollution, not even against war itself. I wanted to be *for* something. But what? Canada? Spirituality? Just plain old peace? Was that enough? I had no group of 500 to walk with, no protest to join, no monks guiding me this time. What was my purpose? *Our* purpose?

Departure day was May 27, 1988. My daughter was celebrating her birthday back home and it was Teoni's birthday too. How auspicious! We gathered at the Grand Parade in Halifax, a famous military square, which seemed an appropriate place to start a peace walk. Our small but enthusiastic send-off was attended by peace groups, representatives from the mayor's office and children from a local daycare, who sat with me and made peace cranes.

One quiet boy, who was sitting some distance from me, asked very seriously, "How do you make friends?"

"Good question," I said. *How DO you make friends?* I asked myself. I looked at all the kids around me, including Desiree, all so innocent, just being themselves, and then it came clear. "Well," I replied, smiling, "when there is someone I want to get to know, I get closer, like this." I scooted along the bench a little at a time towards the child, closing the gap, but not getting uncomfortably close. The boy grinned, as if he thought I was the silliest thing ever. "If you see a kid you want to make friends with, sit down with them. Ask a question, just like you did with me. Before you know it, you might just have a new friend."

The boy looked right up at me and said, "Mr. Youngs, will you be my friend?'

"Of course!" I answered. He threw his arms around me and hugged with all his might, my face stretching into a huge grin.

From this moment our walk had a focus: children. We called it Peace Wave, and we created signs and banners emblazoned with the words: *What about the children*? That would be our motto. It saddened me to think of all the suffering children in war-ravaged countries, and even in Canada, without safe places to live and play, enough food, clean water, or access to education. We would teach that raising children nonviolently was a foundation for global peace. I would send out a newsletter to friends, explaining our mission.

My daughter Christine was due to give birth any day, so we dedicated the walk to my first grandchild. Two days later, on May 29, Kyle was born. Every step I took would now be taking me closer to him. My heart sang out in happiness and pride.

In the first days, I thought about the kilometres that lay ahead. Although my back was holding out fine, I was relieved to have support crew. Most days I spent six to eight hours on the road, the others driving ahead to alert schools and the local media that I'd be arriving soon. It was also their job to scout for that evening's campsite where they could park and I could pitch my tent. (The vehicle was too cramped for two adults and three children.) If they found nothing suitable, they'd seek accommodation in private homes, schools or churches. Most nights, they would have a hot and hearty meal ready for me when I arrived. I've been rather fond of spaghetti ever since.

Teasingly, I nicknamed them the Royal Family. Eventually, as we got to know one another, "Royal" fell off, leaving them "The Family". Later we were simply all *family*. Their dilapidated truck suffered a broken heater, engine trouble, a cracked windshield and a string of bad luck. There were days, I swear, when I saw more of Keith's backside than his face, when the top half of him disappeared under the vehicle's hood, as he tried valiantly to mend the latest breakdown. They were teachers of tenacity.

Sometimes Keith or Teoni and kids would traipse alongside me, with their snow-white dog, Glacier. Even baby Orielle took her first tottering steps on this journey, becoming our youngest peace walker. One day, as I was walking with Teoni and telling stories, I came to the one about working at the steel mill, where I'd decided to add the initial "W" to my name. "I'm gonna call you Derek *Walker* Youngs now!" she exclaimed. The name stuck.

Along the way we were joined by folks from near and far, for hours or days or longer. Matthias, whom I'd met in the Fulda Gap, came to join us for a while. Of course, more people meant more negotiating everyone's needs and wants. We drove each other crazy at times, but I'd ensure we always come together in a circle to talk things out, for if we couldn't do that, we'd be hypocrites. Every day was an opportunity to live our beliefs and learn how to be with each other.

Just as on the Great Peace March, it was necessary to reach out for media attention and financial support, but this wasn't always easy. I loved talking to school groups, but it was different with reporters. I wasn't comfortable talking about myself, and it felt like after a while I was reciting the same old spiel. Teoni, was a natural, though. She landed us print coverage locally along the route and nationally, and interviews on some major radio and TV shows like CBC's *Tapestry, Morningside* and the noon news with Peter Mansbridge. Among other things, Keith wrote articles, canvassed for supporters, and documented our journey with photographs. Renowned Canadian photographer Freeman Patterson donated $600 worth of film to Keith and hosted us for a night, despite just having returned from Africa the night before.

The Family was unflagging in their support, if not always punctual. On several occasions I waited for hours, tired and hungry, for our evening rendezvous. There were no cell phones back then. I would pace back and forth, wondering where the heck they'd disappeared to, my patience wearing thin. I wasn't sure whether to worry that they'd had a breakdown or be angry that they'd forgotten me. Finally, ready to give up and sleep in a ditch, I'd hear the rattling muffler and around the corner rolled the tumble-down truck, arms waving furiously out every window. Peering through the cracked windshield were four grinning Cheshire Cat faces. Fortunately, their enthusiasm overshadowed their tardiness. Keith, camera in hand, would hop out exclaiming, "The light, the light—look, it's perfect!" Indeed, the sky was now a splash of brilliant magenta. How could I complain about that kind of passion?

Some days were lonely. A solitary figure dotting the landscape, I felt exposed, both physically and emotionally. Walking revealed a lot to me about my own mental processes, my assumptions and fears. I got to hone my intuition, that helpful little voice in my head, but the gremlin also made a few cameo appearances. One day while walking along the highway, it hit me how vast and unpopulated Canada was. The scenery was truly awe-inspiring. But after a while it was just tree after tree, hill after hill, lake after lake. I'd never have imagined getting so blasé about nature, or so lonely either. I longed for something interesting around the next corner. One day, in the grip of tedium I spied another lone figure, on the distant horizon. At first I thought, *Oh great—someone to talk to!* As I got a little closer, though, my enthusiasm waned, when I began to wonder what the hell someone would be doing out there all alone. I didn't clue in to what an equally unusual sight I must have been to the stranger.

I could tell the shape was a man. He stood still, which struck me as peculiar. Maybe he's waiting for a bus, I proposed, soon realizing how irrational that was considering the remoteness. Frightening thoughts filled my mind. *Oh God, is he a serial killer? No way to get help. No witnesses....* Each step got slower. I dreaded getting closer, but what choice did I have?

Then I noticed the backpack slung on his shoulder, the tan, the beard, and travel-worn expression. It was like looking in a mirror. As I reached his side, I smiled and nodded. He smiled and nodded. Then, I swear, we said in unison, "What the hell are you doing out here in the middle of nowhere?" Laughing, we sat down at the side of the road, letting our stories unravel.

Buddy was hitchhiking to Edmonton to visit his sister. He looked down on his luck, and I guessed he was coping with alcoholism. He shared some sad tales of relationships gone bad, jobs lost, and even time served at the

Kingston Penitentiary. I knew how to talk to ex-cons certainly, but I didn't want to know about his criminal record, as that serial killer image still lurked in the back of my mind. He went on though, desperate to talk to this captive audience. His story was tragic, with one wrong turn after another, but he was looking on the bright side. He was sincerely willing to make changes in his life.

Then it was my turn and when I finished my story, Buddy exclaimed, "Get outta here, you're pulling my leg! All the way across the country? That's so cool. And for peace? Right on!" He must have quizzed me for a good half hour; it was as if he'd met an alien and wanted to know all about life on Mars. Soon, I heard the familiar roar of an oncoming semi and I turned to face it. The driver was slowing down so I stuck out my thumb for once instead of two fingers in a "V".

The semi stopped for us, and my new friend picked up his backpack. "Are you coming?" he asked. I reminded him I was relying on my feet. He laughed, shaking his head, and then dug down into his dirty blue jeans to pull out a fistful of change. "It's all I have, but it's yours."

"Thanks, friend, but you'd better keep those coins. You've got a long haul ahead of you," I said.

"No way, man," he replied. "I need to do something for peace too. Take it, brother, please."

I couldn't insult him, so I held out my hand and his offerings—including a sticky fuzz-coated piece of candy.—tumbled into my palm. I grimaced at the sight of the gooey gumball. "The money's for peace, but the candy's for being so sweet to listen to my gripes," he said with a laugh. He gave me the peace sign and climbed into the cab of the truck. I watched the semi roll away into the distance. Alone again, I walked on, grinning. You never know who you're going to meet on the road.

Every day on the road revealed something beautiful—sailboats bobbing like white corks on a lake; Aurora Borealis dancing across a midnight sky. I relished moments of solitude when I could just *be*. Of course it was a dance, negotiating space with the others, even out on the long ribbon of highway. Some days I tired of making conversation, of having anyone at all in my physical space. So I'd tell the others I needed to walk in silence that day. I loved the rhythm of my body as I moved through my surroundings, melting with the trees, the sky, the ground beneath my feet, existing purely in the moment. Exhilarating! Without anyone or anything grabbing my attention my mind could rest, and suddenly, insights would spring out of nowhere. I felt so free and so connected to everything. I could sense the wholeness of my body and all its interconnected parts—legs, arms, lungs, heart, brain—working together. Walking had never felt like such a physical affirmation of the wonder of life.

And then, I'd see a beer bottle on the roadside. Or once—an illegal trash dump in the woods, spilling out onto the asphalt. The stench pierced my nostrils. And that was not the least of it. Every part of the country had its share of environmental damage, much of it caused by industries like mining and forestry. In our eagerness for short-term gain, humankind has taken indiscriminately from our planet, wreaking destruction as we go.

It was impossible to turn a blind eye, and I fought to keep a positive outlook at times. Walking alone when I had the chance, was a perfect opportunity to vent my anger about the state of the world. I could yell and stamp my feet without directing my fury at anyone. Eventually, this volatile energy transformed into resolve and hope.

After some time, the emotional pendulum swing began to wear me down. But with every step I took and every extreme I witnessed, a realization began to unfold inside me. Welcome to *life*! It was all about duality, as the Buddhists call it. Of course with every sunny day, showers were bound to fall somewhere down the road. And in contrast to the generosity and welcome we encountered, there were people who turned us away. But amidst the extremes, I could try to be centred. This is what meditation was all about: all the breathing, all the sitting I had done with the monks. This is what I practised for. It was only my attachment to the "positive" aspects of life and my aversion to the "negative" that caused me so much grief. When I let go the stark contrasts blurred.

We all had our difficult moments but learned to take them in stride. In one town, I was refused permission to speak to school kids. "I'm sorry, but I can't allow you to indoctrinate them with your message," said the school official. The next day the local newspaper published a story about an open house at the town's military base. There were photos of children crawling around tanks with blackened faces, holding guns. *Why are we so willing to teach about war, yet so afraid to talk about peace?* I despaired. But Keith and Teoni's energy and idealism, and their children's innocence, kept us moving ahead. In no time we were channelling our anger and sadness into action. Determined not to be consumed by negativity, we responded by planting trees, working in soup kitchens, writing letters, making peace cranes, and picking up trash. We also staged 24-hour vigils in front of factories and corporation headquarters, imploring CEOs to see how their policies were affecting not only our children but theirs. I fasted during UN Disarmament week in October. Somehow it renewed my commitment and lightened my psychological load.

Teoni and Keith's efforts at publicity were paying off. One day, a motorist stopped by the side of the road and got out to talk to me. She had seen us on television and wondered if I could come talk to her class. "I'd love to," I answered. I was always prepared to tell the Sadako story. I also had a slide show, a short theatre piece that the kids could perform and a list of contacts at a school in Russia so the children could have pen pals.

I arrived first thing the next morning, and found my way to the Grade 3 classroom. After discreetly spitting on my hands and smoothing my hair down, I peeked in through the glass window in the door, watching the young teacher in admiration. I knocked quietly and she welcomed me in, smiling.

"Class," she said. "We have a special guest, Mr. Youngs. He is walking across Canada." I was stunned by the hush that had enveloped the room, and I took a moment to scan the small fresh faces. A feeling of warmth crept into my chest as 25 wide-eyed dumbfounded kids looked up at me as if I were ten feet tall.

I explained to them in relative terms how far *across Canada* was, like how many years it would take of walking to school to equal how far I'd be travelling on foot. What was more important to me impressing them with my feat (or feet) was to show them what I was seeing along the way. I had prepared a slide show with many of Keith's photos. It began with a picture of a Great Horned Owl which brought forth some very gratifying *ooohs*. Following that was a photo of a huge moose, and now they sat upright at their desks, eyes glued to the screen. Then I showed a slide of myself, walking alone, dwarfed by cornfields.

Immediately a little boy shot his hand up, waving frantically, as if to stop a bus. He was one of those bright, earnest kids who sits in the front row. "What's your name?" I asked.

"Aaron," he said.

"OK, Aaron, what would you like to know?"

Without hesitation, looking me squarely in the eye, he asked, "Don't you feel a little stupid walking by yourself?"

The question caught me a little off-guard. A couple of kids gasped, hastily covering their mouths, and others at the back giggled, eyeing each other. I smiled and turned to look at the teacher who was now gazing at the ceiling. I guessed she knew Aaron very well. Was I angry or disappointed? Not at all. Adults wonder the very same thing, but having learned about manners, they don't dare ask. Aaron spoke his truth.

Questions reveal much about the inquirer, so I now knew something about Aaron's own self-worth. "Thanks, Aaron." I said, smiling. "What a great question! YES, there are times when I feel stupid! It's not easy to be alone, especially if you're doing something unusual. But I really I believe that what I'm doing is important, and I try not to care what other people think of me. So, if you have strong feelings about something, it's good to pay attention to that feeling. If you want to do something different from everyone else, that's really OK. If you want to say something and nobody else is talking, it's OK to speak up. You might find out that the other kids think you're really interesting!"

I stood for a moment in silence, watching the children's mental cogs turning. There was a tangible shift in their energy. And then suddenly, a dozen hands raised around the room. Aaron had freed the others to ask what was on their minds. "Where do you go to the bathroom?" asked one kid. *A very sensible question*, I thought. It enabled me to talk about recycled paper and composting!

Towards the end of the show, after a few carefully chosen slides depicting scenes from underdeveloped countries, I asked the children what they thought peace was. Hands waved wildly and one by one they shared their thoughts.

"Peace is at night when I look at the stars."

"Peace is when all the guns in the world are melted."

"Peace is safety, like playing outside and not being scared."

"Peace is sharing, like if my big sister doesn't take my toys."

The kids had natural curiosity and compassion that was just waiting to be channelled into action. Falling asleep that night, thinking over those answers, I added one of my own, "Peace is walking with others, when you really wanted to walk alone, and finding a way to truly enjoy it."

CHAPTER 31

GOD

Children continued to be a focus for us on this journey, though not the only focus. I was surprised when God stepped into the limelight. When the subject of peace came up, people often asked if I believed in God. I didn't trust the question. What they really wanted to know, it seemed, was if I believed as they did. Why did so many people think there was only one way—their way? I didn't believe there was one way to peace or one way to understand God. There are as many paths as individuals on Earth, because although we're made of the same ingredients, we're all put together in slightly different ways.

Although I used the word "God" sometimes, I'd never believed in the guy in the sky, the deity who pulls all the strings up there in the clouds. (If you are there, God, and you are more than a bearded projection of our greatest fears and hopes, it's me Derek, and I apologize for not believing in you!)

I had been baptized in the Church of England as a child, but growing up, the only clear religious message I got was that Catholics were bad. We were Protestant, but I didn't even know what that meant. We didn't go to church and we didn't pray. Now, as an adult, I did practise something like praying to connect me with a bigger, intelligent, beautiful *something*, of which I was just a small part. To me, this mysterious something, the universe, and God were one in the same.

At some point I learned the word *agnostic*, which means "not knowing". Despite disliking labels, I did relate to this word. One of my religious friends made it clear that he thought agnosticism was a weakness. To me, *not knowing* felt honest. How can anyone truly know what or who is out there?

I could see that organized religion was a way for people to find meaning in life, but what religions called guidance looked more like control to me. I found it ironic, then, that many of the people I stayed with across Canada were religious. But it also made for juicy conversation.

My younger brother Jim had become a member of the Bahá'í faith, and he arranged a number of contacts for me across the country. I also stayed with Quakers, Unitarians, Jews, and just about every other faith group you can imagine. In the evenings, peppered with questions about walking, I would sing for my supper with stories from the road. Sometimes my hosts would veer off toward small talk, so I would steer the conversation back to *big talk*, asking, "Do you think there will be a future for your children?"

I listened quietly as folks quoted from their literature—the Bible, the Koran, the Torah, the Bhagavad Gita, and so on. I always found a grain of something universal that I could stand behind. "Love thy neighbour"—how can you dispute that? But then they'd veer off, getting bogged down in scripture, away from anything that felt *real* to me.

"Please," I begged, "don't answer as a priest or rabbi. Speak as a parent, a woman, a man! Do you feel any hope for our world?"

"It's all in God's hands," was a frequent and predictable response.

"I think I understand what you're getting at," I answered, "Ultimate control of life is out of our hands. We are small in comparison to the rest of Creation. But perhaps we humans actually embody the very hands of God ourselves. And maybe it's our responsibility to do God's work on Earth and care for each other and the planet by using our gifts of compassion and reason."

Most people agreed on some level that we had work to do. But what the work consisted of was debatable. Doing things in the name of God had gotten us into trouble throughout history.

I often turned to churches for a place to sleep when there was no convenient place to camp. It was rare to be refused, although I did begin to notice a pattern. The bigger the church, the further back into its dark, dusty recesses I was dispatched to lay out my sleeping bag. When I did bump into people back in those lonely corners, they seemed so busy scurrying about doing important work that they didn't have time to talk.

Many mornings I woke up staring up at a cross, Jesus looking down at me where I lay in my sleeping bag on the floor. *What would you say about what we're doing to each other and the planet?* I wondered. I believe if he could see us, he'd shake his head in disbelief. After 2,000 years we are still acting out of greed, jealousy and hatred, and hurting each other in the name of religion. Jesus counselled us to love our neighbours. But how could we do this when most of us didn't even know our neighbours—or worse—were bombing them?

I also stayed with a scientist on my travels. I admire their curiosity and commitment to truth, and I respect that they don't presume to have all the answers. But Dr S. wasn't quite like this. His views were as dogmatic as those of some of the religious people I'd met.

I had told Dr. S. that I wanted to meet people of different faiths across the country. "The idea of a God is nonsense," he scoffed. "Anyone with a brain can see from empirical evidence that humans are driven by biology. God is a myth we've created to assuage our fear of death. In the end, Science can explain everything." He went on for a while in that vein, supporting his argument with facts and statistics.

"Sure," I countered, after pondering his words carefully. "I get that humans tend to project our fears and hopes onto larger-than-life figures. I understand about genes and survival of the fittest. But you can't reduce me to my brain, my blood, and this physical container. How do you know there is no God, when perhaps at this point he or she or it exists far beyond our powers of recognition and measurement?" I enjoyed playing devil's advocate.

Eyebrows raised, the man was about to launch a counterargument, but I wasn't finished. "Don't you think it's a little egocentric to think that there isn't some other form of intelligence out there? The world was proved not to be flat. So I also think there is more beyond the human horizon. More to 'I' than meets the eye. In fact, I am part of you." He rolled his eyes, but I continued on. "As much as I am a speck in this universe, I am also part of the whole. Aren't we all connected on the most infinitely small level, to everything and everyone? It's like in the *butterfly effect*, when an insect flaps its wings and sets off a chain reaction of tiny events that eventually results in a tornado, or—causes someone to smile! I think this is called quantum physics."

Dr. S. nodded thoughtfully and smiled. I grinned back, knowing I'd probably gone too far. What did I know about physics? Wisely, Dr. S. knew we were on the brink of what could have been a long drawn-out discussion, and he switched topics. I hadn't set out to change his mind, but I was glad we'd shared our thoughts. And I was happy to dig into a hearty dinner before I fell into a deep slumber.

In Quebec, we stayed overnight at a huge Catholic monastery. The monks fed us well, and it was good for us all to have somewhere warm, dry and safe to sleep. The next day, one of the brothers, a dear old fellow, took us through their exquisite gardens, quoting, in soft lilting French, St. Francis of Assisi's words about peace. Then, eager for us to come into the huge church, he beckoned us inside. My grasp of the language was not very good, but Keith and Teoni explained that the monks were going to dedicate the mass to me. *Holy smokes*, I thought, *do I really deserve all this?*

We entered the sacred space and sat in the pews, enraptured by the music. Many of the songs were in Latin, and somehow the words conveyed a sense of history, reverence, and mystery, as did the rituals that followed, full of special objects and gestures. Then, the priest began to speak in French. I caught a few words, but most of it went over my head. I felt a little like the dog in Gary Larson's *Far Side* comic strip, listening to its owner. "Blah, blah, Derek Youngs," said the priest. "Blah, blah ... Jesus ... prophet ... Derek Youngs....." I blushed visibly as the priest went on, and now my head was beginning to swell. I sat basking in my ego's glow, as the priest finished his sermon and went on to the next item in the service.

At the end of the mass the priest turned towards us once more. When I heard the words "Derek Youngs, *marcheur de la paix*," he nodded our way, so instinctively I started to rise from my seat. Instead of motioning towards me though, the monk indicated that Keith should stand up. My big head suddenly deflated and I had to laugh. Who had the priest thought *I* was, then? I guess he preferred the young relatively clean-cut father of two as his hero. We didn't correct him, as they'd all been so generous and kind, and had spoken so well of me. Or Keith. Either way, we were honoured.

This was one great lesson in walking that fine line of the ego. It is important to be able to receive praise and own the positive attributes and accomplishments that others notice. However, it's also important to listen to criticism and reflect on what we might change to better ourselves. It's also good not to take either too much to heart. One's sense of confidence must be fuelled from within. At the next Catholic church we went to, they literally closed the door in my face. This was unfortunate, but I didn't feel sorry for us; I felt sorry for them, that they were too ruled by fear to connect with us.

By Thanksgiving, Peace Wave was rolling through northern Ontario. We turned our back on a blaze of golden maple leaves and faced dropping temperatures. By Hallowe'en, the weather turned frigid and blustery, and icicles began to form inside the vehicle. Desiree went out trick-or-treating in the snow that night in a small town. As the walk continued through the cold weather, I grew skinnier, and I no longer looked at my reflection in mirrors or shop windows. Keith and Teoni were running low on supplies. I was always prepared to fast if I had to, but what about the kids?

The family was still comfortable sleeping in the camper most nights, but it was too cold for me to pitch my tent outside, so I'd resort to my standby: churches. Penniless, tired, cold and hungry one late afternoon, I knocked on the door of a United Church in Kenora and was surprised to find someone there at that late hour. It was the minister, no less. His big smile and even bigger heart put me at ease.

"Call me Bob," he said. I shared my story, and explained that there was a very cold and hungry family somewhere down the road behind me. "Come for dinner with my wife Marlene and our kids. We have a spare bedroom so if you'd like, you can stay with us. There's not quite enough room in the house for all of you, so if it's OK, your friends can stay in the church hall." Wow. Warm sleeping quarters and hot food for us all? This was a no-brainer.

Around the dinner table that evening we spent hours in lively conversation. Keith's father was an Anglican priest, so he and Bob had lots to talk about. The following day, the minister and his wife extended their invitation another night. The warmth of this family and their cozy home was hard to resist, so of course we stayed. After three days, though, we all seemed to be skirting a certain question. When would we be leaving? We hadn't told them what dire straits we were in, but perhaps they could see it.

"I've been thinking, Derek," said Minister Bob. "Would you like to deliver our Sunday morning sermon?" Immediately I jumped at the chance, knowing it would afford me a few more days of comfort. And maybe during that time we'd be blessed with a miracle and could afford to continue on.

Bob showed me around the church. It was an old, traditional building, complete with an ornate wooden spiral staircase up to the pulpit. "This is where you'll be on Sunday morning. After the gospel reading, you'll hear the anthem begin, and then you can go upstairs." A knot began to form in my stomach and I suddenly felt very unqualified for the task that lay ahead. I'd given talks and speeches before but never anything so formal, so laden with ritual.

Next, the minister took me to the vestry and opened a closet to reveal an array of long, billowy robes. "Go ahead and choose your favourite colour for Sunday!" he effused. I balked, knowing I'd be overwhelmed just standing way up on that pulpit. The added pressure of a special outfit felt like too much to handle.

"Don't see anything you like? How about this one in navy? It'll look great on you!" The idea didn't *feel* great, though. I'd be an impostor, a hypocrite even. "Or this one in maroon. It's more your style."

"Bob." I interjected. "I'm sorry, but it's enough of a stretch to give the sermon. I just can't do the robes."

"I understand," he replied, but I saw a tinge of disappointment on his face.

Sunday morning, despite my nerves, I found myself up on the pulpit, looking down at a sea of faces. What a feeling of power! I did my thing and talked about walking in trust and faith, confronting my dark side, and getting closer to what I feared. "We must not act out of hate but love for our planet, our children and grandchildren," I said. "The old days of good versus evil, good guys versus bad guys, have come to an end...."

I finished, feeling triumphant and hoping I had inspired the masses. I waited for my usual applause. None came. The huge space was dead quiet. I pulled out another surefire story and continued on. "If we are to have change, it must come from a deep place within...."

Again, no response. I wasn't sure what to do. But then it dawned on me that people don't clap in church. Not sure how to make my exit, I bowed awkwardly, meekly descended the stairs and took a seat with the parishioners. At that point, the minister got up and told everyone that the church was taking up a special collection for Peace Wave. After the service, I was handed a basket with about $200 in donations. This was the miracle I'd been hoping for! We continued on the road, waving goodbye to Bob and his family, feeling incredibly blessed.

I was glad to have risen to the challenge of speaking in church. Getting closer, as always, opened up my fears and judgments for healing. I had now met people of all religious stripes who were devoted to social justice, caring for the poor, and peace, and I could not fault them for the faiths they chose. I didn't think it was their religion that made them good people, though. I saw that religion could be a powerful channel for our innate human qualities of compassion and caring, simple virtues that got corrupted and lost in the trappings of dogma. It was clear to me that religion alone wouldn't bring peace. But nor would science or politics. We wouldn't have peace unless we felt our connection with one another and with this planet. That's what God came down to for me.

CHAPTER 32

RELEASE

Back into the snow we went. It had been falling for days, piling up in great drifts by the roadside. I trudged on, hoping to avoid the logging trucks that rumbled by, stirring up swirling blizzards in their wake. There were no towns along this part of the highway, no campgrounds and not a soul to be seen. One afternoon, I hadn't realized it, but the camper had fallen behind me by 30 kilometres or so. Keith, as he told me later, had noticed something along the roadside and, once again, was on a mission to get the perfect shot: a lone wolf against a backdrop of snow-laden aspen trees. They'd watched it join its pack, which they followed at a distance, as the sleek creatures wove in and out of the brush. Then at one point, Teoni said, "Shouldn't we warn Derek?"

They caught up to me in a hurry, without Keith's perfect shot. I gave him heck for lagging behind and thankfully the wolves—"Wolves?" I gasped—were nowhere to be seen. The sun set early those days, so by 4:00 in the afternoon we had pulled off the snowy road into a narrow driveway for the night. After dinner, I helped Desiree with her homework, and then there wasn't much to do but retire to bed early. Keith invited me to bunk up inside the camper instead of pitching my tent in the snow. It was a tight squeeze, but I was grateful for the warmth.

The next morning before breakfast, I went out to pee in the bushes. Surrounding the vehicle was a ring of huge paw prints, several sets of them. It looked like they had been circling the camper for hours. Keith joked about what a tasty little morsel the baby could have been, in her bundle of white snowsuit just like puff pastry.

On December 5, we arrived in the geographic centre of Canada just east of Winnipeg. The temperature was -15°C. That day local high school students walked with us and we were greeted at the legislative buildings by peace activists. Our arrival was telecast nationally, and we spent the next week giving talks and raising funds, as our finances were once again being stretched. The family was without decent winter clothing, and with a baby in tow, it was neither practical nor safe for them to be living in that truck. Their unreliable propane stove was the only source of heat. I was seriously concerned about their well-being, and after many painful discussions, I insisted that they return home. They reluctantly agreed. I bade them farewell, promising to see them again in the spring.

Alone on the side of that snowy highway, lumbering along in my parka and pack, I was a curious sight. Due to the media coverage, I got many a friendly wave and motorists honked their horns as they zoomed past. But sometimes when I'd stop in at a local store for supplies, the shopkeeper wouldn't know who I was. Of course I'd always mention that I was walking across Canada, and on a few occasions not a hint of surprise would register on the clerk's face. I had to just shake my head and laugh. Some people really don't listen.

The air was so cold now that the sun looked like the moon hanging in the frigid sky. I walked under branches sparkling with crystalline ice. The beauty was otherworldly. But each morning as I set out into the air, I felt like I was stepping into an industrial deep freezer. *Shouldn't my "burning" desire to keep walking be enough to keep me warm?* I thought, but the joke was scant comfort as I plodded the snowy miles, toes and fingers numb. I pictured myself as a statue, frozen solid in mid-gait by the side of the road, snow piled up around me, my two frosty fingers reaching up in an icy white "V" for peace.

All too possible. The truth was, I could not keep walking without another support vehicle. I sent out letters and even put ads in the paper, hoping someone would step up to help, but—surprise, surprise—nobody signed up to drive halfway across the country in the bleak midwinter. I was conflicted about what to do next.

I was willing to be cold and to go without comforts, but if crossing Canada was something I wanted to live for, not die for, I was going to have to adjust. My intuition, and Lani's insistence, led me home, though my pride was bruised.

Back in my nice warm cabin, I snuggled up with Lani. Feeling so comfortable at first seemed a betrayal to the walk, and to my dream, but I counted my blessings after tuning into the cross-country weather forecast. On the prairies, temperatures had dropped to to -30°C, and here I was, with my sweetheart, surrounded by evergreen trees and the ever-blue sea.

When Lani returned to Hawaii for further Reiki training, I made my first serious attempt at writing a book, inspired by meeting my grandson Kyle for the first time. I remember the day, January 15, and I believe it was instant love for us both, as we performed a jolly little dance together at the Vancouver train station. I imagined that some day he would read about my adventures.

Before too long, pink blossoms scented the air and I knew it was time to pick up the thread of my walk across Canada. I was reluctant, knowing spring thaw was only just starting in Winnipeg and that I'd be walking without support until I rendezvoused with the family at some point. Why was I doing this again? If my mind couldn't remember, my body did. Once I got moving, it was hard to stop. There is an addictive quality to walking. Perhaps it's the endorphins, or the thrill of discovering the landscape every day. Or maybe it's something I can't name.

Across the prairies, the driving wind was so forceful at times that I made no headway. If I let go into the bullying gale as it shoved and prodded, I would topple backwards. Collapsed on the ground I'd find a few minutes' relief. But instantly I could find myself in a dust storm, blinded and choking, as the dust whipped across my face.

What left me truly breathless though was the visual splendour of those wide open spaces. The clouds over the prairie are like none you'll see elsewhere. And I will never forget the moment when I glimpsed the first sure sign of spring: a single crocus lifting its head to the sun.

I was encouraged by other signs of life too. Meadowlarks sang out to me in sweet varied tones and prairie dogs sat high on their back legs to watch me pass by. I witnessed a calf's birth. I saw foxes and antelopes, and heard the haunting cry of the coyote. I watched in disbelief as a mother Great Horned Owl tossed her enormous puff-ball babies out of their nest.

One day, I saw another welcome sight—the family! They'd simply driven along the Trans Canada Highway, this time in a Volkswagen van, keeping their eyes peeled for a guy leaning into the wind. Matthias also rejoined us, so after the joy of walking alone, I now had the pleasure of company.

Spurred on by the change in season and the knowledge that the Pacific Ocean was within reach, we were now hitting our stride. After a seemingly interminable march across the flat plains, we spied the distant Rocky Mountains, jagged and still dusted with snow. I felt a jolt of anticipation as we entered my home province of British Columbia. Up we trekked, and down. The memories of snow and wind dissolved in the thick heat. I can still smell the incense of crushed dry pine needles beneath my feet, as I stole bits of shade under gnarled trees in the Slocan Valley.

We were in the homestretch but not flagging. Sometimes Matthias and I, after six or eight hours on the road, would set up our tent in the evening and then he'd look at me and say, "Wanna walk into town?" We couldn't stop.

But we would have to. Soon Peace Wave would come to an end. As we neared the finish, I took time to reflect on the longest walk of my life. Behind me lay over 6,000 kilometres and several pairs of worn-out shoes. The numbers were impressive, for sure, but for me, but was the least of it. More importantly, I had confronted pain and doubt, and I'd seen beauty in the smallest things. I'd *connected*. The openness, warmth and hospitality of folks across the country was unforgettable. We had lost count of all the selfless acts of generosity we'd encountered. People had fed us and housed us, and even lent us their credit cards to buy gas. But they all told us they'd received just as much as they'd given. I couldn't imagine how that could be true, but I had to believe it.

And—what about the children? At the beginning of our journey, children had so aptly reminded us about reaching out to make friends. And we did this all across the country. After the walk was over, I received hundreds of thank-you letters and drawings from all the kids we'd met, in all the different provinces. A couple of them are in touch with me to this day. They now have their own children, who are learning about peace from their parents, learning to appreciate the beauty and sacredness of the Earth, and seeing their own potential to make peace.

My grandson, Kyle, was there on the beach in Vancouver to greet me, as the sea rushed up to meet us all. How elated I was to see him and the rest of my very own family. At our backs stood the glassy high-rises of the West End, the mountains of the North Shore jutting up behind the towers. I was full of joy, but as with all my journeys, there was a bittersweet quality to it.

First, it was hard to say goodbye to everyone after all that time together. And next, there was always the question, *what now?* I fell into the trap of looking too far ahead, wondering where my path would take me. Really, I just needed to be where I was and savour being home. And then, part of me—my ego—was let down. I wanted *more*. I wanted fanfare, I wanted proof, direct feedback that we had made a difference in the world. I wanted to see a direct, clear connect-the-dots line between action and outcome. *Thousands of kilometres,* said a little whispering voice, *and what have you actually accomplished?*

Damn, I thought, *the gremlin is back. Why now?* How, after all this time, with all my family and friends beside me, could I even entertain such negativity? *God knows,* I thought. "Oh, right," I said aloud, reflecting on my own inner dialogue. "God." God had shown up months ago as the true nature of the journey, revealed in the faces of children, in animals, in the northern lights. And if everything was a part of God, so was even the gremlin, the nasty embodiment of my fear. If I could love him as I loved the beauty, I would disempower him. And with that realization, he shrivelled up and disappeared. I felt released.

On that last evening, August 6, 1989, the 44th anniversary of the bombing of Hiroshima, we gathered at the water's edge to make peace cranes. Later, I picked up my drum, and soon, chanting voices joined the drumbeats. I thought of the Japanese monks, whom I knew would be also drumming and chanting this day for peace. I thanked all the people around the world and throughout history, both religious and nonreligious people, who have kept peace alive in prayer and in practice.

Then, at sunset we released hundreds of Japanese paper lanterns out into English Bay, representing the spirits of those who had died when the bombs fell. As the sky grew darker and the lanterns floated away, their flickering lights seemed to extend across the ocean until I could no longer tell where the river of drifting lanterns ended and the river of stars began.

CHAPTER 33

SAINT

Through all my months and years of walking, I had never given up massage therapy. This was partly because it helped fund my journeys, but I also had a deep connection to my clients. It wasn't just a job, it was part of me. But in 1990 I decided to sell the business. I could still work when I needed to, but on a smaller scale, subletting other therapist's clinics for short periods. I chuckled at the thought I could still be a healer when I walked, massaging the Earth, performing global acupressure with each step.

I was back on the road to Japan now, and my first stop was London. As part of a worldwide project, the Nipponzan-Myōhōji monks had built a peace pagoda in Battersea Park—right in the middle of the city.[4] Nagase, one of the monks I had met in Greece, had done much of the construction and was still there, caring for the pagoda and living in a tiny cottage nearby.

Nagase opened the door, grinned, and bowed three times. "Ah! Welcome!" It was like coming home. Before talking any further, we approached a small altar at the back of the cottage and took a few minutes to drum and chant. How good it was to hear our voices and drums together. I felt myself rooting into the floor.

---

4   Peace Pagodas can now be found in Japan, the U.S., India, South Africa, Europe and Mexico.

Next of course came tea. Refusing my help, he brewed and brought in a pot of earthy Japanese tea while I remained seated on a flat cushion. As we drank, I brought him up to date with my walks, and he spoke shyly about his latest dreams. He had long felt a spiritual connection to the Jews who lost their lives during the Holocaust. Because of the political change brewing in Germany he longed to go there, but was unable to. I sensed his disappointment and told him I would be honoured to walk in his stead.

We finished our tea. Then we bowed to each other, and he chanted and drummed as I walked out of the park. "*Namu Myōhō Renge Kyō....*" In the distance I continued to hear the faint sound of his drum, and when I could hear no more, I could still feel the drum's vibration in my body.

After leaving Battersea Park, I returned to Yorkshire to meet my cousin. Fred, my Aunt Mary's son, had been out of town when I'd visited Redcar the first time. He was about the same age as my older brother, Howard, so he remembered me as a tot. Though I had little recollection of him, I picked him out on the street as the bus pulled into town. We shared a similar tallish, slim build, and he sported a full head of salt-and-pepper hair and wide-set eyes like I did. He, his wife and daughters showered me with unpretentious Yorkshire hospitality.

Every day some new relation was brought over to meet the oddball cousin. I was eager to learn about their lives, what they dreamed, what they were passionate about, what they wanted to change. And every day they offered new jigsaw puzzle pieces of family history for me to fit into place.

One day we sat eating winkles from the sea for lunch and I flashed back to doing the very same thing on the beach as a kid. In the evenings we'd sit in the local pub drinking spitz, an interesting concoction of ginger ale and beer, and eating bubble and squeak, or fish and chips. The older folks sat around talking about better days. I was sad to learn that fish stocks were being depleted here, just as they were in Eastern Canada.

Almost any night you could hear live music at the pubs: Yorkshire folk songs played on banjo, pipes, concertina and melodian. And I loved just hearing people talk. It was strange to think that if things had gone differently I'd still have the Yorkshire drawl I found so engaging in my cousin's voice.

Before I left Redcar, I took part in a protest at the nearby Fylingdale radar station. As part of Reagan's "Star Wars" initiative, this local ballistic missile early warning system was slated for huge expansion because of its strategic location. I wonder how many people knew this was going on in their backyard amidst the peace and calm of the North Yorkshire Moors.

Fred and I had our differences, but as straight-laced as he was, I felt respected by him and his entire family. As I said goodbye, Fred choked back tears, while Aunt Mary and I let loose a flood. We knew this might be our last visit, as she was getting on in years.

On April 2, I donned my hat and off I trod down the beach, my face in the sun. Heading south along the beach, the North Sea was on my left and high rocky cliffs on my right. I was alone, just me and the elements—sun, sand, ocean, and clouds.

The beach was littered with rocks and shells, and scattered amongst them were small semi-circular fossils that looked like petrified snail shells. I filled a pocket with a collection of them, later learning that these "Devil's Toenails" are millions of years old.

Atop the looming cliffs were hundreds of white blobs. Moving in for a closer look, I saw that the shapes were seabirds, whole clusters of them, perched on narrow ledges and nesting in small crevices. Away from the ocean's roar, I was now thick in the din of their strange croaking. These were beautiful sleek gannets, whose call certainly didn't match their appearance.

As I returned to the shore, gulls swooped overhead, and a handful of small, spindle-legged shorebirds darted along the tideline, skirting the waves. Their erratic dance made me smile. *Ahh*, I thought. *This is the life.* I stopped to whisper a prayer of gratitude. "Thank you, universe, for creating such a glorious day for me. May you continue to bless me, all of humanity, and all the animals and birds."

I opened my eyes to see a group of those little seabirds scurrying around my feet. Perhaps my steps had stirred up edibles in the sand and I'd been standing so motionless that they didn't know to be afraid. Their antics were delightful, and I quietly began thanking them for their presence. *I'm a regular Saint Francis!* I thought. The patron saint of animals.

My romantic journey continued blissfully along in the sun for hours. I even picked up a long tree branch and whittled away enough bark to make a perfect walking stick. As I went along, I tuned in to the rhythm of my body moving through my surroundings, at one with nature, melting with the sky, the ocean, the sand beneath my feet. I existed purely in the moment. It was exhilarating.

Suddenly, fog rolled in. It was so thick that I could barely see where I was going. The air turned bitterly cold. Rain began to fall, and then—to my utter disbelief—snow. Disoriented, I headed away from the shoreline, but soon the strip of sand narrowed, and the tide pushed me in against jagged rocks. I scrambled up a dirt path, through thickets of brambles, until I was atop the highest seaside cliffs in England.

The dark clouds parted briefly, revealing the lacy black cutout of a ruin against the sky: Whitby Abbey. What a dramatic, ghostly sight, evoking shades of gothic literature.[5] In the 13ᵗʰ century the progressive monastery had housed both men and women; centuries later its shell still dominated the surrounding farmlands. I slept there that night, thinking of the monks and nuns who had lived and worked side by side.

By morning, the weather had improved slightly. The rain and snow had stopped, but it was still blustery. I decided to continue on, choosing not to return to the beach but to take the high route. The wind raced over fields, whipping tall stalks back and forth like waves on the ocean. The path in some places was so narrow that it barely scraped the cliff's edge and I had to fight the gusts that threatened to blow me over the sheer drop. My guts dropped as I envisioned losing my footing, plummeting to my death and being swept out to sea. I'd told no one at home where I was exactly. Why hadn't I called Lani?

As dramatic as this cliff-side walk was, good sense prevailed and I yielded to every opportunity to go inland, taking advantage of rights-of-way across farmers' fields on the moors. These signposted footpaths are a real boon, as long as walkers are respectful, taking their garbage with them and shutting gates properly. Many English people go for a week's ramble on their holiday on this extensive network of trails. After having walked along freeways in Canada and been being blown off the road by the big trucks, this was a real treat.

I came to a weathered wooden stile over a mossy stone wall, past which a flock of sheep grazed contentedly on the crest of a small hill. I was struck by the quiet pastoral scene before me. *Saint Francis would love this!* I thought.

---

5   Indeed Bram Stoker set part of *Dracula* in the town of Whitby, and the novel's title came from a name he found in the local library.

When I clambered over the stile and stood to survey the vista, it was no surprise that one of the sheep looked up from grazing to stare at me. I somehow knew we both sensed we were creatures of God. As it bounded towards me, I opened my arms, and lifted my face to the sky. What a mistake.

A hard, swift blow to the abdomen bowled me over. I lay dazed in the wet grass, the wind knocked out of me and a set of leathery black nostrils snorting in my face. I'd been rammed by a ram! Once I caught my breath and stood up, I looked over to see my assailant, still in the vicinity and eyeing me closely. I made a cautious beeline for the stile and hopped over.

Within seconds I heard the furious honking of geese, a whole flock of them, running at me, wings flapping defiantly. I darted to the nearest stone wall and clambered up on it as a hissing gander nipped at my heels. Fortunately, none of the winged beasts took to the air in pursuit. Now, out of breath and covered in sheep shit, I couldn't help but burst into laughter. "Saint Frankie," I said aloud, "You're getting me into trouble!"

Though I walked alone, I was never lonely. Aside from the sheep and geese, I made lots of friends. I overnighted with a group of Pagans, a family of Quakers, a BBC interviewer, a group of Down Syndrome kids, and even a member of parliament. Every single one of my hosts had a story to share and many chuckled at my tale of my brief sojourn as a modern-day Francis. My dream of walking to Japan earned smiles as well.

On one of my last days in England, I passed through a sleepy little village of 100 people tucked away in the hills and dales. At the post office, Maud, a third-generation postmistress, asked, "*Eer*, what you doin' thousan's o' miles from home, an' where's your car?"

To this I replied, "Don't all people walking from Canada to Japan come through here?" She blushed and giggled. I laughed along with her, immediately endeared. "And do you happen to know," I continued, "a place where this pilgrim might sleep the night?"

"Well," she said, head cocked, looking me up and down, "Why dun't you come stay with me 'n' the mister? It's a tiny house, but there's plenty room on the settee. An' there's a stew on the cooker. You could use fattenin' up!" She gave me directions and told me to meet her after she closed up. I sat down on a bench overlooking the ocean, and closed my eyes.

An hour later I was eating stew with Maud, her husband George, and Baxter, their Jack Russell Terrier. Evening sun slanted through the dining room window. I was explaining about Redcar and Japan.

"Well, you're a proper pilgrim then," George said, through the steam from his bowl. "England has always called to pilgrims, you know," he went on, "an' sent them forth as well. Even from our shores to the rocky coast of Spain, and on to Compostela. Saint Francis himself made a pilgrimage, from Italy of course, along the *Camino de Santiago*." I felt a shiver run through my body.

"And I'll follow in his footsteps," I heard myself saying.

CHAPTER 34

THE LONG WAY AROUND

I was a pilgrim now, heading for Santiago, and ultimately to Japan. But because of my promise to Nagase, I was going to Germany first. I boarded a ferry from England to Holland, trusting that although I had no plans, I would be guided.

Getting off the ferry in Rotterdam, one thing struck me right away: the flatness. The concept of climate change was just beginning to seep into the collective consciousness at that time, so my mind began to entertain frightening possibilities. I wrote in my journal: *THIS LAND IS BELOW SEA LEVEL!!*

The city seemed empty of people and bereft of soul. The Second World War had devastated the city; few buildings of character were left except for City Hall. New shopping malls and futuristic towers had sprung up, all sporting historical names. The irony depressed me and I was ready to get out of there. So I followed the crowd, eventually meeting up with a lively group of university students who were heading for the neighbouring town of Schiedam. There, over 20 environmental groups had come together to celebrate Earth Day. Millions of people were mobilizing worldwide for this huge event. There were musical performances, and speeches, and information booths. I learned about flood control, soil leaching, and wind farming. But the main focus of this year's event was public transportation.

In 1975, the Dutch government started building a freeway from Schiedam to Delft. This area was forested, so work began on clearing a huge swath through the trees. But due to public criticism of the clear-cutting, the project was halted. The stretch of land remained vacant, but over the years vehicle traffic in the surrounding area worsened, so the freeway plan was revived. Now, protesters had an alternative plan. Over 1,000 men, women and children had arrived with shovels to dig a track for an electric tram. And not only that, but they buried an automobile at the track's beginning as a symbol of their stance on the proposed freeway. This peaceful demonstration had the cooperation of the local town councils.

After the event, my new student friends asked if I wanted to come with them to Amsterdam where they lived. So I did. But before I had much chance to explore the place, one of the young women, Barbara, told me she was keen for me to meet her parents in Eindhoven. Again, I accepted the invitation.

We hit it off right away. Both physically and intellectually striking, Marjorie and Peter made a lovely couple, and Marjorie had a mischievous streak, just like me. She was also a Bahá'í, like my brother Jim.

The first evening we spent together, she sat playing sitar while Peter told me about his life. As a yoga teacher he had journeyed to India and other exotic locales. He was also a researcher and lecturer in environmental design at a local university, and would soon be travelling to Sweden for an international symposium. (In the 1970s, Sweden was one of the most oil-dependent countries in the world. In a few decades, it had done a 180 and was now leading the way in sustainability.) A diverse group of 300 academics, engineers, biologists, economists, and architects were meeting in a town called Svedala, to discuss ecological design and technology. I don't know if the term "green" had even been coined yet. "Would you like to come?" asked Peter.

"Of course!" I eagerly replied. I was really on a roll now.

In Svedala, it was refreshing to be immersed in something completely different. How enlightening to glimpse into what seemed like some secret society and their fantastic visions of the future. Even though I didn't understand half of what I saw and heard, I knew these people were dreaming BIG and their dreams weren't nebulous but backed up with data and reports and charts and slides. They worked hard every day to turn their dreams into reality. Like me, they wanted a better world for their grandchildren: improved health, equality, greater opportunities for growth, more happiness. And it could all be sustainable. They didn't equate "better" with more convenience, more material possessions, or ways to extract resources more quickly.

When other attendees asked me what I did for a living, I said I walked. This was met with blank expressions. So I was caught totally off guard when an organizer asked me to speak at the conference. *Who, me? What do I have to add?* I wondered, flabbergasted. I felt conspicuously unqualified, but I had to do it—probably because I was terrified. *Don't think too far ahead!* I reminded myself. I knew if I just stayed in the moment, it would be easier to speak off the cuff than try and plan something meaningful and impressive.

My turn arrived and I took the stage. *How can I speak to them on their level and help them understand me?* I thought. And then it hit me. "Like you," I said, "I have a vision of something I want to create. So, today, I call myself an architect of peace. And although I don't have charts and graphs, I do have a wealth of experience to back up my vision, and I have tools. Instead of instruments, plans, and measuring devices, I have communication tools. With them I help bring people together."

I talked about the Great Peace March and my original goal of eradicating nuclear weapons. Goals were something they could all relate to, being methodical scientific types. "But," I told them, "my goal shifted, and it became a dream of peace, which had no start and no end. After all, even if we do get rid of nuclear weapons, we can always build them again. Weapons aren't the problem; they're a symptom of our deep human fears. And until we learn to trust in life, and trust each other, we will keep building weapons.

"Walking is how I build peace. But there is no zoning or building plan to follow, no maximum height or density. I am free to build as much peace as I can, for the rest of my life."

I could tell some of the audience were just as baffled as I had been, listening to them speak. Most academics had never encountered someone like this before. But for others, my words seemed to strike a chord. I was uplifted by a loud wave of applause as I left the stage.

Afterward, a tiny, white-haired old man with thick Coke-bottle glasses approached me. He looked like a mad genius, with the whole universe behind those thick lenses. He introduced himself as Hans Weil, telling me that he'd been a pioneer in the field of holograph. "Of all the speakers I have listened to so far," he said, "only you did I really hear. You spoke with your heart. You live your talk. You walk your walk."

I loved being an architect for a weekend. Would I go on to become an architect of buildings, or an eco-designer? No. Were the architects who heard me going to put down their pencils and walk for peace? Probably not, nor should they. That wasn't the point.

Sharing who we are with others is like dropping a stone into water. I remembered back to Ontario and my evening spent contemplating ripples in a pond. We all send out ripples constantly, and our most far-reaching effects may be ones we never see, completely below the surface in our lifetime.

After returning to Eindhoven, my new friend Peter told me a story. The more I listened, the more I understood he was out of the box, literally.

He told me that in the spring of 1984, just outside the confines of the university buildings, he had planted a living labyrinth. It was an open air laboratory to test the strength and versatility of living construction materials. At 600 square metres, it consisted of almost 2,000 willow seedlings, planted in a classical labyrinth pattern. Eventually it grew into a kind of spiral forest, an oasis in the midst of buildings and roads, with an electric power station looming on the periphery. Peter told me it was difficult to get people to help prune the willows, which had quickly grown into a thick and tangled forest. So I volunteered.

The labyrinth was more than just a research project. "People often get labyrinths and mazes confused," Peter told me. "But originally, they were one and the same. Greek mythology tells of a maze built to trap the monstrous minotaur. It had convoluted, branching pathways, blind corners and dead ends. It was nearly impossible to escape. Over time, mazes became something more of a game. In Europe during the Renaissance, wealthy landowners built mazes in their gardens as follies. They're still fairly common as an attraction in large public gardens."

As Peter continued, I thought of maze puzzles in the newspaper; I hadn't considered their direct link to physical structures before. "Labyrinths became something distinct," he explained. "Their layout differs in that there is only one path, leading from the outside to the centre. The route is long and circuitous and folds back on itself until it reaches the middle. You can't get stuck or lost. When viewed from above, the pattern is very pleasing to the eye. Medieval European churches built labyrinth designs into their tile or stone floors, and the theory is that the design represented a route to God. It is possible that pilgrims walked these twisting paths in lieu of actually walking to Jerusalem or Rome or on the Camino de Santiago." I got goose bumps again when Peter mentioned this place. "They would recite devotional prayers," he continued, "as they approached enlightenment or salvation.

"There are even ancient labyrinths in Asia, Australia, and the Americas. Two-dimensional representations are found world-wide, so there must be something universal about them. They have certainly undergone a huge resurgence as spiritual tool in modern times."

The labyrinth in Eindhoven was just 20 metres in diameter, but it was so dense with sprawling branches that I could not see, let alone step, through the thicket. Over the course of the next week I walked its entire length, over half a kilometre, pruning as I went along. What could have been an arduous physical task became a meditation.

I mused on the labyrinth as a metaphor. It was easy to live life as though stuck in a maze, searching for ways out—for answers—but never finding freedom. Living life as if in a labyrinth was about relaxing and trusting. This is how I wanted to live.

It's been said that humans, when lost in unfamiliar territory, end up walking in circles. I'd read that a scientific study corroborated this long-held belief. Perhaps it's our primal way of attuning to ourselves and the environment, getting familiar with inner and outer landmarks, so that we might find our way. Perhaps the labyrinth was designed by wise men and women who drew on this natural instinct and shaped it into a tool for self-discovery.

Walking the labyrinth requires slowing down and paying attention to each small step. You can't control the direction of the journey or how long it takes. You just know that in time you will reach the end, and find yourself. This is how I'd been walking now for years: one step at a time, in no straight line but in meandering arcs and arteries, spiralling my way through life. I was in no hurry. Biking to the site each day, or letting my stiff muscles sink into my sofa bed at night, I knew that if I just took my steps and did my job, eventually I would get to the centre. Like I would get to Germany for Nagase, and to Santiago, and eventually to Japan.

I enjoyed the solitude while I worked, but a few days in one of Peter's students joined me. He was excited to practise his English with someone, and I was interested to hear about his pursuits. After a while, though, his enthusiasm for the work began to wane, and he began to complain about issues with his girlfriend, his school, and other matters.

I began to feel cranky. It wasn't that I found his concerns trivial, but neither of us was really present with the job at hand. So, despite concern that I would hurt his feelings, I asked him to be quiet while we worked and to save conversation for break time. I believed the labyrinth was meant to be experienced in silence, so I insisted we carry on this way. And he agreed, if reluctantly.

Every day we showed up with our clippers, making gradual, steady progress, rediscovering and reshaping the labyrinth. As time went on I heard fewer grumbles from Peter's student, and I felt a deep and calm connection to nature. By the end of the week the overgrown labyrinth had transformed back into a living mandala. As we stood quietly beside our completed task, I asked my young friend how he was feeling about his problems. "Oh, right." he answered. "I guess they're not so pressing right now."

And there it was. The long way around, itself, had become the teacher.

THE SPIRAL

The spiral begins
Thoughts spread wings
Toes clutch ground
Body seasons in motion
Tree arms shed autumn
Sky heart feeds winter
Earth legs dance spring
Sun soul fires summer
Balance restored
The spiral leaves

CHAPTER 35

YES

"No Nukes" was the battlecry of every decent peace-loving citizen when I began walking. I had well learned by my fifth year of doing this, though, that it was not enough to be *against* something. What about being *for* something instead? I was still willing to protest and even be arrested, but I was more interested in saying *yes* than no.

No, to me, is a word that suggests contraction, or even inaction; it defines us against something or somebody. It's not a bad word. We must be capable of saying it when something's not right, and in this way we take care of ourselves. But sometimes it's fear that makes us say *no*.

Most of us fear disappointment, rejection, failure, pain and loss. We fear that things won't turn out as we hope. But when we cling to our limited ideas of how things should look, we close ourselves off to life's small miracles, to blessings in disguise, to valuable lessons. *Yes* gives us possibilities, with no guarantee but the opening itself. But if we can embrace uncertainty, we're free.

I don't believe I have to accept every opportunity life throws at me, but I do think it's important to say *yes* to things that will take me out of my comfort zone and down unfamiliar paths. Sometimes I freak out later and wonder what I've gotten myself into, but the important thing is to take that first risk and then follow, one step at a time.

Saying *yes* had taken me amazing places to far, and I wasn't about to stop now.

After restoring the labyrinth, I reconvened with my young friends in Amsterdam, crashing on Barbara's couch. Her apartment was three floors up in one of those classic Dutch row houses that are squeezed together along a street of similar tall and crooked structures. Days turned into weeks and my plans to walk to Germany drifted temporarily into the background. I allowed myself to be seduced by the culture of coffee, canals, and cycles. It wasn't the easiest city to walk in, with bikes whizzing everywhere, but there was an order to it all, despite the mayhem. Everyone had a bike like everyone has a car in North America. It wasn't a question of cost; bikes were simply the most practical and efficient mode of transportation. For the first time since I was a kid, I hopped on and began to tootle about.

One day I cycled to the local laundromat to wash my meagre collection of clothes. Since I didn't have enough items to fill a whole machine, I asked the young woman next to me if I could throw my things into her washer. Amused at my forwardness, she motioned for me to go right ahead. Later, I laughed out loud, having to extract two bras and seven pairs of knickers from my trousers and t-shirts. This moment of intimacy was my introduction to Lucile and the beginning of a great enduring friendship.

As we sorted socks, we chatted and found we had something in common. She was studying to be a physiotherapist, which in the Netherlands includes a large component of massage. My shoulder was in a lot of pain from carrying a heavy pack, so I inquired if she'd be willing to work on it.

Lucile was shy and did not seem confident about her skills, but I told her not to worry, that any kind of attention to my shoulder would be better than nothing. So she gave me a treatment that was very good technically, but tentative. She lacked the intuition that would come not just from years of practise, but from connecting deeply with people.

I invited Lucile to walk with me. She was frightened but intrigued, sensing a once-in-a-lifetime opportunity. Her curiosity won out, and she planned to meet me after her school term ended in June. She would be my guide through the Netherlands.

In the meantime, I accumulated more walking companions. I was saying *yes*. Barbara wanted to join us for a few days, as did another friend of Lucile, and a new acquaintance, Fenris, from Canada. A lost soul with an open heart, he just needed a little encouragement in finding himself.

In the week before we embarked, I was enjoying one of my last lazy mornings in a real bed with a comfy duvet. I lay in a beam of sunlight, contemplating the journey ahead.

The shape of the trip had not quite materialized in my imagination, and I was OK with that, but things always got a little complicated when other people were involved. Perhaps it was time to ask for a little guidance from spirit, which I did silently as I fell into slumber. *Let me know if I'm getting myself in too deep, OK?*

Deep in dreamland, I was walking in a field of flowers, birds singing from the trees, feeling the sun on my face and the breeze in my hair. Then, *bzz, bzz … bzz, bzz …* a large bumblebee flew right past my ear. *Bzz, bzz …* around to the other side of my head. The high-pitched double buzz continued until I realized I had to wake up and answer the phone. Maybe God was calling with his reply to my request. "Hello?" I answered, laughing aloud.

"*Ja, hallo,*" a nervous but deep baritone voice responded. "Are you *de* peace walker that I read about in the newspaper yesterday?"

"That's me," I chirped.

"My name is Karl," he said. "I would like to walk with you."

"Well, it seems you're not the only one," I replied, biting my lip. "But—sure—the more, the merrier!" It seemed the universe wanted to make sure I had enough company on the walk.

"Thank you. Good," said Karl. "I will also bring my wife. And my farm."

"Farm?"

"Is that OK?" he asked.

"Uhh … um," I stammered, intrigued but wary. "Yes," I answered, less than confidently, but at least it was *yes.*

"Tell me where you are staying and I'll see you there tomorrow morning." I did just so and we said goodbye. That night, I had dense and confusing dreams, in black and white.

The next morning, as light filtered into the bedroom through gauzy curtains, I heard a noise from the outside. I rubbed my eyes and headed for the window, drawing the drapes sleepily. Down in the middle of the street sat a tractor. It had a huge bouquet of flowers on its hood. Perched on the tractor's seat was a smiling, muscular young woman wearing a vivid rainbow headband and cutoff shorts. Behind the tractor was a huge covered wagon that seemed to be held together by a complex system of string, rope, wire, and miscellaneous hardware. A ladder, canvas bags, tent poles, and an assortment of pots and pans hung off the sides. A long crooked stovepipe poked up through a well-worn tarp on the roof. I threw on some clothes and ran downstairs.

There was more to see. Behind the first wagon was another, in vivid blue, with a gigantic, six-foot long wooden replica of an audio cassette tape on its front. In this wagon lay an enormous pig, grunting contentedly. A bright pink sign read "Caroline". Behind that wagon was a small trailer, labelled "Alfa Romeo". It strained under the weight of an enormous brown and white cow, whose head was constantly in motion as she chewed her cud. The result of all this chewing was dumped unceremoniously at her discretion. Tied to the starboard side of that last wagon was a shabby, bearded goat, her full udder swaying. Two beautiful ponies were tethered to the port side: a young pinto whose tail swished with an air of indifference, and a creamy white older mare. A wiry young man with spiky hair, a deep tan and bright orange wooden clogs popped out from behind.

"*Hoi!*" he called, striding towards me.

"You must be Karl," I said, and he nodded in agreement. "I almost thought I dreamed our conversation yesterday," I added with a smile, trying not to betray my incredulity. Karl just grinned. I gathered he was a man of few words. "It's nice to meet you," I said, taking in the whole spectacle. As odd as it was, I was charmed by the menagerie.

"Hi, I'm Kirsten!" yelled the rainbow-headbanded driver cheerily, as she hopped off the tractor and joined us.

"I'm Derek," I said. "You're really on the *moooove*, aren't you?" They smiled uncertainly at my pun. "I hope that you're not expecting to start walking at this very moment, though. I still have a few things to take care of."

"No, that is fine," said Karl. "We will meet you and the rest of the walkers when you are ready." We arranged for a rendezvous and said goodbye. I watched the farm clatter away, tattered flags fluttering. There would be no one but myself to blame if the whole thing went totally haywire.

Soon, arrangements were complete and I set off with Lucile and her friends. We strolled for several days through the flat Dutch landscape, admiring quaint brick houses with white lace curtains in windows especially dressed up for passersby, along canals straddled by windmills and busy with boat traffic. And then we met up with the farm.

That day we had an agenda: walking to Ginkelse Heide for a protest rally. This place consisted of 2,000 acres of wilderness in the centre of the country. Many people used this area for hiking and recreation, but it was under threat of development. In the Netherlands, much of the area where people live and farm is actually reclaimed from the sea by systems of dikes. This land, with its natural meadows, heath and forest, was a rarity. The Dutch army wanted to fence it in and exploit it by driving tanks across it, detonating explosives, and playing war games there.

It enraged me how military bureaucracies had become so powerful that economics seemed to play a bigger role than protection of citizens did. Huge profits could be in the making, testing, and sale of weapons. And like all businesses, enormous amounts of money and energy were spent keeping products current and attractive to customers. With the threat of the Cold War fading, I didn't see any need for military expansion into this wilderness area. Even the local government in the area was against the plan.

We started walking at 5:30 that morning. I took my place in the caravan and off we all paraded down the road together. As we passed by, strangers stopped mid-step, turning heads and pointing fingers. We must have looked like a modern-day Noah's ark on wheels. In no time at all, two or three carloads of police officers pulled up alongside us, lights flashing. "*Halt!*" they barked out the windows. We waved and continued on. This angered them, but we were only trying to find room on the shoulder to pull over safely. When we stopped, the officers jumped out and began to clamber over the wagons, exclaiming loudly, pulling apart anything that wasn't attached. Meanwhile, we tied the ponies and goat to a tree and let them graze. Then we got out our food supplies.

We invited the cops to join us for juice or tea, but they lectured us furiously, saying we'd have to dismantle everything. We'd breached a multitude of laws and they would have to charge us with a list of infractions. With a moderate amount of sincerity we apologized for not keeping up to the standards that were required for a travelling farm and began to dissemble the wagon train. We untied all the equipment and piled it on the roadside. Then the animals needed to be dealt with. But Alfa Romeo and Caroline were reluctant to come out of their wagons, and no amount of pulling, shoving or cajoling would get either of them out. The frustrated police officers went off in a huddle. A while later one of them came over and in a quiet voice said, "Just move on."

This became a routine in the days to follow as we made our way slowly through the countryside, and we learned to anticipate the daily interlude. Upon hearing the approaching sirens, Karl would holler, "Lunch time!" and we'd untie the animals, get out our sandwiches, and wait for the show to begin.

On the day of the protest, however, we had no leisurely afternoon ahead of us. We were due there at 3:00 and were going to have to hoof it—pun intended. We walked, jogged, took turns on the tractor, and even rode the poor ponies. At 2:59 we pulled into Ginkelse Heide, dirty, sweaty and exhausted, but in time to join the thronging crowds and get onstage to make our impassioned speeches.

The protest was a success, attracting the media and getting the word out. Later, an environmental study was undertaken, the transfer of land was stopped, and a tragedy was prevented. Of course, our eccentric entourage alone couldn't have accomplished this—it was thanks to the groundswell of public support for protecting the area. But it was encouraging to think that our very peculiarity had helped to tip the balance.

Mission accomplished, we walked on towards Germany.

We were an odd lot indeed, but less odd as we got closer. And less shy, and less judgmental. Everyone had something to contribute: music, foot

Yes

rubs, food, or just a smile. Eventually, our dedicated and motley crew approached the border of West Germany. Only Lucile, Fenris, and I were continuing on, so it was time to say goodbye to Karl and Kirsten and their rolling peace farm, and the others. The hugs and tears wouldn't stop. But then it really was time to go.

"Derek, your back pack is too heavy," said Karl, matter-of-factly. "Your shoulder is damaged." He took the reins of the elder pony. "Please accept Mary as my gift to you. She can carry your things in saddle bags."

More than a handful of concerns passed through my mind, but how I not say *yes* to this beautiful gift horse? I looked into the animal's big brown eyes as I took her reins, and I felt her ask me to take care of her. *Yes*, I told her, silently. And in reply, I believe she told me she would walk me to Berlin.

As Fenris, Lucile, and I set off together, waving goodbye, Mary gave a soft *whuff* and matched her pace to mine.

CHAPTER 36

WALL

I could never have imagined having such a dignified and graceful companion as this gentle white pony.

We got off to a smooth start, Mary taking the new arrangement in stride, not fazed by leaving her family behind. Once at the border crossing, though, we encountered our first hurdle when the guards were willing to let everyone but Mary cross into West Germany. They demanded to see her papers, but we didn't have any. This wouldn't stop us, though. I asked Lucile to cross back into the Netherlands and find a veterinarian, which she did. He drew up a very official-looking letter, stating that the pony was fit and disease-free. We presented it, they stamped it, and we got in.

Mary and I developed an easy walking rhythm and soon we had a sixth sense about each other. I'd had experience with a horse as a delivery man, but this was different, more intimate. We relied on each other day in and day out. I tried never to ask her for more than she could give, and I know she did the same. She carried my things in saddle bags and I found her the juiciest pastures to graze in. Every morning she greeted me with a friendly whinny as I peeked out my tent door. Our mutual affection grew into unconditional love. I nicknamed her Peace Pony.

Lucile and I got along well, too. She spoke German fluently, which was a great help in securing us places to stay for the night. Our first night across the border, she found us a farm where Mary had her own stall to sleep in with other ponies. They followed her around as if she were their own mother. The rest of us were invited into a lovely warm home to enjoy hot showers and home-cooked food.

During our time together, Fenris would go off walking alone for hours at a time, and eventually for days and weeks. Ours was not an easy relationship, as fond of him as I was. After one long absence, he never returned. When Lucile needed to return home to attend school, it was just Mary and me. This was a real test, as I had no plan, and didn't speak German, but Lucile had written me a list of useful phrases:

Guten Tag, mein Name ist Derek.
Ich bin von Kanada.
Ich brauche einen platz für die Nacht
um mein Zelte auf zu stellen.

My first night alone, I nervously recited my script. The householders, if taken aback at first, were hospitable and my fears melted. In the next few weeks though, there were misunderstandings. People thought I wanted to leave the pony with them over the summer, or that I wanted to camp for weeks at a time. But it always got sorted out and most people were very generous. I did my part by helping out with dish washing or other tasks. Once I got to pick grapes in a vineyard.

After a while, Mary's saddle bags began to prove troublesome. They were unwieldy and would swivel under her belly, which I'm sure made her uncomfortable. I tired of trying to straighten them out and the leather straps were stretching to the breaking point. As soon as I made a repair, they'd break in a different spot.

As we walked into one town, the saddle fell right off. I sat right down on the roadside, feeling defeated, and then imagined Lani saying, *Is this pony really a gift?* I had grown so fond of Mary and didn't want to give her up, so what could I do to change the situation? I needed better bags or a better system entirely.

I heard another voice now, out loud. "*Brauchen Sie Hilfe?*" I looked up to see a stout man towering above me. I had no energy to try and communicate in German.

"Do you speak English?" I asked.

"Of course," he answered. "Would you like some help?"

"Yes, please," I said. "As you can see, I am in a bit of a bind."

"My name's Müller. Please come with me—I live just around the corner."

The man picked up one of Mary's saddlebags, I picked up the other, and off we went. Ten minutes later Mary was grazing in his backyard, and Mr. Müller and I were eating lunch: cheese and pickles and meat on thin slices of rye bread. I was ravenous.

Afterward, we went outside and he opened the door of his garage. "I think you need something like this," he said, pointing at a small hand-built cart with wheels, the kind that kids ride around in. We looked at each other, grinning. Six hours later, he had transformed his son's cart into a perfect wagon for Mary, complete with a new harness. But pulling a wagon wasn't necessarily a natural thing for a pony to do; it took practise.

By the time we left the following morning, Mary was trotting happily down the road, pulling the wagon. "Thank you, Mr. Müller!" I shouted and waved. Everything was now working perfectly. In a few days, though, the harness began to detach from the wagon, and then a few hours later, *crunch!* Off fell a wheel. A driver stopped next to us and took me to a nearby town to see the bicycle repairman, Mr. Schmidt.

Mr. Schmidt, a white-haired man with a sun-weathered complexion, was seated in the shop amongst a group of other white-haired men, drinking coffee. He rose, looked the wagon up and down and threw his hands up in the air. "Catastrophe, catastrophe!" he railed. "This is a serious problem, but you have come to the right person. You will not find wheels in this world that will fit your contraption. So I must make them. You must wait a few days." I was uneasy about being at the mercy of this fellow, but what choice did I have?

He took the wagon apart and waved parts in the air with disgust. At every given opportunity Mr. Schmidt would remind me, and all his friends, about the severity of the situation. Sometimes I'd catch a twinkle in his eye and the flash of a smile before he picked up his tools with a flourish and returned to his work. This man was a performer.

It took four days for Mr. Schmidt to perfect his new wheels. They were beautiful, but even more attractive was the hand-painted sign that his grandchildren had made on the side of the wagon. It had colourful doves and flowers, and read: *Canada—Japan.*

"Thank you, my amazing magician," I said.

"*Es ist mein Vergnügen,*" he answered. "My pleasure."

When people offered us help from the heart, I could feel it. But the sense of duty in this country felt almost oppressive, and I didn't like to accept anything when the giving felt false. But I had to watch that my attitude wasn't *holier than thou.*

We mostly walked on the shoulder of small roads. Some drivers zoomed right past Mary and me without so much as a glance. Some would do your classic double-take. And a very few would stop, eager to find out what this long-haired stranger and his pony were doing.

I passed into East Germany without incident. This was a critical time in history with the fall of the Iron Curtain in Eastern Europe. It was 1990 and the Soviets were pulling out of East Germany, the communist state was dissolving, and reunification was underway.

One day I sneaked into an old Russian military installation that was in the process of being decommissioned. Walking in the shadows amongst the rusting shells of old fighter jets and the big hollow hangars gave me the eeriest feeling. I snapped a whole roll of film only to discover, when I had it processed, that all the shots were double exposures—ruined. But I didn't need pictures to remember the haunted quality of the place.

As Mary and I walked along, we drew far more openly curious onlookers than we had in the West. Folks stood in doorways with mouths open in shock, staring at the two of us as we ambled along. When they learned what I was doing, some people would cry.

Peace Pony had a way of communicating with people that transcended words. Once, when we met a group of mentally disabled women, I watched her in awe as she stood patiently, letting the women throw their arms around her neck and kiss her. "*Liebling, liebling,*" they squealed with delight.

One evening I stayed with a church pastor. Dieter, and his wife, Sigrid, both spoke English very well, which was uncommon in Eastern Germany. Over dinner, they shared their thoughts about reunification. "You, Derek, are doing something that was absolutely forbidden up until very recently," said Sigrid. "For someone to travel in this manner, and so openly for peace—we just didn't have that kind of freedom. If you had family members just over the border you would need special permission to see them."

"We are very excited," Dieter explained, "about the changes, but the situation is far from stable. Life under communism was hard, but it was predictable. We didn't have much, but every family seemed to have enough. Now, we don't know what to expect. West German money is pouring into the East for reclamation and restoration projects. But what about regular people? How will they make their living now in a capitalist system? How will this be fair? Easterners are flooding into the West, too, desperate to see the land of progress they have been denied for so long."

"With communism," said Sigrid, "we feared that even our closest friends and relatives were informants for the government. We couldn't even be frank with our own family! You could trust no one. Can you imagine how nervous this made us? And if anyone had real subversive things to discuss, like helping family escape to the West, we would go to nearby secret caves to speak in private."

"Everyone welcomes *glasnost*," said Dieter, using the term for the Russian policy of openness, "but it will take time. We need to learn how to trust again."

Sometimes the hardest thing about *glasnost* is talking about it," said Sigrid wryly.

One afternoon, I stopped to watch a huge van pull up on a side street. Without warning, people emerged from houses, cars, and the woods, to gather quietly around the van. The two truck drivers hoisted the back door open and I saw box upon box of bright golden bananas. Faces lit up and I heard several excited gasps. Just months earlier, bananas had been a black market commodity, a luxury that most people couldn't afford. Silence and order returned as everyone filed along to fill their baskets, and within half an hour, the truck was gone, and the street was empty.

As I neared Berlin, I found a place to board Mary for a while, and Lucile rejoined me to enter the city. Our timing was impeccable.

The place was buzzing. Many of the checkpoints in the Berlin Wall, which separated East and West, had been opened officially, and citizens on both sides were crossing freely. I could see stunned looks in some people's faces and euphoria in others, as they crossed the border on foot and on bikes. Hordes of them ran back and forth enjoying the sheer novelty of it.

But now, something even more exciting was happening. The wall itself—the monolithic symbol of oppression, which had stood since 1961—was coming down. This did not happen in one fell swoop. The process had started in November 1989, with individuals smashing out small chunks, but often these sections were repaired by officials. After a while, though, chaos reigned, and now crowds were surging towards it with picks and hammers. We followed them and watched as everyone—teenagers, doctors, businesspeople, homemakers—joined in dismantling the wall, hammering and chipping, laughing and chattering over the din. There was something cathartic in this destructive act and somehow it made the new freedoms more tangible.

During this cacophony I began to hear not just hammering but drumming. And not just any drumming, but the familiar, primeval pulse of the monk's drum. I thought for sure it was coming from my own heart. Was I hallucinating? Maybe, but I yelled to Lucile, "I have to go!" and ran excitedly through the crowds, following the sound until I arrived at the Brandenburg Gate.

Then I saw him. Kijima. In classic stoic tradition, he sat, hardly glancing up, still drumming and chanting. He looked exhausted. After some minutes he put down his drum and stood up, and we bowed three times to each other. He told me he was on his tenth day of fasting for peace at the gate. As I pulled my from my backpack, a small grin spread across his face. And then he resumed, and I joined him: "*Namu Myōhō Renge Kyō….*"

When we finished, bowing three times to each other, he whispered, "Thank you for sharing your energy, Derek."

"Walk in peace, Kijima," I said, as I walked away. He continued to bow.

After Berlin, Lucile returned home, and Mary and I continued on through East Germany, just the two of us again. This was good. I needed time to be alone and process some of the changes that had taken place in my life. Lani and I, although we were still very much committed to each other, were undergoing a transition from partners to friends. She was still busy travelling and practising Reiki, and it was logistically difficult to stay in touch. We shared an uncanny sixth sense, though. On the odd occasion I phoned out of the blue, she'd answer after only one ring. "I was just thinking of you!" she'd say.

I was honest with Lani that Lucile and I were becoming more intimate. Lani and I both knew that however this evolved, things would work out because we trusted each other. I would never make a decision without involving her and she was always the first to know my feelings about anything. Of course I didn't know what would happen with Lucile. My priority was walking and hers was school. We knew we would see each other again, but not when or where.

As Mary and I neared the border of Czechoslovakia, we attracted our usual array of puzzled spectators, some of whom were concerned with more than just our general welfare. Wondering how we planned to cross the border, they recited lists of various official papers and documents we'd need.

"Thanks for your concern," I told the strangers, "But I'll worry about the border when I get there. Now, could you show me the road out of town?"

CHAPTER 37

LEARNING TO FLY
PART TWO

"Ah, you and Mary, you don't follow rules!" says Charlotte. My pony lets out a good chortle, seemingly in agreement.

"But she is *très charmant,* so you can get away with it," says Danielle. "Besides, I think that good fortune follows you everywhere."

"Perhaps," I say. "But have you ever heard of the phrase, 'Shit happens'?" They look at each other quizzically.

In the 1960s and '70s, if you were a fully accredited, died-in-the-wool hippie, it was mandatory to plaster your rundown car or VW van with bumper stickers. Starting with *Make love, Not War* or *Flower Power,* you'd gradually fill your bumper and then begin plastering your windows and even the sides of your vehicle with more conspicuous statements, like *Save the Whales* or even *Impeach Nixon.* Like a kid on an Easter egg hunt, I'd rush into the local record shop, passing the LPs and black-light posters, and frantically rifle through rows and rows of stickers, looking for that special one that both expressed my true feelings and let the world know how deep my thoughts were. My favourite was a quotation from J.R. Tolkien: "Not all who wander are lost."

In 1980, still shopping for bumper stickers (was that me?) I came across a new one: *Shit happens.* I laughed. But a decade later, the sentiment took on deeper significance.

Mary the Peace Pony's wagon had no bumper stickers, but it was painted with the words *"La Paix"*. We were in East Germany, heading south. The two of us walked in comfortable rhythm, side by side down a long country road. The sun was gentle and forgiving, and had pushed aside the young morning clouds. Oak trees lined the roadside, and we ambled in and out of their cool shadows. It was peaceful.

The daughter of a family who had just hosted us was walking alongside us. Eleven-year-old Constantine had fallen in love with Mary, as did most young girls. After pleading relentlessly, she persuaded her parents to let her walk, and we arranged for them to pick her up later in the afternoon. We walked and grinned, but spoke very little.

As the day wore on, I noticed Constantine's smile fading, a small frown taking its place. Obviously, her energy was flagging, so I motioned to the wagon and invited her to climb on board. She smiled shyly, nodding her head, and I lifted her up onto the wagon. Seeing her relief and pleasure, I impulsively picked her up again, and set her on the pony's back. This is something I never, ever did, out of respect for Mary. But I was delighted to see Constantine's jaw drop, her eyes brighten, and her head begin to bob like a marionette's. We both laughed and Mary didn't even break stride.

Moments later, I heard the loud roar of a car from behind. I turned to see a Mercedes speeding toward us down our side of the road. I realized then that I'd broken another of my rules—to never walk with traffic at my back. But the shoulder on the other side had been much too narrow to walk on. However, I was confident that the Mercedes driver could see us, and sure enough, he slowed abruptly, either out of consideration or possibly curiosity at seeing the pony and wagon. What nobody anticipated was the tailgating two-cylinder rust-bucket that flashed around the passenger's side of the first vehicle, leaving no room for the Mercedes driver to give us a wide berth. He panicked, hit the brakes and skidded directly into our path.

First, there was an ear-splitting crash, and then a lull. Suddenly, I felt a blunt shock to my lower back and was lifted high into the air. I flew in slow motion, watching in horror the blurred image of Constantine sailing slowly past me. And then, as I had in my motorcycle crash—my first flying lesson—I entered an eerily silent, timeless state of almost-bliss, where I wondered with strange detachment if I would simply remain aloft. I didn't.

We hit the earth, rolling over and over in tall grass. For a brief few seconds I was at peace until pain engulfed me. And then darkness. I awoke later and looked over to see Constantine lying beside me. I stretched out my hand, barely reaching her. I touched her head and whispered, "*Gut, oder nein?*" She nodded—good. Then I moved my hand to her belly, arms and legs, repeating, "*Gut?*" She continued to nod. She was uninjured. I sighed in relief and then blacked out again.

Sounds began to filter into my consciousness and I heard distant voices speaking frantically. The words had no meaning. I opened my eyes and saw the Mercedes driver standing above me. "Where's Mary?" I asked, desperately. He said something in German that I couldn't comprehend. I looked over and in the distance I saw Constantine running down the road after Mary. With a surge of adrenaline I jumped up and tried to follow, but my body refused and I fell to my knees.

I surveyed the chaos around me. My belongings were strewn across the pavement, along with shards of the wagon. Constantine returned with Mary and I was relieved to find only one shallow cut on my pony's left hind leg. Somehow, despite the sharp pain in my side, I located some rope amidst the rubble and tied her to a tree. The driver of the Mercedes and his two friends stood motionless, watching me, and then asked in broken English whether I needed a doctor. I nodded *yes*. And again my body shut down.

When I regained consciousness once more, I asked Constantine to get my sleeping bag and cover me up. Then she sat with me and held my hand. Whether this was for my comfort or hers, I don't know, but tears came to my eyes as she looked down at me. It was not fair for her to have to care for me, or to witness any of this.

The next word I heard was *passport* and I looked up to see a police officer who was standing with the driver, talking about the accident. I felt a sudden urgency and rush of adrenaline. What was he telling the officer? I needed him to hear the story from my perspective. The driver offered to interpret for me but how could I trust him?

"*Schnell, Schnell!*" I screamed, gesturing wildly to the cop. Why did drivers try to risk passing each other at such great speed on narrow country roads? I had seen this before, East German against West German.

Constantine's father arrived next. Smiling gently, he took my hand, and thanked me. *He's thanking me?* I puzzled.

"If you hadn't put my daughter up on the pony, and if you had been walking *towards* traffic," he said, "the two of you might have been hit head on."

"I guess you're right," I answered. "Perhaps the universe was taking care of us after all." Maybe even my own rules were made to be broken. I reached up and put my arms around them both, crying, as paramedics loaded me into an ambulance. Someone assured me that Mary would be taken care of.

I was taken to a hospital for the first time in my life. In the sparse, decrepit emergency ward, I felt almost like a prisoner. In fact, my insecurities verged on paranoia, and I fought the nurses' attempts to get me onto a hospital bed and sedate me. Instead, I sat in the hallway with my torn and bloody clothes, plotting my escape out the window. This seemed quite rational to me at the time, but I see now that I must have been in shock.

They treated me as best they could, but my escape plans continued for days until I was coherent enough to walk myself out the door, despite a splitting pain in my head. On my way out a young doctor noticed me and blocked my exit.

"Where are you going?" he demanded.

"I don't know," I replied, "but I must get back to my pony." Local folks had been boarding her for me, and I was anxious to see her. "We need to start walking again."

The doctor shook his head in bewilderment. "Oh no, you don't! You are coming home with me," he ordered. "You can barely stand up for a few minutes at a time, and you're in desperate need of rest and recuperation. My wife is also a nurse. Please stay with us until you can walk again." I didn't really have the will to refuse. After staying with them for some time, I was then taken home by Ellie, a friend from Berlin. Lucile took time off from school to visit me as well.

During my convalescence, I had lots of time to mentally deconstruct the accident. I wanted to devote as much energy as possible to healing, but I seemed to need to obsess for a while. I'd felt so in harmony with everything and then the situation had flipped so dramatically. What had I done to deserve this? Was this some kind of message? Eventually the answer came: *Shit happens.*

The universe is filled with shit happening and we can't control it. When once I might have bought the popular New Age saying that "everything happens for a reason," now I did not, and that came as a relief. There are reasons, of course—everything is cause and effect on some level but not always a *personal* level. I also disagree with the idea that we "create our own reality." These beliefs seem misguided and egocentric to me. They cause people to blame and pressure themselves, especially when it comes to things like getting sick or being robbed. "Why me?" they ask. Or if they don't win the lottery: "Why not me?"

We are a tiny part of a complex system,—an objective reality—that's full of variables: other people, objects, invisible energy and forces as simple as gravity. Everything influences everything else but not always directly. Perhaps some highly evolved individuals *can* change the weather, but I'm not talking about them. Maybe on some deep level our souls have control over our experiences. Regardless, what matters to me is that I can control my subjective reality, the choices I make, my attitudes, thoughts, and reactions or responses. If I dwell too much on what is fearful or difficult, I will cause myself more suffering and discomfort. If I spend my thoughts on gratitude instead and take positive action, I will be happier. We are co-creators of our lives. But if we think we can control our objective reality, we are in for a shock. Shit happens.

Miracles happen too. We were all *alive* after that accident, when the outcome could have been horribly different. For some reason that day, Constantine, Mary, and I were spared. This could have been totally random luck. Or perhaps, as Constantine's father suggested, we lived *because* I had broken the rules. Or did someone or something intervene?

I don't know, but I have a sense that miracles happen when we've done our best. And then, all around us, unseen forces play their parts, and everything falls into place, like a lock springing open when the numbers line up. No one single person holds the combination, and while anything is possible, it's not necessary probable. At any rate, I was happy to be alive!

The accident did take a toll, and not just on my body; it also made a big financial dent. I had to get a new wagon built for Mary, and there were medical bills and other expenses. Initially, the Mercedes driver had apologized and seemed willing to help cover costs. But after exchanging a few letters, the correspondence suddenly stopped. Perhaps he was afraid I might sue him, but that isn't my way. I don't believe in entitlement and revenge, so I had to let go. If this person was not willing, on a small level, to help, then I would not resent him; I would wish him the best and hope that he would learn from the incident, just as I would.

When I was able, I joined Lucile in Amsterdam. If I couldn't walk for peace, then I would sit for peace. I went to the statue of Gandhi on Churchill Avenue and sat fasting for a week, sharing thoughts with the spirit of Gandhi about the impending Gulf War.

A few months later Mary and I were on the road again—and not just any road. We were on the very same one of our misfortune. As we passed the accident spot, Mary flinched, raised her head, and let out a fierce whinny. I kept a tight hold on her reins, and we continued our journey through East Germany.

Now, whenever I see a *Shit happens* bumper sticker on a stranger's car, I wonder about the story behind it.

CHAPTER 38

ALONE

My body shot bolt upright. Through my sleep, I'd detected a change in my environment. Now, rubbing my eyes in the half-darkness, I pieced together bits of sensory information. A ray of sunlight beamed through a tiny hole in the lightweight tent canvas. I heard birds chirping. I hadn't heard birds in days, only a wall of noise—which had stopped. My mouth stretched into a grin as I realized what this meant. "YES!" I whooped aloud.

For five long days and nights it had been pouring and I'd been stuck in my tent, the rain's incessant drumming driving me mad. It was a loud, confined, soggy hell. I leapt up and unzipped the door. In the growing light, the glistening trees seemed be stretching themselves awake and gently shaking off the wet. The deluge was over. Mary turned her head slowly to look at me, swishing her tail gently to and fro. She was happy too, and surely champing at the bit to get on the road, just as I was. No time for java this morning; I threw the soppy mess of a sleeping bag and tent into the wagon, hitched up Mary, and we were out of town while the streets were still empty.

After a few hours on the road, the impact of five days of virtual solitary confinement hit me. I was angry. I'd been camping in a playground, smack in the middle of some town, and not one person had stopped by to see if I needed anything. Not that it was anyone's job, I tried to remind myself, but I wasn't used to this degree of isolation. When knocking door-to-door, I was usually able to disarm people pretty quickly with a smile, a binder full of newspaper clippings, and Mary's charm. Though I'd seen townspeople lurking on the edge of the park, no one had been brave or interested enough to approach me this time. Sometimes, I thought, people just didn't enjoy having their ordered lives shaken up by a stranger. Besides, I told myself, folks were still wary of each other—friends, let alone strangers.

As I walked on, anger morphed into self-pity. *Why am I doing this? Who cares? I miss my family. I miss my friends. I miss speaking English. And I'm in pain!* I had weathered worse storms, literally and metaphorically, but I was weary, and the constant strain on my feet, hips and knees was eroding both my body and my confidence.

On one occasion weeks earlier, at the end of a day's walk, I'd noticed that one of my shoes had turned an interesting shade of dark brown. I stopped to take it off and found a bloody mess inside. My right big toe had been smashed to a pulp. Mary had stepped on my foot again, for perhaps the fourth time, and I had simply blocked out the pain. And now I could see that if I faced north, my big toe pointed west to match the other one pointing east.

That night though, once I was off my feet, a bigger hurt took over. My heart began to ache for a human companion once more to lift my spirits. The next morning I placed a long-distance call to Lani but I couldn't reach her. I thought about trying Lucile but knew she'd be at school. My family, my friends, and even my dream of walking to Japan seemed very, very far away. I didn't mind being alone, but this was different. This was *loneliness*. I felt like weeping, but the tears wouldn't come. I stood there for some time, with no will to move on.

I led Mary to a nearby field, unhitched her, and tied her to a tree near some tall grass where she'd be happy to munch away for a while. I slumped down with my back against the tree, breathing a roller coaster of sighs. What I did next surprised me. I prayed, to capital G-O-D, God. Not exactly my style, but I figured it couldn't hurt. I didn't literally think that God was up in the sky, but this is where I now looked, craning my face upwards as I began my rambling plea.

"Please help me God," I said. "I'm so worn out. I'm so lonely. I want to cry but I can't. Do you think you could send someone my way?" I was silent for a moment, witnessing my own desperation. "And God?" I continued, "I don't need pity. I just need companionship. They don't need to do anything to change my feelings or my situation either, because I know I need to work this through."

I paused, continuing a mental inventory of pleas. "Just one more thing," I went on, "I don't want to be picky, but I do think I should be specific here—God, I'm really hoping you'll send a human companion. You see, I love my pony, but I'd really like a hug right now. Someone to hold me. I'll accept anyone—an old man or a child, but, if I have a choice—and I'm sure you know what's coming next— could it be a woman? I don't need her to be young or pretty. It's just so much easier to cry on a comforting soft bosom." I half expected the big finger of God to appear out of the sky and—ZAP!—there she'd be, next to me. But nothing happened. And that was OK, because somehow I'd regained the will to walk. I hitched up a very contented Mary and we set forth, my prayer forgotten.

About six hours later on the crest of a hill, I spied a small village ahead down a quiet road. *I hope there's a shop open,* I thought. I could pick up some fresh supplies for dinner and then find somewhere just past town to set up camp before sunset. I rifled through my satchel to make sure I had some money handy, and when I looked up, I was taken aback. There was someone in the middle of the empty road ahead of us. A woman stood, arms folded lightly across her chest and a soft smile on her lips. How old she was, I had no idea, but she was pretty, with big brown eyes and long raven hair. At that moment I remembered my prayers at the tree and smiled in disbelief. She smiled back.

As I approached with Mary, the woman motioned towards a small stone cottage. We walked towards the building and I noticed a tiny barn behind. She pointed to it, nodding, and then to Mary, before disappearing into the house.

It took some time for me to unharness Mary and perform her usual bedtime routine. I brushed her down, got her some fodder and sat with her for a moment before saying goodnight. The evening ritual complete, I went to the cottage, knocked timidly, and peeked in.

Seated at a tiny wooden table, the woman smiled and gestured towards a wooden chair across from her. I sat down. Atop a flowered tablecloth was a huge steaming bowl of stew and hot dumplings, a loaf of brown bread still warm from the oven, a glass of water and a small pitcher of wine. We sat in silence and shared the simple meal. After months of bread and cheese, this was a banquet. Finishing a second helping of stew, I cleaned my bowl as the monks do, swirling a little water from my glass and then drinking the remains. We sat in the fading light, and then the woman led me up a narrow wooden staircase, to her bedroom.

She got into bed, and I climbed in beside her. But this was not about sex. I cried, and she held me. She rocked me and stroked my hair, continuing for the longest time, holding me until my sobbing stopped. I slowly lifted my head, which by now was resting on her warm chest, and looked up into her gentle eyes. I noticed a tiny tear begin to well up, and I watched as it slid down her dark lashes, fell onto her cheek, and gradually trickled past her nose, off her chin and onto her neck where I stopped its path with my lips. This uncontrollable gesture on my part brought about a flood of tears from her. I sat up, put my arms around her, rocked her and stroked her long hair. When her wailing stopped we looked deep into each other's eyes once more.

Just as I had prayed for, she could not give me advice, listen to my lament, or tell me she was sorry for me—we couldn't speak a word of the other's language. But we could still communicate. After a while, we drifted off, our bodies curled up together, hands clasped under soft eiderdown quilts, moonlight streaming through the window.

The next morning we sat again in silence, our elbows planted firmly on the table, cups of steaming coffee nestled in our hands, just looking and—knowing. Looking and knowing. Every few minutes we'd smile, put our cups down and gently stroke each other's hands. Then we'd shake our bewildered heads and raise our cups to our lips. It was the longest and sweetest breakfast of a lifetime. Eventually we both knew, without any words, that it was time for me to leave. I pushed back my chair, opened the wooden door, and went to get Mary.

Once ready to leave, we paused outside the cottage door where my new friend reappeared. We hugged, reluctant to hold on too long, as tears were close to falling. She accompanied us to the road and then I signalled to Mary to move on. I turned to look back, but the woman was gone and the road was empty.

I walked on for days, sustained—almost inebriated—by the innocent love we had shared, and I was feeling no pain for the first time in ages. And though I was alone again, I was not lonely.

I thought back to the early 1980s and the Long Dances I had taken part in with Native Americans, celebrating the solstices and other cycles of the earth. I remembered one such occasion vividly. In the ceremony, as drummers kept a steady beat on the sidelines, men and women formed separate circles, one inside the other, yin and yang. The women's dance was hip-driven, as they undulated in a counterclockwise circle around the centre. The men moved up and down in a clockwise direction around the outside. Dancing, I felt like a young buck, and with a surge of energy I began running. Approaching a kind of bliss, I didn't want to stop. But suddenly I felt tears run down my cheeks. The thought occurred to me, though I was surrounded by friends: *I am alone.*

No sooner had I been struck by this revelation, when two women appeared at my side, running in step with me. And then there were three of us, performing the male dance in absolute harmony, the women expressing their own yang with me. It was a conversation without words. *I am not alone*, I realized.

Through the night and into the next day we danced in the round. Nothing and no one else existed to me at that moment, and I began to sing unfamiliar words and a strange tune I didn't know. But I understood it was my own song. I sang to the universe and more tears fell. Again, I was hit with the depths of my solitude. Then I found myself in the middle of the women's circle, surrounded with yin energy, and beside me was a woman chanting. We did not acknowledge each other's physical presence but continued together in rhythm. I felt deeply a part of the people around me. Inseparable, yet completely free.

The Long Dance continued throughout the weekend, until the sun rose on the day of Spring Equinox. As a rosy pink began to bleed from the horizon into the brightening sky, the slow pulse of the drums began to pick up speed. *Boom, boom, boom!* they echoed and the drummers picked up speed, energy mounting. And then suddenly, everything went still. A sliver of sun broke over the hilltops, and insight flooded my tired muscles as light filled the sky.

We dance solo. And for a time, we dance together. Then we part. But we are always a *part* of the great whole as well. The Circle in action. Now, on the road with Mary, this remembrance and the lingering warmth of my encounter with the woman on the road were a comfort, dulling the pain in my feet, easing my legs into striding forward, and causing me to smile at my faithful pony. Words formed in my heart and came to my lips, and I walked on, repeating and jumbling the words until they blurred together into a mantra: "Alonealonealone ... alone ... a lone ... *all one.*"

CHAPTER 39

WEAVING

It's the height of autumn, 2014, and I've taken a break from writing to walk in a park not too far from home. It's silent here but for the hiss of fir needles falling like gentle rain. I am surrounded by conifers, oaks, and maples, whose leaves are splashed with crimson. A huge yellow maple leaf wafts down from the sky right in front of me. *Hello, Derek!* I think. He would have loved it here.

I keep walking, thinking about this journey of pulling Derek's stories together. There's excitement in finding a journal entry or letter with that one missing detail I've been looking for, but at times I doubt that a cohesive book will ever emerge from the material that's strewn across my desk. I am torn between my urge to document Derek's entire life and my desire to keep this book simple. *After all, it's not a biography, it's a memoir*, I keep reminding myself. At some point, I will have to let go.

Suddenly a diamond glint catches my eye. Sunlight filtering through the canopy, has caught in a string of glistening dewdrops on a spider's web. I stop to look more closely. The web is gossamer light, yet incredibly durable. It strikes me that the book can be like this web. The threads need to be strong and linked, but loosely woven, with room to breathe, room to ponder. Suddenly my task is clearer.

Walking to Japan

I return to my desk at home, and take a good look at the threads. There are stories of him performing weddings, swimming with dolphins, walking on fire, and a tale of him stranded naked in a remote village in Mexico. There are whole countries, walks, and important life events that I need to omit. I am learning that while it's important to be thorough, it's equally important—and even more difficult—to leave things out.

At the same time, there may be readers who crave continuity as I do. If you are one, then here is what happens next: Derek continues walking through Europe and is especially charmed by the budding new tourist destination of Prague—the beauty of its architecture and the openness of its people. He becomes an overnight sensation on local TV, and the news presenter tells him, in front of a greatly excited audience, that he is on par with the outrageous avant-garde performer Frank Zappa (one of the country's greatest musical heroes, bizarrely) who had graced their stage only months earlier.

Despite this warm reception, the ache of loneliness begins to creep back into his heart. "Don't go to Prague without a lover," he writes to a friend.

Soon, it becomes evident that he won't be able to continue walking at the same pace. He is in pain and his hips are still torqued from the car accident, which affects his gait. So, he accepts the need for rest and recuperation, and stops walking for the winter. Mary needs somewhere to stay, though, so he makes a plea for support in the media. This garners help in a jiffy. He leaves Mary in expert care with a family who own a retired racehorse.

Derek's returns home are always bumpy, but never more so than after Eastern Europe. Everything he could need or want is practically at his fingertips. But this gives him a kind of spiritual indigestion after the lean conditions he's become accustomed to. He and Lani inevitably have gone through personal transformations that leave them on different wavelengths, and it takes much talking to get back in sync.

From what I gather, 1992 is a time of beginnings and endings. With the help of friends who assisted with editing and producing illustrations, he produces a self-published children's book, *Peace*

Weaving

Pony. His daughter Pauline gives birth to her baby girl, Chamille. He and Lani separate, intentionally, celebrating 20 years of friendship with a vacation to California. Derek invites Lucile to live in Canada with him, but she changes her mind. They don't see each other for a few years.

Now based in Vancouver, Derek helps organize Walking Home—a trek of almost 1,800 kilometres—with his friend Linda Bassingthwaighte, a massage therapist and peace activist based in Vancouver. One night Linda has a dinner party and I meet Derek.

Linda B. is a friend of mine and I arrive early on the afternoon of the dinner party to help prepare the house for her guests. Later, she walks through the door accompanied by a fellow wearing baggy purple sweatpants. He has a salt-and-pepper ponytail, a big nose, and a sparkle in his eye.

At dinner, he tells us about walking across Canada. I am utterly amazed. I have always loved walking, but it's never occurred to me that someone could make a life out of it. I know in that moment that one day I will take a long-distance walk. This inspiration simmers on the back burner of my mind during the years that follow.

For Derek, this year marks another crucial event in his life....

CHAPTER 40

FLOWERS AND BLACKBERRIES

I was in my mid-50s when I decided to count the number of days I'd been alive. It turns out they added up to almost 20,000. But how many of these days did I truly remember?

So many experiences seem to evaporate quickly, quietly, like hot vapour into cool air. But certain moments from my past refuse to fade over time. When I close my eyes, there's a time that springs to life in full colour, rich and detailed, charged with emotion. I can slip right back into it like walking through a door.

It's 1992 and I'm sharing a clinic with several other health practitioners in Vancouver. My morning begins with a survey of my schedule. I sit down at the reception desk, filtering out the noise of co-workers as they exchange morning greetings and check messages. Suddenly from behind, rousing me from deep concentration, lilts a soft English accent, floating over the bustle and chatter.

I turn around and in front of me stands an angel. I swear I see a halo, but, shaking myself from my dazed state, I realize that this figure is a woman whose head is silhouetted by the lamp behind her. I don't notice the colour of her hair or what she's wearing, but I can see her eyes, and it's all I can do not to stare. *I could drown*, I think, *in these blue, deep-as-the-ocean eyes.* A shiver shoots up my spine, and goose bumps cascade down my arms. I'm almost dizzy. *What's happening?* I ask myself.

She continues to stand there smiling at me and I'm speechless. It's not a gregarious smile, nor a shy smile, but it's natural and warm and captivating. *Oh crap*, I think. *She's just said something to me. What should I do?*

"Please forgive me," I squeak. "My mind was somewhere else for a second." *A second? It could have been half an hour. I'm in another dimension here! Focus, Derek, focus!* I tell myself.

"You must be Derek," she says, as I blush. "My name's Lin. Linda Ward. I'm new here, working with Dr. Chan." Her voice is like music, wafting over me in gentle waves.

"Yes, uh, right." I hear my stilted voice and cringe inwardly. I feel like everything's in slow motion. "I'm, um, pleased to meet you, but … I'm sorry, I have to go get ready for my first client. See you around the office!" I force my mouth into what I hope is a natural smile and walk down the hall to my treatment room. My heart's beating a mile a minute. *What did you say to her, you twit?*

I think about Lin all day and after work I somehow gather the courage to ask her out on a walk. She accepts my invitation. We walk and talk all night, and from then on we're inseparable. We walk on our lunch breaks, and in the evenings we chat in cafés until the wee hours. I am smitten, and apparently she is too.

There are two energies to an intimate relationship: the Lover and the Friend. The Lover is passionate, mercurial. The Friend is more stable. In a friendship, agreements can be made, conditions can be set out, and boundaries established. Lin and I feel both the Friend and Lover strongly, but we try to keep the latter at bay, for once it's unleashed there's no controlling it. It's no use, though. Eventually the Lovers are loose.

Though we have become a couple, we do not make a commitment. Walking is still my priority. And Lin, when not busy at work, spends every moment studying for her degree in Traditional Chinese Medicine. That is her passion. She admires my walking but has no inclination to travel herself, except for her career.

Every time I leave the country, Lin and I embrace, and look deep into each other's eyes. We see trust there. Lin understands, respects and supports my dream to walk to Japan, and I support her dream to become a doctor. For her to stop working as a healer would destroy the essence of the woman I have fallen in love with. And were I to stop walking, it would erode the spirit of the man she adores. We agree that it would be unwise to make a commitment because of our differences and my absences. If we are meant to stick together in the long term, then it will happen. So over the next two years we repeat our agonizing separations.

Enduring months of lonely nights apart, we spend hundreds of dollars on teary long-distance phone calls. Because of the difference in time zones, though, we don't always connect. Once, when Lin is out, I leave a message on her answering machine, calling back over a dozen times in succession, using a different accent on each recording—Scottish, Japanese, Swedish, etc. I love hearing her laugh. Sometimes, though, when we do talk, the conversation feels heavy. We both dread hanging up.

One day, on the outskirts of a small town half a world away from Lin, I am poised in a public phone box. Desperate like never before, I'm almost afraid to call. But I dial the number.

"Hello—Derek?" she answers, sleepily. Her voice is balm for my aching heart. However, the slight time lag between my words and her replies makes our conversation difficult. Our words get crossed and then there are long pauses filled with nothing but longing. I push coin after coin into the slot, crying and confessing how much I miss her. Between my sobs I hear her whisper tenderly, "Derek … let go … trust me … trust *us*."

She's right. We had agreed to this. As I hear the echo of my final coin dropping down the phone's metal gullet, I yell out, "I love you, Lin!"

We have another phone date the following week, while I am stationed at a friend's house. I grab the phone off its cradle practically before it even rings. Now it's Lin in tears. She says she thinks of me constantly and has trouble concentrating at work. "I just don't think I can keep this up."

Trying to soothe her, I repeat to her what she'd told me about trusting and letting go.

"OK, I'm alright now. Really. I'll be fine." The melodic lilt in her voice confirms it. We both feel strong again, but days later I call her back, desolate once more. This happens with predictable regularity, either she or I feeling the separation more intensely.

A month later, I find myself planted in another phone booth, tears already welling in my eyes as I get out my coins. Lin answers, and I'm about to tell her how much I miss her, but she interrupts, the sweetness in her voice now absent. "I can't do this anymore, Derek. Obviously we talk about letting go, but we're not really doing it. So either we're in this relationship, or we're out of it. And if we're out, we have to stop calling each other. It's too painful otherwise. As for me, I'm in, which means I am *committed*. Now, what about you?"

I'm stunned at her tone, and at the ultimatum. I stumble over my reply. "Wow ... umm ... you're right ... I guess I need to think about this. Give me some time and I'll call you in a few days. OK?"

"Fine," she replies in a curt tone I've never heard, and hangs up. I am rendered numb by her last single word. The phone booth feels like a big block of ice with me trapped inside, my hand frozen to the receiver. Why hadn't I said YES? What was I so afraid of?

I lie awake for hours in my camper van, bathed in a cold sweat. What did Lin mean by commitment? What more did she want? Could I handle being with someone so sweet and forthright and trusting? What if I hurt her? I toss and turn and pray for the answer.

In the morning, it was clear. *It's so obvious,* I write in my journal. *I don't need days to figure out what I already know! YES, YES, YES, YES!*

I drive to the phone booth and dash inside, stuffing my pocketful of coins down the slot. It rings just once before Lin answers and before she speaks I blurt, "I'm in, I'm in, I'm in!" We cry together until my money runs out.

On my return home, I stop over to visit dear friends from the GPM, Shoshana and David. They live near the gardens of the Self-Realization Fellowship (SRF) Ashram in Encinitas, California. It was here that Paramahansa Yoganada wrote *The Autobiography of a Yogi*.

I explore the garden, which sits on the edge of a cliff above the crashing surf. Exquisite floral scents waft in on warm ocean breezes. Lush foliage envelops me like a womb. Beyond a dense thicket of palm trees stands a white temple with a golden roof where meditation students emerge to perform their silent walking practice. My own mind I cannot still, however, as it returns again and again to thoughts of Lin.

Leaping up, I run wildly through the trees, into the temple and down the hallways in search of a telephone, disturbing meditators along the way. Finding it, I am delirious, like a child on Christmas morning. I dial Lin's number. After an eternity, she picks up and I hear a small gentle in-breath. But before she can say anything, my words come gushing out. "Oh, Lin—I'm in this beautiful garden. It's sacred, magical. I really need you to be here with me. Could you just do something crazy and come down here, now?" The music in her voice sings to me over the line. It sings to me through the night and into the afternoon when she steps off the plane and into my arms. We go straight to the gardens.

I take Lin along a winding path, an undulating carpet of tiny magenta flowers caressing our feet. Ducking under a canopy of palm fronds, we brush past a cluster of lilies to a secluded corner where we sit on a stone bench beside a fish pond. At the pool's edge, a gentle waterfall spills out sparkling diamonds into the water, where a dozen huge dappled koi swim lazily. We sit in silence. Every breath feels like a lifetime and nothing exists but that very moment. I turn to Lin and whisper, "I feel so connected to everything right now. Especially you. I want to feel this forever. Will you marry me?"

Lin smiles, her eyes bright with tears. "Yes," she says. "And will you marry me?"

We wed on August 26, 1997. Lin's birthday. I recite these vows at our ceremony: "Lin, it has been five years since we first met. It was truly love at first sight for me. It was also a time where I chose to walk alone in life, so I struggled for some time with holding on and letting go of you. Today, on this, your birthday, and with my heart full of joy I release this struggle. Today in the presence of these wonderful witnesses I say to you and the whole world: Yes. Let us continue our lifetime journey of laughing, crying, learning, picking flowers and blackberries, and growing old together."

Yes. We continue to repeat this, day after day, week after week, year after year as we reaffirm our vows. Imagine the rewards in the constant reaffirmation, the joy of hearing, "YES, I want to be with you!" Our marriage can only be authentic if we have freedom with our commitment.

Each evening we make time to cuddle and talk—about our days, about our dreams and fears, and about *us*. We learn to speak the unspeakable. Because we had created a Circle of love and trust, there isn't one thought, doubt, or concern about our lives or our relationship that we can't share out loud. This keeps us united while we're apart, and draws us even nearer when we come together again.

As Lin and I are both very strong-willed people, with a lifetime of experience already, we each have habits. So we must stretch in order to live harmoniously. But this happens organically, without either of us imposing our will on the other.

Eventually, my walking changes, as I become less focussed on the outward expression of my calling. I go away for shorter periods and Lin feels more a part of my journeys. She helps me with my talks and fundraising, she fills my packsack with herbs and health potions, and she dashes me off to the airport in her little red hatchback. She writes to me daily, *to Hubby from Wifey*, with tidbits from home, stories about her hikes with the dog, her puttering in the garden, and even her delight at finding a perfectly ripe apple for lunch. When I am far from home, I pull out a thick bundle of dog-eared letters to find comfort in her familiar looped script and words of love.

I am humbled by the absolute faith Lin has in our relationship. She bestows her blessings when I spend time with female friends and travelling companions, saying, "I'm so glad she's taking care of you because I know you'll return home to me safe and sound." On every walk, I let everyone know that Lin is my highest priority. We make a pact that if she ever needs me to come home I will drop everything immediately and catch the next plane home.

It takes effort to live in a committed relationship, but we relish the dance, the to and fro, the intimacy and the solitude. On our anniversary and Lin's birthday we sing each other a song I learned many years ago. I can't remember who taught it to me, but we share it with all our friends:

Happy Birthday to you,
Happy Birthday to me,
Every day we are born,
And every day we are free.

For us both, it feels that each day spent together is one to remember. And we hope there are at least 20,000 more.

CHAPTER 41

A PLEASANT DIVERSION

And now we arrive where this book began, on the road in France. It's the summer of 1993, and I am walking with a new lilt in my step thanks to Lin.

Mary the Peace Pony and I have reunited and are heading for the *Chemin de Saint Jacques*—or—the *Camino de Santiago*. It was now my time to walk the ancient pilgrimage route through Spain. But two lovely young women stop us on the road and I regale them with stories.

"Japan is a dream and not a goal," I say. "So I have a lifetime to get there and the whole world to walk through." The girls nod, smiling. "You see, I am a pilgrim, and for me it's the journey that is more important than the destination, and—"

"But Derek," says Danielle, brow furrowed, "We understand that now. But where are you going TODAY?" Her sister echoes her inquisitive looks.

"Oh," I laugh, caught off guard. "I guess we'll walk until we're tired, and then Mary and I will look for somewhere to bed down for the night."

"Where will you stay this evening?" they query in unison.

"No idea. Any suggestions?"

"*Oui!*" says Charlotte. "Would you like to stay at our farm? It is not far, and we have horses and donkeys, so your pony will have good company."

How can I resist? I'm tired and I haven't had a comfortable sleep for some days. The sisters hastily sketch a map to the farm and promise to meet me there later.

The map led me high up into the hills. In no time, Mary was slick with perspiration and I was short of breath. We drew strength by stopping periodically to marvel at the view of the valley below. After a while, I began to wonder if I was going the right way, so every so often I'd knock on a door, waving my tattered scrap of paper. Folks nodded and just kept gesturing up the hill. *Not far?* I thought, shaking my head. I should have known. The sisters, in their car, had not grasped how long this would take on foot.

Many hours later we reached their village, which had an extraordinarily long name for such a small place: La Neuveville-devant-Lépanges. Down the road, nestled in the hollow of a mountain, was the farm, La Verdine. It seemed tranquil until barking dogs brought everyone out to greet me. I was welcomed warmly, with handshakes, hugs, and kisses on both cheeks. Charlotte introduced me to her husband, Marcel, who reached out and stroked my face gently. I was taken aback until I realized he was blind.

Elizabeth led Mary to a lush pasture, where she promptly began her evening ritual. Staring intently downwards, she turned a few circles and then scraped at the ground with her hoofs. Next, first bending her front two legs and then her hind ones, she lowered herself onto her back, and rolled deliciously in the grass. I felt a twinge of envy.

After a brief tour of the farm, Charlotte declared, "*Bien, mon ami,* you have a choice of where to stay tonight—the house, your tent, or—*voila!*" She pointed to an old covered wagon under a huge oak tree. A number of other wagons dotted the surrounding field.

"Yes, please! I said, eager for the novelty.

"Please make yourself comfortable," she said. "There's a bed set up in there, and you can wash up in the house and then join us to eat in the back garden."

Dinner was served around a long table behind the house. Floral scents filled the warm air. As the first round of wine was poured, Marcel stood theatrically, raised his glass high, and toasted my arrival with a booming, "*Salut!*"

My new friend was not only blind but could speak no English, so the sisters translated for us. When I spoke, Marcel would "see" me by letting his rough, yet incredibly sensitive fingers wander through my beard and over my face and clothes.

After sharing my tale of acquiring Mary, I asked my hosts the question that had been simmering since my arrival. "What's with all the covered wagons in your field?"

"Ahh, it's our circus," Danielle explained. "For the last several years, we teach 'special' children how to work together and perform."

These developmentally and behaviourally challenged kids, she said—some of whom lived in foster and group homes—needed a sense of belonging and purpose. Every winter, the sisters and Marcel taught the kids to juggle, mime, clown and perform magic acts. Then, in the summer they'd caravan through the countryside by horse and wagon. Each evening, villagers would be treated to a *Spectacle Extraordinaire*.

"Can I join your circus?" I exclaimed.

"But of course," the trio cried. "You must!"

"Then I will!" I whooped.

At the meal's end, a plate of cheeses was set before us, and a long baguette was passed from hand to hand. We each tore off a chunk of bread. I smeared mine with a gooey white cheese that was tangy, nutty, and sweet. Then Charlotte brought out an ornate bottle of liqueur and poured us each a small glass. I loved the convivial ritual of the whole meal. "Derek," she said, before I'd taken a sip, "in order to join the circus, you must first pass a test."

"Oh," I said, slightly worried. "What is it?"

"You must drink this."

The first taste seared my tongue. But there was no stopping. I poured the rest down my throat and it burned the whole way down. All eyes were on me as I held my breath and let the tears roll down my cheeks. As the fire inside slowly flickered out, I knew that I had passed the test.

But what about walking the Camino? This was a serious hitch, because with the circus beginning in two months, I wouldn't have enough time for the pilgrimage first. Spain would have to wait. I decided that Mary and I would walk the perimeter of Alsace and return in July, in time to turn my little-boy dream of running away with the circus into reality. And off we went.

CHAPTER 42

DRAGON AND DEER

If you look at a map of Alsace, you will see a mountain range called the Vosges. When I looked up at the massive undulating shapes in front of me, I saw the mist-shrouded outline of a dragon sprawled across the land, with the highest peak as the head. I immediately dubbed the range the "Dragon's Back" and thought of each summit in relation to that great beast. The Dragon's Head loomed steadily closer as we climbed, and I anticipated our triumphant and breathless arrival.

Tourists would drive up a winding 25-kilometre road to this peak, but we ascended slowly on foot. The day we reached the very top of the Dragon's Head, I'm willing to bet that the tourists took more photos of a white-bearded man and his white pony than they did of the distant snowy-white Alps.

After descending the Dragon's Back, we entered a valley where medieval abbeys and ancient castles sprang from rolling vineyards. The fat, ripening grapes must have worked some kind of spell as we traversed the countryside, because it seemed nearly every winery on our route invited us in for the night. Each evening, guests gathered around a large wooden table. Then, the vintner, with a bow, would present several bottles of his best vintage.

Speaking French—and often a French-German dialect I could barely understand—he'd explain what went into the grapes, and I would imagine each detail: the content of the soil, the weather, the changing emotions of his family. I sensed generations of pride in his voice. This was not just a bottle of wine he was holding but his family's life: its past, present and future. As the guest of honour, I was expected to taste every variety and inevitably it took great effort to locate my tent after these festive evenings.

At breakfast, the vintner's family would request that I recite all seven of the Alsatian grape varieties, which I'd endeavoured to remember. I'd be sent off with an armful of bottles and kisses on the cheek. Mary and I would set off through the valleys, sometimes venturing along paths in the forest where deer, pheasants, and wild pigs wandered. Each small town was different from the last, but equally charming, with half-timbered buildings and narrow winding streets. In the evening I'd find myself with another family of winemakers around a table in a pleasant garden or cool stone house. After some weeks I considered jettisoning my clothes to make room for all the unopened bottles of wine.

Mary was like the Pied Piper. In villages we'd accumulate a little throng of kids who walked with us, talking to the pony and petting her the whole way. In the town of Orschwihr, we met a teenage girl named Julie, who told me how much she loved her neighbours' ponies. It was nearing the end of my day so I asked her if these folks might let me set up my tent in their field.

"I am sure they would," said Julie. "Mary will love the ponies, too. Come with me!" She led me up through an expansive valley dotted with pastures, graceful horses grazing on both sides of the lane, and down a long driveway to a small, pretty, wooden house. She knocked on the door and a young couple answered. "Mimi, Marcou," said Julie, "I would like to introduce you to Derek." They looked at me and I at them, and goosebumps broke out on my arm. I felt a kinship, knowing somehow that we were family, *soul* family.

Marcou, an artist, spoke only French, but his facial expressions were so animated that I had no trouble comprehending him. Mimi, a teacher, spoke English well, luckily for me, and understood when I explained that I needed a place to stay for the night. Immediately, they invited me to stay indefinitely, and we laughed, sensing that this long-lost family had much catching up to do. Later they introduced their son, Loic. We enjoyed lazy days together, with mornings out in the dewy meadow tending horses, and evenings spent cooking up a storm.

One morning, out for a jaunt with Mimi and Marcou along the country road, I felt a digging sensation in my gut. Not a physical pain, exactly, but an intuition. I asked Marcou if he would cross the road and see if there was anything amiss on the other side. He did, but then shrugged his shoulders, yelling, "*C'est Bon!*" Something still felt wrong to me, so I asked him to check again. He shook his head, puzzled, but he obliged. I felt a little foolish, but I couldn't continue walking without knowing what was wrong. I stood waiting, and then heard Marcou let out a cry.

Mimi and I ran to his side. My heart sunk. In the ditch lay a deer, wounded and close to death. I scrambled down and sat beside the buck. His eyes looked deeply into mine and his chest heaved erratically. I put my hand to his chest. It was at that very moment I felt a single, lurching heartbeat, and then nothing. My eyes watered. How was it that I came to experience a death like this for the second time in my life?

The three of us held hands in a circle and cried. I felt such sadness and anger knowing that a car must have struck it. The roads seemed so full of drivers intent on getting from here to there, unaware of the destructive path they cut through nature. I prayed for the magnificent animal, with its four-point antlers and gentle eyes, and the rest of the day I walked in silence.

I left a few days later. It was hard to say goodbye to my new *soeur* Mimi and *frère* Marcou, their son and their animals. But—I had a circus to join.

CHAPTER 43

LEARNING TO SING

Verdine was bustling with strangers fixing props and tents, their saws, hammers, and paintbrushes flying. In the distance, I glimpsed children running about, but my friends were nowhere to be seen. The farm had metamorphosed into a construction site. I stood on the periphery, stunned, and then heard a shriek. "Derek!"

Charlotte and Danielle ran towards me and enveloped me in a flurry of hugs, kisses, and chatter. Over the next hour, they introduced me to each of the 30 children, who were practising magic and other feats, and to the 15 adults who were their caregivers.

After dawn, and an official farewell from the mayor, dignitaries, and families, the covered wagon train snaked its way out of town. Mary obediently took her place, pulling her own little painted cart in line with the big wagons. She was in her glory.

That morning, like each to follow, we passed through villages with names like Epinal, Fays and Chamdray. Some of the children would travel ahead on unicycles, scooters, and bicycles shouting, "*Le cirque, Le cirque!*" Each afternoon, the wagons would be parked in a circle, and the adults would put up the red and white striped Big Top tent. Children, in a last-minute frenzy, ran to and fro, fetching props and donning costumes. Arnaud and Stephanie sat under a tree, adjusting the delivery of their comedy routine. Others—Kevin,

Christophe and Alexis—practised their new-found juggling skills. No time for perfection; dropped juggling clubs simply became part of the act. There was a show to put on!

The evenings saw throngs of people at the Big Top's entrance, rising on tip-toe to peek in. Sometimes a child outside in the shadows would dare to lift up the heavy tarpaulin flaps and sneak inside for free. The show began when Marcel emerged into the spotlight. The ringmaster did not appear to be blind. He played the crowds, strutting, and whipping the trailing cord of the microphone as he announced, "Spectacular events never seen before in this town!"

The children were magnificent. Fabian, who had Down Syndrome, performed sleight of hand with two empty jugs, which involved materializing water from one of them. The crowd would go wild, giving him a standing ovation. If you listened carefully you could hear his shriek of delight as he walked out of the tent with arms outstretched to the sky. The recognition and affirmation all the children received was transformative.

Exciting as the performances were, I was also impressed by what took place between shows. Fabian, who, at 15, had the mind of a five-year-old, had difficulty with words, but his communication was uncanny. One day, a caretaker reached her breaking point and began to scream at some misbehaving children. Where another child might have seen a "mean" adult, Fabian sensed her frustration and pain. He walked over to her and gently touched her face. I saw her flinch, but she then relaxed and let him cradle her head in his hands. Her whole body softened, and then she smiled. Fabian squealed gleefully and then ambled away.

It was Fabian who inspired me to introduce the First Nations *talking stick* to the group. This was something that certain indigenous peoples used back home in Canada. "You know how the circle of the Big Top creates a special feeling, right?" I explained. "It's a place for magic. Well, if you gather outside the Big Top, you can create another kind of circle where you are safe to talk about anything," I explained. "You pass the talking stick around from person to person, and everyone has a chance to speak their piece." (Or peace, as it were.) I knew this tool might help create more understanding and acceptance, and at the same time rein in some of the difficult behaviour of adults and kids alike.

Once, on a particularly trying day, the caregivers were fuming at each other over organizational matters, which set off a chain reaction with the kids. I suggested the adults hold their own circle with a talking stick, while I did one with the children. It took the grownups much longer to calm down.

Each night towards the end of the program, Mary the Peace Pony and I stood patiently outside the Big Top, inhaling wafts of popcorn and sawdust, waiting for the children to finish performing. I can still picture her standing under the moonlight, draped in the beautiful white blanket that Mimi had sewn for her, which was embroidered with the words "Peace" on one side, and "*La Paix*" on the other. Her hoofs were painted jet-black and her mane was adorned with flowers.

When I heard clapping and saw the silhouettes of children moving backstage, I knew it was our turn to enter the ring. Despite weeks of nightly performances, I was almost just as nervous the last night of the tour as I'd been the first. "Ladies, gentlemen, and children!" Marcel announced in French, "Now—a special guest! We are proud to introduce the Unusual Traveller, a man who walks the world. He has crossed deserts, scaled the Alps, walked on fire and swum with the dolphins. Tonight he is here in your village to show you the ways of peace. Please give Monsieur Youngs and his faithful pony, Mary, a big hand." Finally, as the pipe organ let out a musical flourish, we would enter the hot and crowded tent. I would tell a few short stories that were translated for the audience. We always got a big round of applause, but I give Mary credit for stealing the show.

On the last night of the circus, I had something different planned. As I entered, I looked up into the rafters where strings of delicate peace cranes dangled near the trapeze. The children had made them just for me. The sight gave me courage, as did Mary, standing so calmly beside me. "You have heard some of my brave tales," I said, "but now you will witness the most courageous thing I have done yet. I am going to sing to you." I truly was terrified. I wasn't a singer by any stretch of the imagination. The tent was hushed, all eyes in my direction, and for a moment I considered jumping on Mary's back and riding out of there. I took a deep breath. The words slowly poured out in a shaky voice. "All we are saying is give peace a chance. All we are saying is give peace a chance...."

I felt so vulnerable. *John Lennon, if you hear me now*, I thought, *please give me the strength*. In the next moment I felt a child's warm soft hand clutching mine. I looked down and there was Little Nathalie shyly looking up at me. As I smiled, she began softly singing with me, and before the next verse started, I felt someone else take my other hand, this time more firmly by Fabian, who joined in without any hesitation. Slowly, from the back of the tent, one by one, we were joined by the rest of the boys and girls. None of them spoke English, but I am certain they grasped the meaning and power of the song.

Then, out into the audience they went, teaching and encouraging everyone to sing. As Mary and I began our exit from the tent, we turned and looked back. The performers and the entire audience were now singing in unison and holding hands. As I waved goodbye and left the tent I could still hear them singing.

While spectators filed out of the Big Top, I hitched up Mary to her wagon, and found a quiet place to sit and gather myself. After some time, I opened my eyes. Around me all 30 children sat in a circle, sitting absolutely still. My eyes welled up. In turn, each child came to hug and kiss me, before quietly walking away. That spontaneous ceremony was the perfect parting. If I close my eyes, I can still feel every hug—and beyond that—Nathalie's and Fabian's hands in mine in the Big Top. And I can hear the children's voices as they join the song: "All we are saying is give peace a chance…."

CHAPTER 44

GREEN

"If we are not gentle with life, the garden within us dies."

- from *Song of Waitaha*, by Barry Brailsford

I opened my eyes to sunlight slanting through the camper van window, illuminating the corner behind the passenger seat. Faded yellow flannel was wrapped around a bulky object I hadn't had the chance to examine properly the night before when I'd crawled into the foldout bed, exhausted.

Now I reached over and pulled the soft fabric back. What I saw underneath was green. Being colourblind, I'd only ever seen shades of grey and brown instead of green, but now somehow I *felt* it. Varied, subtle, translucent green, so soft that it took a long moment to register that this object was actually very solid. It was stone. *Pounamu.* Also known as greenstone or jade, it was a gift from my friend Barry, an enormous chunk bigger than both of my hands. It was not a gift to take home, though. It was my companion for this journey.

For thousands of years, jade had been sacred in this land, playing a crucial role in ceremonies and rituals. Wars were fought, and arduous negotiations were conducted over pounamu, which was now a protected national resource. This chunk, I discovered, when I sat up and hefted it, must have weighed at least five kilograms. Its surface was uneven, yet smooth, as if centuries of hands had caressed it.

The stone brought a solace my night's sleep hadn't—a physical blessing for my journey on the green islands of *Aotearoa*.

It had been over two years since my first trip to New Zealand. Back in 1992, Lani and I, still fast friends though no longer romantic partners, had attended a conference of worldwide indigenous cultures. She gave a spiritually-inspired dance performance and I did storytelling. The highlight for me of that energizing gathering, though, was meeting Barry Brailsford, an affable "kiwi" scholar. Short in stature, with curly hair and a grey beard, he was a real-life leprechaun, complete to the twinkle in his eye. But when he spoke it was with the gentle authority of a learned author and anthropologist. Barry intrigued me with tales of the ancient tribes of Aotearoa.

Barry had been honoured by elders in the indigenous Māori nation of *Waitaha* and granted the responsibility of documenting their history and traditions. Two hundred tribes of Waitaha were believed to have lived in peace for over 1,000 years, in harmony with the life-sustaining land and waters. They were known as the Water Seekers, the Stone People, the Star Walkers and the Wind Eaters. In time, their peace was disturbed by another Māori nation that invaded from the north. Collectively, the Waitaha decided it was more honourable to die in peace than to live in war, and they humbly bowed their heads to the warriors' clubs. Stories tell of how the rivers, shores, even lagoons turned red. Those few who survived the bloodshed were assimilated, but they kept their traditions and beliefs alive through song. This history was being recorded by Barry in a book, which he was close to finishing.

Barry shared some of the stories with me, and one in particular caught my attention. There had been a Peace Trail, *Te Huarahi o Rongo-marae-roa*, on the South Island. The Waitaha would gather pounamu to carry on this gruelling path over the Southern Alps. Over 100 years ago, Barry told me, blood had been spilled on the Peace Trail in violence. Visitors were then barred from the trail, which had remained off-limits until recently.

I felt a stirring. "This trail is calling me!" I blurted. Barry listened quietly, not interrupting, like a father listening to his excited son beg for a new red bicycle. "I'd be honoured if you could walk it with me, but if that's not possible, I'll do it alone," I declared, naïvely.

Naïveté has taken me to some amazing places, but thank goodness Spirit recognized my foolishness this time. In retrospect if I had walked this trail alone I surely would have died. Barry cautioned me that to do this journey right, I would need to go with a group of people who understood and accepted the old ways. This would take time to organize.

Two years later, I arrived at the Auckland airport on New Zealand's North Island. I joined my fellow travellers in the passport line with resignation, awaiting the usual bureaucratic rigmarole. The ritual display of authority at borders had always seemed tedious and irrelevant, but since being arrested in the U.S. for protesting and walking on government-restricted land, I'd become a little nervous at border crossings. I began to feel guilty, as always, but couldn't dredge up a single good reason for it.

Eventually my turn with the customs officer arrived, and he ordered me to turn over my tent and boots for inspection. Ugh. The last thing I needed was this kind of hassle after a 13-hour flight. *Honestly, do I look like a drug smuggler?* I felt a wisecrack working its way from my brain to my mouth and instantly shoved it back inside. This customs officer had the power to make my life a living hell. In the past I'd been strip-searched at borders for drugs, held at gunpoint, and had my bags torn apart. I knew the routine.

With a groan, I dragged myself and my gear over to the tiny inspection room, let out a sigh and sat down. Two other officers had already taken my tent apart. One was busily scraping away at the tent pegs, the other gouging out dirt from the treads of my boots. Seeing the look on my face, one of them explained that they had to test the soil for foreign bacteria.

They went on to tell me about the sensitive ecology of New Zealand. Pines from California, possums from Europe, rapidly spreading gorse bushes from Scotland, and countless insects from far-flung lands were all wreaking havoc on local ecosystems. Now I understood. Across the planet, the introduction of foreign species has seriously upset the delicate balance of nature.

Eventually, my tent and boots passed the test, and I was given entry. This gave me pause for thought. I had to admit I felt a sense of entitlement to be anywhere, that all citizens of the planet ought to share this place freely with one another, while respecting others' privacy, values and history, of course. I balked at anyone giving me permission. But now, something had shifted. I could see how humans were damaging Mother Earth in the name of "growth" and "progress". Corporations acted as though they were entitled to resources. But what about me? My wanderlust was not entirely innocent. Jet fuel had been burned to get me here.

I felt a nagging in my stomach. Was I being self-indulgent? Maybe I should just quit rambling and go to Japan. This feeling was heightened as I thought of the amount and quality of trust that Lin extended to me. I didn't know if I deserved it. That night of my arrival, part of me was still weighing the words that I had inked in my journal somewhere over the Pacific:

LEAVING VANCOUVER: SUNNY

LAST BREAKFAST AT
WALKING IN ENGLISH BAY, BALANCING
ROCKS. EAGLE FEATHER FROM TEONI
SLIDES FROM KEITH. COLOURS OF 4 DIRECTIONS
CRYSTAL FOR CLARITY. HOW MANY TIMES
HAVE I DONE THIS. WHY IS THE
EMOTION NO LESS AND VERY DIFFERENT.
I LOOK OUT OF THE PLANE WINDOW. VANCOUVER
IS CRYING. PAULINE IS CRYING, LIN IS CRYING
I AM CRYING. MY CONNECTION TO LIN IS
OVERWHELMING. I LEAVE A BIG PART OF ME
I FEEL A HOLE IN MY BEING.
RAW

I knew I could not take for granted my being here. This was especially sobering, knowing I had even more permission to wait for. Barry told me that not only did the Waitaha elders have to agree to grant access to their sacred land in order for a walk to take place, the land itself would have to agree—the mountains, rivers, streams, oceans, and from the Grandfathers and Grandmothers—spirits of the land. What this would look or sound like, I was not sure.

Now I was lying in the bunk of Barry's camper van. He was off doing a book tour and we planned to rendezvous in several weeks to prepare for the walk over the Peace Trail. And I was missing Lin. I reached out to pick up the greenstone. Its solid weight in my hands was comforting. To someone accustomed to the increments of footsteps, there is a dreamlike unreality to travelling by plane. Perhaps everyone feels this, that niggling sense that it really isn't possible to be so far from where you were just hours before. Was I really here? The jade in my hand, so hard yet almost liquid, seemed to pulsate, voicing the contradictions within it. *Of course you are here, Derek. You are meant to be,* whispered the sunlit stone, in the almost audible voice of its dark depths and glowing surface. I laid it gently down on the flannel.

I am not the most patient man, and it could have been a real test to wait for Barry and our permission. But with this home on wheels at my disposal, I didn't have to sit around. There was so much to explore: geysers, volcanoes, wildlife sanctuaries, things that made New Zealand unlike anywhere I had been before. I wanted to see it all!

Barry's van was perfect for travel and had everything I needed, despite the compact quarters. In fact, compared to many places I'd stayed, it was sheer luxury. I even had space to set up a little altar where I laid the greenstone besides some small precious stones I'd brought from home, along with my shaman's medicine pouch and some photographs of my family. Barry had named the camper "Tardis", after the time machine in the British TV series *Doctor Who*. This made me think of Lin, and the gulf between us. Sadly, Tardis could not take me to her. I pulled out my video camera and began to film, so that Lin could explore my temporary home with me.

I panned the camcorder from my cozy bed out the window to the open road. "Hold on to your seat, Lin!" I quipped. "Your peace pilgrim is about to become a peace tourist! And you're along for the ride!"

I was driving on the left side of the road now, like they do in England, and it was easier than I'd thought it would be. More difficult was understanding the New Zealand accent and slang, but soon I was wishing everyone *Kia ora* (the Māori equivalent of *aloha*.)

As I made my way around the North Island, I was blessed not only with new sights, but new friends. As always I was torn between my love of people and my desire to explore, but it was even more acute at this quicker pace. I didn't have the time to linger, to cultivate deep intimacy with people and the land as I did through walking. I was somewhat unsettled by this, though it was my own choice. I kept moving on, even stopping at roadside plaques like a proper tourist to read about important places and historical events. One such sign was in honour of the early settlers from Scotland, and as I read the long list of names, I noticed they were all men. What about the women? Without them, there would have been no settlements. I shook my head, wishing that there was more of *her-story* in history.

Humans in New Zealand are outnumbered 20 to 1 by sheep, the locals were proud to inform me. I didn't doubt this, as every path, road and field I came across on the North Island was littered with them. On one of my first nights camping, I was visited by a huge shaggy ewe. I froze, thinking anxiously of the sheep who had bowled me over in Yorkshire. "Hello, sweet thing," I said soothingly. I wouldn't play saint this time, though. Instead I backed slowly toward Tardis. My path was blocked by an equally shaggy, monstrous pig. After a few uneasy minutes it was clear that the creature was merely curious, and not hungry.

New Zealand's bird population also beats the humans'. At the seaside I encountered gangs of tottering penguins, and also huge colonies of Kakapu. These birds are born blind and featherless, but after four months they take to the air in a mass migration. It must be an awesome sight. As I sat very still on a black volcanic beach, a Weka bird (a kind of rail) ran up and nipped at my feet. My favourite bird, though, was the Tui, or Parson bird, which is named for its costume of iridescent black, with a small lacy white collar of feathers adorning its neck. Tuis are known for mimicry and can be trained to talk like parrots. I enjoyed their natural calls from the forest canopy, which sounded like a percussive overture for woodblock, rattle and slide whistle. And in the evenings, I heard the haunting cry of the Morepork (a type of owl), hooting, "*Ruru, ruru...*." *Good night Derek, all is well.*

I stopped for lunch one afternoon in the cool shade of a gigantic Morton Bay Fig tree. Its huge aerial roots hung down like long drips of candle wax, and at the trunk's base, massive roots spread out along the ground like fins or legs. They were nearly half my height and at least 30 feet long. I felt as though I were sitting in the lap of Shiva.

Another afternoon I stopped the van near a trail to the beach. When I got down to the sand, it was deserted as far as the eye could see. So I "doffed my togs" and ran naked into the ocean, soaking up salt and sun on my wet skin, feeling inexpressibly alive.

Exhausted one evening from a full day's driving, I lucked out with a campground that advertised hot springs, and it was my first intoxicating dip of many. I learned that the whole coastline, all 10,000 kilometres of it, was riddled with geysers and hot springs. The hot, mineral-rich water welling from the earth felt as different from a warm bath in city water as sunlight feels from a flashlight. A healing, sustaining force worked its way deep into my body. Oh, if Lin could only join me now.

Just when I had comfortably settled into my role as a peace tourist, it was time to reunite with Barry. At first I barely recognized the man I'd met the year before. Our long hug gave me a chance to feel his energy, which was very low, sapped of vitality. He told me how demanding his book tour had been, and the toll that the five-year process of book writing had taken on his life and relationships. I could relate to an extent. This felt like some kind of cautionary tale to me and I filed it away for later.

My friend gave me a copy of *Song of Waitaha*. It was almost as heavy, and almost as precious, as the greenstone itself. What a treasure.

Barry had secured permission from tribal elders and selected 12 individuals to make the journey. The night before our departure, we huddled together in a darkened room and Barry spoke in grave tones about what a physically dangerous undertaking this would be. This wasn't Everest, but it wasn't a walk in the park, either. That sleepless night I spent pondering what lay ahead.

In the morning we gathered again and drove to the foothills. Before we began walking, we blessed one another with a traditional Māori saying: *Mate aroha tatou e putikitia:* "May love bind us one to the other."

In my pack I had the greenstone. The night's worries melted away in the sunshine, and I imagined myself skipping along in blissful harmony, flowers at my feet, the wind at my back and the warm sun in my face. And that was exactly what the trek was like, too. For about an hour. Then everything changed.

Suddenly there was a mountain in front of us, and we were going to scale it. Up we climbed. Soon, my back cried out in pain. The pounamu, which had been such a gift, now became a burden. I knew it would be sensible to give the stone to someone else to carry, but I couldn't let it go. It not only meant I was not fit enough, but that my heroic story would be tarnished. *There goes your ego again,* I thought, *flaring up with your back.*

I had no choice but to surrender my pride and the jade, feeling the sting of humiliation as I passed it into the hands of Gail, a slight 11-year-old girl. But as the stone left my grasp, I heard it say, *There are no heroes in peace, Derek, only people working together.* As we toiled uphill, each person took the stone in turn. And somehow, the jade, so soft, yet so solid, was how I needed to be—strong but not rigid.

The steeper the terrain, the more frightened I became and the shakier my legs got. I needed to stay in the moment. If I looked up I might freeze in fear of what lay ahead, and if I looked back to where I'd come from, I might lose my balance. So my task was to just focus on one step at a time.

Hours later, we reached the summit. We all cheered, but of course, having achieved that height, the only way ahead was down. Perched on the thin edge of the mountaintop, I waited in nervous silence for my turn to descend the other side. I was sure that the rest of the group could hear my heart racing. I dreaded the first step, but knew I had no choice. "Derek, you're next," said Barry. "Just take a good grip of the rope and reach out with your left leg."

"OK," I said. But I could not move.

"See those footholds that have been hacked into the ice below you? Just lower yourself down and put your left foot into one of them."

He's crazy, I thought, feeling a tremor in my arms and legs as I looked down the seemingly endless drop. *I could die.* But then these words came to my lips: "*Hoka Hey*," the war cry of the great Lakota leader Crazy Horse. *It's a good day to die.* Indeed it was a good day to die, and consequently a good day to live. I grabbed the rope and stepped down.

I uttered those words, *Hoka Hey*, again that day as we forded a river, linking arms in a chain to avoid being swept away by glacial torrents. My relief was palpable when we all reached the other side in safety, but my guts lurched again each of the half dozen or more times we had to repeat this effort over the course of a day as we continued down the path. The Peace Trail was one challenge after another, physically and spiritually.

It was a mystical reality both familiar and utterly new. We learned how the old ones navigated, without compasses, radios or GPS to guide them safely. Instead they followed birdsong, cloud formations, wind direction, and air temperature. We learned how to recognize and enter seven sacred doors, which are energetic portals. Only after we had meditated, waited, and watched would each open in its own time. This was another form of permission.

After six days, we reached the end of the Peace Trail. Gail passed me back the precious jade. As she did, I heard the stone again. Not in words, but in an ache for home that echoed my own ache for Lin. My journey from here was utterly necessary if the lessons of the Peace Trail were to sink past my own surface and become part of my core. And it was not just about me—I knew I must take the pounamu back to its source. Somewhere in my journey around the South Island, I would find it a home.

Before we parted company, we held a ceremony and recited the "Traveller's Prayer" in Māori:

Ka u ki Matanuku
Ka u ki Matarangi
Ka u ki tenei whenua
Hei whenua,
He kai mau te ate o te tauhou.

I arrive where an unknown earth is under my feet,
I arrive where a new sky is above me,
I arrive at this land,
A resting-place for me.
O spirit of the earth! The stranger humbly
offers his heart as food for thee.

Physically exhausted but emotionally strengthened, I felt I had earned permission to keep walking.

CHAPTER 45

RETURNING HOME

I called the South Island walk my "One Earth Pilgrimage". Before setting off, a group of wonderful new friends held a circle with me where we exchanged small pieces of greenstone, and all took a turn holding and blessing the large chunk of pounamu. We shared prayers and sang a song that had been written for the occasion:[6]

> *I come from ...*
> *May I fall in step with you?*
> *We can walk in peace together,*
> *sharing stories, sharing love.*
> *We'll walk for those in hunger,*
> *We'll walk for those in fear,*
> *We'll walk for all our loved ones,*
> *and the earth we hold so dear.*

Other walkers joined me for a few hours or a few days, and I was even lent a beautiful white pony named Frosty. I renamed him Trusty as a reminder

---

6   (Clem and Janet McGrath, printed with permission)

to have trust and faith. In many respects, the whole experience reprised my time in Europe with Mary, from the enjoyment of the bond we had, down to the comedic struggles with saddlebags and wagons and help from strangers when I most needed it. There were also echoes of the fear and loneliness. But I knew how to cope. At times I sat with the feelings, and other times I knocked on doors.

For several nights I stayed with a young couple who ran an organic farm. I liked Gil and Frida and their two rambunctious children right away. They were eager to show me their crops, greenhouses, solar energy system and water wheels. They made delicious food and sang songs at sunset. But by the end of the day, I could see the masks coming off, not intentionally but probably from exhaustion. Rarely had I come across such a gentle couple, but there was also a sadness about them and their connection was tenuous.

It saddened me to see couples drifting apart. Often I'd hear about friends who suddenly broke up—apparently out of the blue—one partner leaving overnight to the other's complete shock. *Jumping out of the circle.* This can happen when partners don't know they're in the Circle, let alone understand they need to cultivate it. I couldn't tell Gil and Frida to stay together, but at least they could come to a decision together.

On the second evening, the three of us sat outside on the earth, with them facing each other. I asked them to look deeply into each others' eyes. They were timid at first. I talked about how revealing our vulnerabilities can actually be our strength. I talked about creating an energy field of love, where they would be safe to share anything. They both began to weep, falling into an embrace. Then, as I faded into the background, they began to reveal their true feelings. They discussed their long days of physically demanding work and agreed they had let their relationship stagnate. But now, they would begin to tend it—together.

As rewarding as it was to make deep connections and to feel of service, one of the most significant relationships on this journey was with the pounamu. I had imagined its voice from when I first saw it, but the more that I carried it, travelled with it, took in its surface and its depth, the less this felt like imagination. Of course, stone had long been an important symbol for me, of my father. But this was beyond symbol. The greenstone, my teacher, was speaking to me, and it wanted to go home.

Returning Home

After months of tramping—as they call it in New Zealand—we came to a place on the Otago Coast where huge spherical rocks emerged from the sand at the water's edge—the Moeraki Boulders. They looked like half-buried marbles in a giant's playground. I stood for a long time drinking in the delightful picture before clambering up on one, and hopping from boulder to perfectly rounded boulder.

Tethering Trusty to a scrubby bush where the sand met shallow cliffs, I hoisted my piece of greenstone out of the wagon. I perched atop one of those perfectly round boulders, pounamu in my lap, and looked out at the endless sea, waves slowly rolling in like long gentle breaths. I looked down at the greenstone, and again I was mesmerized by the translucence of the jade as it caught and refracted the sunlight in its outermost layer. It gradually became darker and more opaque, until at some indefinable depth, light could no longer penetrate. Silently, I asked if it had anything to tell me. *Yes,* I heard. *This is the place.*

I searched among the boulders until I found a hidden hollow where a fissure deepened into a tiny cave. I wedged the pounamu securely in place, my chest expanding with gratitude for all that my journeys with the stone had taught me. Stepping away, I took one last look at it, in deep shade but for one corner that glowed where sun came into the fissure. I smiled. It had returned to where it belonged; I could feel it. I reached out a finger for a farewell touch. The surface was smooth and warm. *Derek,* I heard it sigh, *I am home.*

Now it was time for *me* to go home. Time to leave the land of greenstone for my own green land of towering fir trees and beaches. And time to be with Lin.

After returning Trusty to his owner, I said my goodbyes and got on the plane. I watched the islands recede through the small, blurry window. And I heard the pounamu calling—*Mate aroha tatou e putikitia:* May love bind us to one another.

CHAPTER 46

THE NOTE

Back home in Vancouver, I enjoy a blissful reunion with Lin, and then, inevitably, we both must to return to work.

Before meeting my first client of the day, I often like to take myself out for breakfast on Granville Island. It's the perfect spot to people-watch: art students, tourists, fishermen, the whole gamut. I sit with a newspaper, drink coffee and soak up the city vibe before heading off to my quiet massage studio to help people unwind.

One such morning in a trendy café by the water, I sip my latte with a hint of cinnamon. I glance up from my newspaper, and notice a charming young Asian woman at a nearby table, smiling nervously at me. I smile back politely and return my gaze to the usual sensationalized, depressing stories of the day.

Sometime later I look up again, and the young lady once more catches my eye and smiles at me. How flattering! What a beautiful young fresh smile it is, and just for me. What an impression I must be making. My male ego still loves being noticed by a pretty girl, more so now that I'm nearing retirement age. I smile again in return, now feeling a little flushed from the attention. I continue reading, but I lower the paper just a bit to gaze over top and check to see if she's still looking. I watch as she reaches into her purse and pulls out a small electronic translator. Then, she begins to jot something down on a scrap of paper.

Suddenly, she is walking towards me. Still smiling, she drops a folded note casually on my table, nods, and walks away. I take the note and pause, relishing the moment, and watch her disappear around the corner. *Wow, I think to myself. Such a pretty young thing attracted to me? Yup, I've still got it! What'll I do, though? I'm flattered, but I'm also very in love with my wife.* I sit there, the note still clutched in my hand, and I ponder my response. I can't wait any longer. I unfold the note, and read the following words:

Excuse me sir. You pants is broken in the middle of pants. I am sorry to bother you.

I look down. Oh God. My fly. It's undone. And—I don't wear undershorts. I quickly do up my zipper and crumple up the note. I keep it, though, to remind me of my vanity. And I consider buying a pair of boxers.

CHAPTER 47

CAMINO

I walked up the stone steps and knocked on the heavy wooden door of the farm house. It opened, and a man and woman stood there for a moment, looking dazed. "Derek—*Est-ce vraiment toi?*—Can it really be you?"

I hadn't told my friends Marcou and Mimi that I planned to drop by. Six years had passed since I'd left my pony with them in Alsace in 1993, and since then I hadn't been in Europe at all, let alone France. Mary the Peace Pony was now enjoying a contented life of equine leisure with two companions, Rebel and Plume, out in their back pasture.

I preferred to keep visits like this spontaneous, to spare everyone the emotional buildup and potential letdown if the course of events were to change. More often than not, this tactic paid off, as it did now. Our reunion was joyful, the hugs and kisses upon the cheek were copious, and I was faced with a barrage of eager questions. But first I needed to see Mary.

I felt strangely reticent. What if she didn't remember me? Or—what if she did and was angry with me? I took a deep breath and walked out the back door into the field where she stood in the distance. Suddenly my heart felt too big for my chest. How noble she looked, like a smooth marble statue, standing in the cool shade of an oak tree.

I walked up to her slowly. Her spirit was as strong as ever, but I could tell her body was weary. I had never known Mary's exact age, but figured she was close to 30. I needn't have worried; she knew me. We stood silently together for the longest time. I softly pressed my face against hers and held her head in my arms, just breathing her in. When we'd walked across Europe, every evening ended this way. After setting up camp, I would feed Mary and then brush her silky mane. While watching the sky's brilliant colours fade into soft shades of indigo, I would ease her head toward me, and she would close her eyes, falling asleep in my arms.

Once my visit with Mimi and Marcou came to an end, the difficult part came—goodbyes. We knew we would see each other again, but I realized with a deep ache that this was my last visit with Mary. I went out into the field one last time and took her head in my arms. After some minutes I felt a heavy weight as her head gave way to my support. I could have stood there forever. But, slowly, gently, I released her head from the cradle of my arms and retreated. Stopping at the fence, I turned back to call out a farewell, but my throat tightened and I choked. I closed my eyes, and, under my breath, whispered, "Goodbye my old friend. We walked well together." Once more, she was teaching me to let go, trust, and love.

Now I had another journey to complete. Years ago, I had planned to walk with Mary along the Camino de Santiago de Compostela in northern Spain, but we'd been diverted by the children's circus. Now it was time to embark on this famous route.

Camino means "road" or "way" in Spanish. And Santiago—he's Saint James. In his lifetime, this apostle of Jesus is said to have spread the gospel in Spain. Forty-four years after the death of Christ, James died at the hands of King Herod and his body was cast adrift on a stone boat. As legend has it, the boat landed on the shores of northwestern Spain, where his followers collected and buried his body. In the 9th century, the remains were discovered by a hermit, guided by a field of stars (*compostela*). Soon after, visitors began travelling from afar to this special place. The veracity of this tale is debated to this day, but the Camino remains one of the most important pilgrimages in the world. In fact, centuries ago, Dante wrote that the title of "pilgrim" belonged only to those who journeyed to Santiago.

Putting aside its religious roots, there had always been something so compelling to me about the idea of following in the footsteps of not only the famous pilgrims of old—Saint Francis of Assisi, Queen Isabella of Spain, Charlemagne—but more recent ones as well—Paolo Coelho, Anthony Quinn and Shirley MacLaine (who would soon write a book about it). This is not to mention the thousands of nameless souls through the centuries who trod the way without modern conveniences like hiking boots, sleeping bags, or water bottles. Perhaps James truly is buried at Santiago and perhaps not, but for hundreds of years, seekers of transcendence and transformation have used nothing more than their own power to reach this place.

Accompanying me on this journey was my friend John Mills from Vancouver, who had walked the Camino on two previous occasions. With our combined walking experience, we felt ready to guide a group of ten pilgrims along this ancient route. Because of time constraints, we offered a two-week walk across the last quarter of the 800 kilometre trail in the region of Galicia. Two hundred kilometres, we thought, wasn't that far.

Nothing could have prepared me for the difficulty of our undertaking. But this had little to do with the severity of terrain or weather, blisters, or overstuffed backpacks—and we had all of these. The challenge lay mostly in group dynamics. John and I had set out to accompany fellow pilgrims on a journey of personal change. It seemed that many of our pilgrims had come expecting a guided tour.

John and I made great efforts to ensure ten people were cared for and satisfied, but a pilgrimage isn't meant to be easy. Now we heard otherwise: the days were too long, the weather was too hot, or too wet, and the meals were too unfamiliar. After having walked in Greece with watermelon as my only fuel, I had little patience for pickiness. When people started complaining about the beds being too hard, I expected Goldilocks to round the corner any minute. But this wasn't a fairy tale; it was a pilgrimage! On a door in one of the pilgrims' hostels there is a sign that states: *A tourist demands; a pilgrim receives gratefully.*

When we reached Santiago, there's no doubt I felt a moment of triumph and gratification. But I also felt depleted and I swore never to return.

But—something called me back to the Camino. Despite the popularity of the pilgrimage, Northern Spain seemed untouched by the endless stream of pilgrims, except for well-worn sections of trail where millions of footsteps have eroded the path, sometimes to a depth of over eight feet. It calls to mind hollows worn into ancient stone stairs, only here the centuries of countless footfalls have worn away the earth itself.

The Camino crosses through several distinct cultural areas of Spain, each with its own customs, music, food, and dialect. In Galicia, you can hear the region's Celtic lineage in bagpipe music that wafts out the doors of bars and cafés. Equally captivating is the language of Gallego, which sounds like a form of Portuguese, though much of its vocabulary has Celtic origins.

On Galicia's eastern horizon, snowy mountain peaks serrate the sky. The Camino unfurls between them, meandering alongside creeks and cutting through fields that evoke the rolling hills of Ireland. In misty valleys sit stone churches covered in moss. Roadside altars to Saint James dot the dusty roadsides and cows saunter down main streets. Townspeople along the way still dress in traditional garb. Men proudly sport the ubiquitous black Spanish beret called the *boina*; even farmers who toil with scythes wear them with their proper button-down shirts. Women lean out of kitchen doorways in checkered aprons. It is a step back in time.

The following year, my dear friend Lucile and I were planning to walk from the Netherlands to NATO Headquarters in Belgium in late spring. She mentioned that the timing could dovetail perfectly with another go at the Camino and suggested that she co-lead another group with me. I reminded her of my frustrations with the Camino as tour, but decided it was worth trying again.

This time, we set more realistic and clear expectations for the group. Our pilgrims were happy and we felt much more rewarded than drained. The two of us continued taking groups every spring for six years, growing exponentially as friends and leaders on each occasion. We were like shepherds, guiding people not just on the physical journey but the emotional one. There was something so humbling in being of service, learning every year how to exert ourselves less, yet give more. This helps me now in my "normal" life now as I get older, knowing that I can do less, but still *be* more.

Each morning on the Camino, Lucile and I would meet with our group in a circle, sharing prayers, worries and intentions for the day ahead. Then, arming our pilgrims with small hand-drawn maps, we'd send them off. We knew each would experience moments of triumph, panic, joy, revelation, communion, and humour. I insisted that each person try walking alone at least once, but most folks found this challenging, and ended up clumping together. Along the way, Lucile and met up with our pilgrims periodically to make sure they were alright. Occasionally one or two would go astray, but we'd always track them down.

At day's end, after walking up to 30 kilometres, our group of ten would sort out packs and bunking arrangements at the *refugio* (pilgrims' hostel), and spend time attending to personal matters: blisters, provisions, laundry, etc. Later, around the dinner table at a local café or tavern, we'd debrief, sharing stories of the many small miracles we'd witnessed along the road. One pilgrim recounted his story of hunger pangs after a missed breakfast, miles of lonely countryside, and his shock at the sight of a ragged old crone suddenly blocking his path. His worry turned to rapture when the woman offered him savoury pancakes to fuel him for the road ahead. Another walker told of watching a newborn calf being licked clean by its mother.

A hearty evening meal in our bellies, and sometimes too much *vino tinto*, pilgrims wandered off to their bunks, and Lucile and I would hug goodnight. Afterward, even when mentally or physically exhausted, I liked to spend time sitting alone in the café making notes in my small journal before retiring.

One evening, I was alone with my notebook when a small throng of Italian pilgrims approached me. "Are you walking the Camino?" they asked.

"Oh yes, it's my fifth time." I remarked, casually.

"Oh, that's fantastic. We didn't know that! Are you writing?"

"Yes, I'm writing about the Camino, actually," I said.

"Oh, really? A song of the Camino!"

"Hmm, yes, I guess you could say that," I answered.

"The music of the Spanish northwest is very Celtic, is it not?"

"Yes, that's true." I wasn't a music expert by any means, but this much I did know. I found the line of questioning a bit odd, but didn't dwell on it. I knew to expect the unexpected on the Camino.

The group seemed very keen to get acquainted with me and questions continued for some time before I finally excused myself. They looked disappointed to see me go, which left me feeling vaguely unsettled. But I was too tired to investigate that sensation.

The next morning, I told my own group of pilgrims about the encounter, and a young woman in my group, Elaine, started laughing. It turned out that earlier the previous day, she had been approached by an Italian pilgrim who'd asked, "This man, with the long grey ponytail and the red bandanna—he looks familiar. Who is he?"

"Oh, him? That's Willie Nelson!" Elaine had quipped in jest. So there I was, famous, thanks to a case of mistaken identity.

Lucile and I pared the pilgrimages down, with my aim to offer a taste of what I'd learned on my own walks. Time has a way of stretching out at a walking pace, so I figured that ten days could offer both the exhilaration, as well as the integral physical and emotional hurdles. Away from the hurtling pace of ordinary life and its everyday distractions and demands, they could step past their comfort zones.

Early on in the planning process each year, I could sense resistance in some folks. On one level I understood this. New things can be scary. Some people said they were going to the Camino but never took the steps to actually get there. It was like me at the steel mill. Another year would roll by and they were still no closer to making their pilgrimage happen. I got better and better at identifying who was really interested and willing to do the work, and who just wanted to talk about it. I eventually stopped responding to the latter but hoped that one day their Camino would happen for them.

Months before each walk was to begin, I'd be inundated with questions from excited and anxious pilgrims. It was understandable, but some people wanted to know everything ahead of time. "How many kilometres? How big a pack? What can you tell me about the weather?"

"I can tell you one thing about the weather," I'd say.

"What's that?"

"There will be some."

"But I need to know what kind of shoes to buy, and whether to bring a raincoat or a poncho. And while we're at it, how far between bathrooms? Just what can I expect? How hard is it going to be?"

Oh boy. People seemed to want to plan all the fun out of their journey. So this was my answer: "How long is your list?"

"Well," they'd say, "there's my sleeping bag, and two pairs of trousers—two for hiking and one dressier pair, and a pair of shorts. And then the tops—undershirts, an intermediate layer, a sweater and a rain jacket. But you see, now there is no room for—"

"OK," I cut in. "I don't really need to know exactly what's going in your bag. That's not the point. How about if I tell you how *I* pack?"

"Oh, yes please."

"Make a pile of all the things you think you need," I'd start. "Then split it in half. You'll need even less."

"But how can I do without *such and such*?"

"The bigger your pile, the longer your list, the less time and the less room there is to see and feel and breathe the pilgrimage," I answered.

"But," they'd say in defence, "I want to be prepared."

"Believe it or not," I'd answer, "it isn't your *stuff* that prepares you. In fact, it can get between you and the Camino."

"Ohhh . . . ." they'd say, with a glimmer of recognition.

"Less truly is more, and more is less. If you succumb to the urge to pack your bag for every unforeseen circumstance—with clothes for all weather, every possible first aid supply, maps, journal, extra shoes, books, camera, a tripod for the camera, etcetera—then you have one heavy pack and one very busy mind. Consider that less clutter will let you experience more.

"Obviously it's smart to be in shape and to have proper clothes for the climate," I continued, "but your mental outlook is what really counts. Give a thought to letting go."

It's a human instinct to want *more*—more things, more information, more status, more food—more, more, more. We possess a natural drive to accumulate and achieve. It keeps us moving forward as a human species. But when this drive gets out of control, we become like addicts, ultimately never satisfied by what we get.

Compiling a list or amassing things can be a way to soothe our fears. It makes us feel safe and in control. But this can equate to the clinging attachment the Buddhists talk about. Just as problematic is aversion, when we're adamant about what we *won't* do, or have, or think. But we can learn to tolerate discomfort instead of pushing it away. I am not saying this is true in every case, but when we can live with something we dislike and reach the point where it no longer disturbs us, we have already let it go. I had already learned in so many ways that I was happiest when I let go. If it was true for my own life, it was true for a pilgrimage.

When we led Camino groups, Lucile and I seldom had time to walk on our own, so I made the most of an hour of solitude one day, sauntering along in my own quiet little sunny world. As I walked, I began to hear something in the distance behind me, a low-pitched hum. As it grew louder, I realized it was music. Suddenly, two figures sped past me, singing in heavily accented German, and disappeared over the next hill. I wouldn't have been surprised if they reached Santiago by nightfall.

That evening, our group sat at a long wooden table, joining other pilgrims from at least half a dozen countries inside a low, stone tavern. As not everyone shared a common language, music was the way for us to connect, and people began sharing fun rhymes and tunes from their respective homelands. I couldn't recall a single Canadian song except "If I had a Rocket Launcher", an activists' call-to-arms by Bruce Cockburn, but it seemed too political. Why couldn't I recall something like "I's the B'y", a Newfoundland folk song that every Canadian kid learns at school? I'd grown up in the U.K. of course. I sighed, feeling embarrassed at having nothing to offer. Suddenly a tiny, compact young woman with dark eyes stood up and started singing in Portuguese. Everyone went still. A huge voice filled the room, sensuous and impassioned. I didn't understand the words, but I knew they mourned a lost love. After the singer's last note, she sat down demurely. The room was silent.

The spell was broken when the big wooden front door burst open and two figures tumbled into the room—the guys who'd passed me on the trail! The husky fellows were flushed, smiling like crazy, and holding hands. My curiosity piqued, I had to ask them their story after they took off their packs and sat down. "We're brothers!" they announced proudly. This was their first time together after a 30-year separation. As they walked, their childhood melodies, locked away in memory for years, had been unleashed, rekindling a fraternal intimacy they had also lost.

There is always love on the Camino, which is revealed in different forms. In the village of Furelos, there is a small stone church. Inside hangs a crucifix like no other I have ever seen. Instead of showing Jesus with both of his hands nailed to the cross, his right arm is extended downwards, as if he is offering help and comfort to the people below. To me, this is the spirit of the Camino.

As much as the Camino can bring out the best in us, it can also sometimes bring out the worst. The pilgrimage triggers fears of physical challenges, loneliness, the unknown. But it's how we react or respond that's important, and, after years of walking and leading pilgrimages I noticed that we tend to fall into categories in terms of this. I'm no expert on Jungian archetypes, the Enneagram or astrology or any of that stuff, but I found it interesting every year to see who would fit each role. Everyone is unique of course, and that's what makes us so interesting, but there were definite types, with their respective positive and negative traits.

Inevitably there would be a drama queen, or king. These people can be some of the most sensitive and loving individuals, but there is often something deep within that needs healing, beyond what a ten-day walk can accomplish. The drama queen needs to stand out in the crowd and knows how to get attention. She may become the life of the party, may repeat stories of personal achievement, or may complain. I'm not saying I required stoic pilgrims, but there's a difference between sharing and complaining.

I would watch the drama queen, and notice the other pilgrims gradually becoming annoyed and avoiding her. Although I believed that our pilgrimage was a chance for people to work out their differences together, I didn't want to see this happen at the expense of anyone's personal well-being. I wanted to create opportunities for intimacy, not separation.

Nick was a smart and generous man, endearingly eccentric. He wore an enormous floppy hat with a long peacock feather. Obviously he liked standing out in a crowd, but that in itself was nothing to complain about. However, he didn't remove his hat in the churches we entered, which was of great concern to some of the elderly Spanish gents and ladies. Neither did he take it off at mealtime in the crowded cafés. He came close to poking people's eyes out with that feather. At night he had a habit of hanging the hat on the rail of his bunk bed, and invariably it would get knocked off when someone brushed past it. This gave Nick the excuse to yell at some unsuspecting pilgrim. This happened every night.

I took him aside at the end of our fourth day on the road. We sat in the corner of a quiet field, watching a parade of colourful chickens scratching for grubs in the dirt. I could tell Nick was already feeling defensive, having been pulled aside, so I broached the subject of his hat very carefully. But he blew his top, yelling, calling me a fascist who wanted to trample his freedom of expression. I didn't react. I recalled talking to the ex-cons, and I remembered Dhiravamsa, and the monks who'd set such a great example with their unflappability. It was important to not react, which would escalate matters. Instead, I responded slowly.

"What do you really want me to know, Nick?" I asked, quietly. In an about-face, he looked at me, tears welling up in his eyes. I could see something of the child inside him.

"You've turned everyone against me," he said, as he began to cry. I felt an enormous surge of compassion, and suddenly I knew, without being told, that he'd been abused as a kid. It didn't seem like the right time to ask about his past, though. "I am not driving anyone away from you, Nick. Can you see how your behaviour has affected others? I am not trying to control you, though I would prefer if you could control yourself. Does that make sense?" He nodded.

"Just because we don't like the hat, it doesn't mean we don't like *you*." I said. He swallowed hard, trying to regain his composure. "Can you understand your attachment to the hat, Nick?" I continued. "You've been using it as a shield. We all have masks, we all have idiosyncrasies. But whatever pain and fear you hold inside—you don't have to bear it alone. I am available any time you want to talk and I can also recommend other capable ears."

"Thank you, Derek," he said softly, drying his eyes. I knew he was beginning to dismantle the wall he had built between himself and others. From then on, he wore his hat only when he was walking, and he removed the feather. He made a concerted effort to consider others and stop blaming them for his loneliness. He made friends. We kept in touch after the Camino, and a few years later he revealed the story of his abusive uncle. I wept upon reading this, but sadness turned to joy when I learned that after undergoing counselling he'd met and married the woman of his dreams. Their honeymoon was on the Camino.

On the Camino, or any long walk, something happens after a while. Your body slows down, and so may your mind. You start to really take in your surroundings. You begin to appreciate the beauty of the tiny yellow flower that's reaching out to the light from between two mossy rocks in an ancient stone wall. You can hear your own heartbeat in the hush of an ancient church, as you gingerly cross the threshold from the hot sun into the cool dampness of the dark sacred space.

What can also happen is that the momentum of your fast-paced life, the life you've left behind, creates a kind of spiritual backdraft. It's like walking on the side of the road when a big truck passes you. Seconds later you're engulfed in the suction of a big whoosh of air. On the Camino, you could be sitting alone in a meadow of wildflowers, enjoying a picnic of bread, wine, and cheese, feeling on top of the world, and suddenly, you're overwhelmed with tears. *Why is this happening?* you ask yourself. *Why now?* It's because you've allowed yourself this time to do nothing. Space opens up, and into it floods new thoughts, ideas, insights. But all the frightening, negative, self-critical thoughts and feelings you've been keeping at bay for years can rush in. This can be a shock, but it's also a great opportunity.

People walk the Camino because they are hungry for transformation, for transcendence, for magic, for a "spiritual" experience. It's the same longing that can lead us to sign up for meditation retreats and self-improvement seminars. We want to be changed. But "getting changed" is passive. We must actively participate in changing and this can't happen unless who we accept who we are. There is no escaping ourselves. We do the Camino as we do life.

We don't have to travel to Spain. Lasting transformation does not happen overnight, at least not often. But a pilgrimage can be a start. If we are open, and willing, and mindful, we can see ourselves with greater clarity. The real change, though, comes when we return home and bring that new awareness into our daily lives. At first, things won't seem to fit. Our old habits and our new visions will clash. Then the work begins.

Every May 10th was the last day of our 200 kilometre pilgrimage. Having scaled mountains, tramped through green valleys, trudged and slipped along muddy tracks, strolled through tiny hamlets, and navigated industrial suburbs, we arrive in Santiago. Gathering my flock, I lead them through the narrow cobblestone streets as a distant bagpiper's drone beckons us through a portal. Step by step, we round the corner to be met with the great cathedral's ornate façade. Some pilgrims weep for joy, others let out a cheer and then we all lie down on the cool stone of the courtyard to gaze up at the magnificent spectacle.

After taking in the sight, it's time to participate in an ancient tradition. Filing into the entrance of the cathedral, each of us wait in turn to touch the marble column of the Tree of Jesse. In the column is a deep, discernible hand print. One by one, we each press a hand into the smooth hollow. The imprint is cool, but, under the steady stream of hands, not as cold as the surrounding marble. It feels like touching the souls of all those pilgrims who have gone before. For some, this is the end of their journey, but for others, the pilgrimage has just taken root.

CHAPTER 48

ANOTHER WALL

Sweat poured down my brow. The heat—45°C—was almost too much to bear, but we pushed onward through valleys filled with cactus, groves of silver-leafed olive trees, and fields of chickpeas. My friends and I were on an ancient pilgrim trail through Israel to Jerusalem. It was our second such walk, in 2002.

Every morning before dawn, we set out while it was still cool, with a local camera crew who were filming a documentary. I was impressed by the head cameraman who walked just as far as we did, backwards and barefoot, with a 10 kilogram camera on his shoulder. I was also amazed that they all willingly risked their lives by crossing into Palestine with us one day.

A clandestine trip took us into Ramallah to visit Palestinian President Yasser Arafat's compound. It had been under siege for months, much of the compound reduced to rubble. Our guide led us calmly through the wreckage, pointing out the gnarled remains of a vehicle that had been a gift to Arafat from U.S. President Clinton. As we talked, she looked up at a shattered window and said, "The president is asleep in there."

When I asked if I could see Arafat himself, she smiled politely and said, "Only if you stay for a while." We declined her offer, as we were already feeling nervous about getting back across the border before the 7:00 p.m.

curfew. A few days later Israeli tanks once more bulldozed their way into the compound.

Israel was one of the most challenging places I had ever walked. Palestinian suicide bombings were a constant concern, and the everyday sight of teenagers in army fatigues with machine guns slung over their shoulders was chilling. Many people said, "This is just the way it is." Others talked about change, but there didn't seem to be much willingness to compromise. I don't believe it's necessary for opposing sides to agree on everything, but I do believe they can come to a place of mutual respect based on the sanctity of human life. To me, our humanity supersedes nationality, religion, and politics.

One afternoon we emerged from a meeting, warm with connection and shared concerns, to the news that a bomb had exploded in the road—ten minutes after we had driven through that morning. Fifteen people had been killed. I began shaking uncontrollably, then was filled with the need to smash something. I looked at my companions, who were clearly feeling the same helpless rage. It was if we were all feeling aftershocks from the bomb that had ripped buildings and bodies apart. I don't know which of us began to shout, but we stood there wailing together, in wordless lament for the lost lives and for our helplessness to change the tragedy.

Each time we heard news of another act of terror, we confronted our own knee-jerk reaction: what if we just went home? We may have felt like fleeing, but we chose not to. Leaving would have seemed like betrayal, and it was important to bear witness. Our eyes were opened, sometimes painfully, and I was never more aware of the privilege of living peacefully in Canada.

Every day, people shared their stories of living with violence. We met a Palestinian man who'd been paralyzed trying to rescue his children, an Israeli who refused to complete military service in the Occupied Territories, and parents grieving the loss of their 18-year old daughter in a suicide bombing only two weeks earlier. I was particularly moved by a former political prisoner, a soft-spoken man who, two weeks after his release, lost his legs in a bombing. He sat in his wheelchair, his two-year-old son quietly creeping into the room and onto his lap while he spoke. The young boy's dark eyes were downcast. I made him a peace crane. I didn't know what else to do. Sometimes there was nothing to do but listen.

Years earlier, I had experienced this in South Africa when I attended some of the hearings of the Truth and Reconciliation Commission (TRC). After centuries of racial segregation, oppression and abuse, fighters like Steve Biko (a hero of mine, who died in 1977 as a result of police torture), Nelson Mandela, and many other hardworking crusaders and ordinary citizens, had paved the way for the TRC. Reparations for the crimes and injustice were now underway. I was greatly touched by victims of violence and discrimination who were courageous enough to come forward and speak their experience of apartheid. Not everyone who spoke at the TRC was able to forgive, but again, I could sense that healing had begun.[7]

Now, once we reached Jerusalem, we came face to face with a massive barrier. I looked up at the high concrete wall and tears rolled down my cheeks. My head crumpled into my chest. *Another wall?*

Construction of a wall to separate Israel from the West Bank had begun that year and the structure was still growing. At eight metres high, 60 metres wide in places, and 700 km long, it was to be four times as massive as the Berlin Wall. It would be state-of the-art, complete with patrol vehicles, electric sensors, thermal imaging, video cameras, unmanned aerial vehicles, sniper towers and razor wire.

Standing there, I felt a sense of déjà-vu. As in Germany, this wall would separate citizens on both sides not only from each other, but also from things they needed to live simple ordinary lives—land and water resources, businesses, health services and even religious facilities.

In all conflicts there are different versions of the truth. To some, this new wall was a "security fence" built to prevent terrorists from entering Israel; others saw it as a land grab designed to humiliate and destroy the Palestinians. To me it just looked like a wall of shame. I did not want to live in a world where people were not free to go—peacefully, and respect-fully—where they wanted. But I guess I did live in that world. Humanity is at its worst when we rely on outer strength instead of inner strength to resolve differences. I dreamed that this wall of Jerusalem, like the Berlin Wall and the ancient walls of Jericho, would eventually crumble too.

---

7   Derek would have been happy to know that Canada birthed its own TRC, to address a history of systemic abuse of Aboriginals in the country's school systems.

There are walls closer to home as well. Sometimes we call them borders. I once did a walk into the Nevada Test Site in the U.S. It is one of the most bombed and radioactively contaminated places on Earth since the government expropriated it for missile testing. Along with my friend Linda Bassingthwaighte and other protesters, I crossed hundreds of kilometres of desert to get there. In my hand I clutched my permission, a slip of paper given to us by elders of the Shoshone Indian tribe, granting us the right to walk on their land. We were confronted by a sea of dark sunglasses: identically dressed law enforcement officers staring at us while they tapped their batons. We couldn't see their eyes or spark any glimmer of human understanding. I looked down at a thin line that had been scratched on the ground between where we stood and the cops stood. I realized that by standing on "my" side, I was confirming our separation—the "us and them" mindset. So it was not out of defiance or anger or protest, but just out of my humanity that I simply took one step across that line towards the cops.

And then I was in handcuffs. I held up my permission paper, but they pushed my hands down and swapped my paper for another—an arrest slip. I looked at the cops and saw myself: my own fear and judgment mirrored in them. Once again I realized I had a choice. I could create an enemy or not. As we rode off to jail, I wondered about the officers, and how they might shake their heads at the end of their own long day. Just as we were doing what we had to do by drawing attention to this ravaged part of Earth, the officers were doing what they felt they had to. Would a day ever come when we agreed, rather than facing off over that line in the dirt?

If that day is to come, I know that it starts here. I'm just as good at building walls as anyone, but that the walls I build to protect myself end up imprisoning me. The more distance I create between myself and others, the more I stand in judgment. The more I judge, the more I fear. The more I fear, the more justified I feel in harming, exploiting and vilifying others. It's a vicious circle.

Physical walls can be torn down, but walls between people have deep foundations that can't simply be knocked down. They have to be dissolved organically. For this to happen, I must have the courage to be vulnerable and to get closer to what and whom I fear. And that's when I'll be free.

CHAPTER 49

HEART

My feet were numb. I wasn't imagining things. It was more than just my mangled toes; my feet were losing sensation. I'd also begun to feel a loss of strength in my hands after years of working as a massage therapist. I wasn't alarmed, but it was getting worse. I was losing my ability to grip things and my calves were slowly beginning to atrophy. My balance was off and walking had become a challenge. I continued to watch these things without giving them too much attention.

Several years of Lin's insistence led me to a neurologist. His cursory examination consisted of poking and tickling my feet and hands. Then, in the classic gesture, he lowered his eyeglasses down his nose to peer over them. His head began to bob up and down while he murmured, "Hmm … hmmm. I would say it's peripheral neuropathy."

I looked over at Lin beseechingly. She was a doctor, too, after all. She looked at him squarely and asked, "So what can we do?"

He explained to us that there were a myriad of possible causes but no cure. "It's a progressive wasting disease of the extremities. The symptoms can be extremely debilitating," he explained, finishing with, "I'm sorry, but you will likely end up in a wheelchair one day."

In the car on our way home, Lin and I talked very little about the diagnosis. We weren't in disbelief or denial, but I suppose we were letting it all sink in. At the same time I also felt that it was just one doctor's opinion, which wasn't necessarily a capital "F" Fact.

Later that evening in bed Lin asked me how I was feeling about the news. I thought for a moment and then said, "Is my penis considered an extremity?"

"No, you silly man," she replied, right on cue, with a sparkle in her eye. "It's only your hands and feet that are disappearing, thank goodness. Now you'll be even more powerless to my charms...." We snuggled into each other's embrace.

But how about the irony? Here I was, a walker and massage therapist, losing the sensation in my feet and hands.

Ram Dass, spiritual teacher and author of *Be Here Now*, was an inspiration to me when confronting this condition. After suffering a massive stroke in the 1990s, he found that everything slowed for him—his walking, writing, speech. He took it all in stride, accepting every new challenge as another opportunity to grow. I wanted to do the same. Neuropathy was not a path I would have chosen, but I was on it and had to learn to navigate. Lin and I joked that if my extremities were disappearing, eventually I would just become a heart, and maybe my friends could carry me around on a little red pillow.

I have come to understand that whatever hand we're dealt in life, we can't foretell how those cards will play out. So, whenever confronting the unknown, I let myself imagine a range of outcomes, including the "bad" ones, giving myself at least five possible scenarios. Now, I could just shrivel up, but if I had friends to carry me around, that didn't sound so bad after all. Or, I could become a miserable grouch. Maybe another doctor could tell me it was just a food allergy, or, I might just die in a plane crash and render it all moot. Or, despite my diagnosis, I would walk to Japan, or roll there in a wheelchair. Some possibilities were more, and some were less, likely to happen, but I wasn't attached to any. In looking at a variety of choices, I empowered myself and did not become a victim. With my imagination, it's possible I may never be truly shocked by anything because I have already allowed it into my consciousness.

Now I get around more slowly, and with a walking stick, but I don't feel there is anywhere I can't go, given time and determination. I believe that walking is the true speed of the soul. If we're not mindful we race too far ahead. So I embrace my slower way through life, and the pace of my body and spirit feel very well matched.

CHAPTER 50

FLAMINGO

While walking in Israel in the fall of 2003, I received an email from one Carolyn Affleck, asking if I recalled meeting her at a friend's house years before, and if there might be space for her in the upcoming Camino group. Having recently lost her father, she felt it was the right time for a long walk.

I did recall a dinner party and an effervescent young woman who never stopped asking questions. She was definitely a person who would understand the difference between pilgrim and tourist. I accepted her application without hesitation.

May, 2004: I stood atop a high hill, overlooking the route of the pilgrimage to Santiago de Compostela. This stretch of road was three days into the pilgrimage. My seventh time leading, I was attuned to the group's pace and was sure I wouldn't see anyone for at least another hour.

I blinked; down the long valley a pilgrim was moving quickly my way. The long-legged, loose-limbed figure was wearing a pink hoodie. It was

Carolyn, looking like a camera-toting flamingo. There was a lightness in her step, and every now and then she stopped to compose a photograph.

Watching her, I knew exactly how she felt: absorbed in the landscape, surrounded by the beauty of nature, totally alive. In recent years, my neuropathy required that I pay a lot of attention to my footing and balance. Carolyn reminded me of days past, when my head was in the clouds and my feet had a life of their own. In no time, she had reached the bottom of the cliff. As she began to stride up the steep trail, I had a flash of knowing. She was to be my protégée. I had no idea what that would mean in practical terms, but I knew it to be true.

When she reached the summit, I hugged her and asked how she was doing. "Fantastic!" she effused, barely out of breath. I mentioned the flamingo image. I don't think she found it very flattering, but she laughed anyway—an unrestrained, infectious giggle.

Within days, Carolyn and I developed an easy rapport. As much as she was a woman who gave things a lot of thought, at times to the point of getting stuck in her head, I recognized her as someone who lived from the heart, like me. We spent a day together after the pilgrimage ended, and I learned that at the same moment that I'd stood on that hilltop and had my intuitive flash, she'd had her own. Approaching the cliff, she'd seen me standing there with my rain cape and my white beard and thought, *He's my Obi Wan Kenobi!* I got a good chuckle out of being the cloaked, white-bearded Jedi Master from the movie *Star Wars*. This meant, I guess, that she was my Luke Skywalker. She liked that better than the flamingo idea.

CHAPTER 51

HOW TO TAME A FLAMINGO

Carolyn as protégée was a delightful surprise on that trip. She surprised me more, though, after returning home.

People had often shared their snapshots of the Camino and I'm ashamed to say I developed a bit of a *been-there, done-that* attitude. But I almost always accept these invitations, if reluctantly. In June, Carolyn suggested she come up to visit me and Lin where we were living on the Sunshine Coast, north of Vancouver, to show me her photos from the trip. We sat down at a café, she pulled out a huge album, and I groaned silently. *Oh great,* I thought, *this is going to take a while. How many pictures of pilgrims in hiking boots and blue rain jackets can I tolerate?* From the first page, though, I was awestruck. In years of walking the Camino, I hadn't seen a fraction of the things she had captured in her images. Even though she'd walked briskly, she noticed details that everyone else overlooked. She was a true artist, revealing the spirit that exists beneath the surface of things. Protégée? Perhaps, but not just that. I sensed that I had things to learn from her, too.

Carolyn and I acknowledged that we wanted to walk together more and work together, although we weren't sure what form that would take. So we needed to take a few steps and see what kind of doors opened up for us and, of course, this would need to happen in the Circle of my marriage. Over the next few months, she came to visit us regularly and became family.

At some point, I suggested that Carolyn meet Lani and her husband Peter, who also lived on the Sunshine Coast. On our way over to their house, I talked about Lani's and my enduring relationship, and referred to the health clinic we'd run back in the '80s. Suddenly, Carolyn's eyes lit up. "Was it on Main Street?" she asked.

"Yes, up near King Edward Avenue. Why? Did you ever go there?

"Go there?" she shrieked. "I took first-level Reiki there from Lani almost 20 years ago! But her name was Launa then, right?"

"Yes!" And in a flash, I remembered. Carolyn and I had passed each other in the doorway of the clinic.

With each visit Carolyn made to the Sunshine Coast, an idea took shape. Lin, though not much of a traveller, always threw her heart into helping me follow my calling, and before we knew it, the three of us had planned a 40-day trip for Carolyn and me to take across Canada. We would revisit some of the places I'd walked 14 years earlier, and she would help me do my slide presentation along the way to schools and peace groups.

Two months later, Carolyn and I set off in her second-hand camper van, with Lin's blessing, and the familiar ache in my chest at leaving her.

How affirming it was to show Carolyn the very places I'd walked, rested, gotten lost, and to share with her the lessons I'd learned along the way. As support driver when Carolyn took off on foot, I quietly contemplated and reflected on my younger self with what I hoped were wiser eyes. Then Carolyn, after walking, would jump into the van, breathless, full of observations, and we'd slip into lively conversation.

Occasionally our conversations were more roiling than bubbling. It was only a couple of days into the trip, driving down the highway, when we had our first row.

"Let's write a book," I said.

"Huh?" she said. "What do you mean?"

"We talked with Lin about doing something creative and productive on this trip. Let's start!" I grinned.

"But we can't just—write a book—just like THAT!" Carolyn said, clearly shocked. "I've done some writing, but I'm not a WRITER!"

Her words echoed mine from years before, so I was sympathetic, but I questioned her resistance.

"What's going on here? What are you afraid of? We've lined up only a few slide shows. I need us to do more to justify this trip."

She shot me a piercing look. "But you can't just spring this on me. It has only been two days! Can't we just have some fun first? Can't we talk about this later?"

"This IS later, Carolyn!" I said, my anger stirred. "Fun is not enough." Tears welled up in Carolyn's eyes. "Cut it out!" I snapped.

She sat, still and silent, looking straight ahead, her face expressionless. I pulled the van over to the side of the highway and drew a long, deep breath. "Carolyn, the silent treatment doesn't work with me." She stayed quiet, almost frozen. "You can sit there if you want," I said, "but it's not fair to me. I need you to tell me what's going on in your mind."

"Fair to YOU?" she shot back immediately, tears streaming down her face. I'd never heard her raise her voice. "What about me? How is yelling at me fair? And how is walking not a good use of time? You've totally hurt my feelings."

"I can't hurt your feelings, Carolyn," I replied, my voice raising a notch. "You're the one choosing to let yourself get hurt. You're reacting, not responding."

"Hey, you yelled first! But you wanna know what I'm thinking? I think you're just worried that other people will think you're having an affair with me."

Her words gave me pause. I didn't care much about what others thought of me, but I did care about how my behaviour reflected on Lin, personally and professionally. "You're right," I said quietly. "And to tell you the truth, I really do want to play on this trip. But I think we could have fun writing. What do you say we give it a try?"

"Sure," Carolyn continued. Her face softened.

"Are you OK?" I asked. "Are *we* OK?"

"I think so. But you really scared me when you yelled. My brain just shut down and I wanted to run away. I totally get your point, but how you say something is just as important as what you're saying. If I don't feel safe with you, we're not going to get anywhere on this trip or in our friendship."

That hit home. I was used to *gestalting*, but not Carolyn. "Maybe you can help me to contain myself a little more."

"It's a deal," she answered, a warm smile lighting up her face. "And maybe I can learn to argue. I need good communication just as much as you do. But the delivery really makes a difference."

Carolyn trusted me enough that I introduced a technique Lin and I had come up with years earlier. It was brilliantly simple: "Do we want a five-minute argument or a five-hour one?" Most of the time, we'd end up laughing and choosing the five-minute version. But sometimes issues needed to be hashed out, which gave us both the opportunity to stretch ourselves.

Carolyn agreed to start writing. She wanted me to write about myself. I didn't. So we began a novel. Our protagonist was a young woman who gave up her job on a whim and met a wizened, road-weary peace walker. You get the picture. Eventually we tired of this and started a blog, which was more rewarding for Carolyn, and the daily efforts at collaboration taught us how to work together.

After our return home, I showed Carolyn some of the stories I had written years ago about my walks. I hadn't so much as glanced at them in years. "These are wonderful," she said. "Why did you stop writing?" I told her the story of how I stopped reading, and about my encounter with the screenwriter. "You know, we really could write a book if we had some more stories like these."

"I wouldn't even know where to begin," I said.

"Oh Derek," she said. "You don't have to. Just take a step and I'll help you. One foot in front of the other!" I smiled, hearing her echo the very thing I'd told so many people over the years.

Although Carolyn's and my values were compatible, our personalities and working habits were very different, so it took us a while to learn how to collaborate. Although she was a very *feeling* person, when it came to writing she was more about *fact*. I was convinced she was an uptight detail-freak. She thought I was a melodramatic flake. I'd be going on about how magical something felt and she'd retort, "Yes, but where were you? What year was it?" This drove me crazy. I prided myself on living in the moment, but perhaps this was because I had a terrible memory. Carolyn, with the instincts and determination of a detective, hammered away at me until one day I cracked, and details of long-forgotten stories came spilling out like candy from a piñata. "Wait, wait!" she said, furiously trying to take notes as I rambled on. But it was too late; I couldn't hold back.

Carolyn couldn't write fast enough. Later, she had a mess of scribbles to transcribe. She gathered them up with old half-written tales and we began to string everything together. There were gaping holes and dangling modifiers but the Grammar Queen took care of that. Carolyn magically polished up all the W's—the *whos*, the *whys*, the *wheres*, the *whens*—and transformed my clumsy prose.

The book developed in waves, a deluge of inspiration followed by a long lull. In our creative periods, we could spend hours working on one page and feel totally fulfilled. But at some point, excitement turned to obsession. What had once seemed casual and fun now felt like hard work. I was serious about the project, but there had to be some sense of enjoyment in what I did, and I couldn't feel it any longer. Everything we wrote left one or other of us dissatisfied. We slipped into old roles: the dreamer and the perfectionist. "This isn't bloody *War and Peace*, you know!" I barked at Carolyn. "We'll never be finished!"

"Well, this book has to be good," she screamed back at me. "I don't want it ending up in some thrift store bargain bin!" Our working honeymoon was over.

By now we were working in the same room, side by side, and at times it was just too close for comfort. After arguing for what seemed like hours, I reached my limit. "If this isn't fun, I'm out."

"Oh yeah? Well, me too!" Carolyn retorted. Arms held tightly across her chest, she fixed her eyes on me and I glared back defiantly. It was a standoff. Several minutes of strained silence ticked by. Soon, Carolyn began tapping her foot in annoyance. I did my best to ignore this, but then something caught my attention. I looked down, and to my surprise, I found my own foot had joined hers in tapping. Carolyn's eyes widened in disbelief. *Oh crap,* I thought, *I didn't mean to mock her.* But I couldn't stop. Our feet were out of control, and, in spite of us, they were doing a Fred Astaire and Ginger Rogers routine. A grin spread across Carolyn's face and I couldn't help but smile too. We burst into laughter. The standoff was broken.

"I'm sorry," we whispered in unison, and hugged. It was now obvious that in our enthusiasm to make this book a reality, we had been seduced by the goal and had lost the dream. How ironic. That day, we gained a new understanding of the difference between dreams and goals. Agreeing to stay focused on the process and not the end result, we let go—of our expectations and need for control—and jumped back in with all four feet.

CHAPTER 52

LEARNING TO SLEEP

The Canada trip was pivotal for me. I discovered I had a lot to learn about letting go.

My first letting go was about my prime obsession, walking. There was only so much time in a day to spend on foot if we were to keep to our schedule. I whined at first, but this didn't work for Derek, which meant it didn't work for *us*. So then we talked. And talked. I'd always been the emotional, talkative one in any close relationship and having the tables turned was discomfiting.

Derek was absolutely clear about unconditional love, but I learned that there was no such thing as unconditional like. In such tight quarters there had to be conditions, so that we'd both feel comfortable and respected. Our occasional, if dramatic, clashes were a crash course in self-improvement. Sometimes I felt chastised by him, but he was most often correct in his observations of me.

Once I let go of my expectations around walking and began to witness the restless sensation in my body when I craved it, I could then respond. I learned to breathe through my restlessness, which made me a much easier person to live with. And I still got to walk. I'd saunter off down the road, and later, Derek would pop up mysteriously like the same wise shepherd materializing out of nowhere on the Camino. He was always there at the right time, when I was lost or lonely, tired or hungry.

I treasured every minute of walking through my beautiful country. There were so many images I never captured with my camera though they stuck in my memory, like the long Vs of geese flapping and honking a path across the sky as they practised for their autumn flight south. I heard the trees whisper and saw where small animals made their homes—things I completely miss from the car.

Though I only got a taste of what it must have been like for Derek all those years ago, I learned it wasn't all about beauty and connection with nature. I felt the loneliness of the highway and the jarring impact of my feet against pavement, and I tried to imagine Derek doing this for nine months. I braced myself for the buffeting backdraft of every speeding long-haul truck, closing my eyes against the sting of debris whirling in its wake. Walking those long empty stretches of road was exhilarating and enlightening. I also felt, in a way, that Derek was passing me the torch.

But being on the road, even with someone so wise and capable, brought up fears I didn't even know I had, like walking into a gas station and asking for directions. Instead of merely brushing my irrationality aside, Derek encouraged me to indulge my deepest fearful fantasies and to entertain as many reasons as possible for not walking into that gas station. It felt silly at first.

"I'm afraid of going in there to ask directions because—what if I get tongue-tied? What if people laugh at me?"

"You can do better than that," he said, gently goading me with a smile. "Come on, I'll show you how it's done: I, Derek, am afraid of reading my poems aloud because—it will be obvious that I'm a high school dropout. People will laugh so hard that I'll run out of the room in shame, and as I'm running out, I'll trip and land on my face, and then blood will be spurting everywhere, and I'll not only ruin my new white jacket, but I'll stain the floor, and the venue won't be insured for blood stains, and they'll have to re-carpet the whole place, billing me for the cost, and the whole incident will be written up in the local paper, and then the national press will pick up the story, and then Lin will find out about the whole thing and realize she married the wrong man."

I burst into laughter. He was teaching me that fearful thoughts are like a runaway train. "It's a waste of time," he said, "to be thinking about thinking about thinking about...." I did a lot of that. It's what worriers do, batting around the same little fear in our minds until it becomes a huge problem. Derek would draw attention to the times when I seemed to be off in my own little world, *thinking about*, and he'd bring me back to the present. At first I'd feel irritated and resentful. But then I was relieved. Letting go of irrational fears made actual problem-solving much more productive.

Our first night on the road was a case in point, and a revelation. The camper had two bunks, upper and lower. I took the top. As I climbed up to the top bunk, Derek's eyes opened wide as he took inventory of all the gear I employed to help me sleep better. On the front of my pyjamas I had attached a tennis ball, so that I would wake myself up in the middle of the night if I rolled onto on my chest (which was bad for my neck). I also wore a large padded neck brace. Next I donned a pair of bright orange ear plugs. On my forehead was a dark purple shade to pull over my eyes. When Derek said goodnight I'm sure all he heard in return was a muffled, "*Gurrgigh.*" I couldn't enunciate properly, due to the mouthguard I wore as protection from grinding my teeth. I must have looked a fool.

For a while, I shuffled and shifted around in the top bunk, but I just couldn't get comfortable. My thin camping mattress, which I'd laid out on the bunk, was sliding across the velvety surface of the camper's upholstery. After an hour I began to settle down, but despite my earplugs I could now hear Derek's snoring from the bottom bunk and the wind howling through the thin canvas of the camper's pop-top. I tried to sleep, but the more I tried, the more alert I became. Derek had assured me that if I needed anything, I should just call down. Eventually I swallowed my pride. "Derek," I said, hearing a snore break off abruptly, "I can't sleep."

"Why don't you try doing without some of your gadgets?" he suggested. "Don't they just get in your way?"

"Hmm," I said, popping out my mouthguard. "I don't know if I can. Maybe just one or two." I put my mouthguard back in its little container. I hadn't slept without earplugs in ten years, but I took them out. The snores began again immediately from the bottom bunk. I lay there, for maybe half an hour, enduring the sawing, and feeling increasingly uptight.

"Derek," I said eventually, an unmistakable edge to my voice. "You're snoring again and I can't sleep."

"Oh sorry," he replied. "I'll turn over. But how about taking off some of your gadgets?"

"You already suggested that," I replied, "and it didn't work. I'll try again, though." I really hated to complain, so off came the eyeshade. After another half-hour of lying there, watching shadows play across the canvas roof, I had to pee. *Great*, I thought. *Now I'm really awake.* I climbed down from the bunk and slid open the door of the vehicle quietly. I wasn't sure if I'd woken Derek or not, but when I returned, and closed the sliding door behind me, he was definitely awake.

"Not sleeping?" he said.

"Um ... no," I admitted. "I usually sleep really well at home, though. I promise it will only take a night or two to adjust."

"I know that I'm probably snoring again, and I'm really sorry. Lin has learned to live with it and I'm going to challenge you to live with it too. It's a good opportunity to learn how to let go! You know if you just lie there trying to block out the sound, you'll only be focussing more attention on it. Try instead to let it into your ears and don't resist it."

"Oh," I said. "I hadn't thought of it that way."

"Why don't you just come down here and snuggle up beside me?" said Derek. "Just let your body relax."

"But then I'll be even closer to the snore!"

"It's true. But perhaps your body is more attentive to sounds than it needs to be. I can just hold you while you let yourself relax."

"I don't know," I said. "Are you sure this is a good idea?"

"What are you afraid of?"

"I know Lin is OK with us cudding. I guess I just really like to have my own space."

"Space shmace," he said. "Just try it on, like a new coat in a store. If you don't like it, you don't have to buy it." he told me. "What's the worst thing that can happen? Seriously."

"Well, I suppose—not sleeping. Which is not so bad, I guess. It's not like I have a job to go to tomorrow."

"Right," he said. "And even if you're just lying there, your body is still resting and that's a good thing." he said. "But get rid of all those appliances! If you ask me, that's your real issue. Come on, just trust me."

I sensed in that moment that this was one of those times in life when a door opens. If you choose to go through it, your life can change forever. So I trusted. I took off my neck brace and removed the tennis ball from my pyjamas and crawled under the covers with my friend. Derek suggested that instead of struggling to shut out all the unfamiliar sounds and ambient light, to instead let it all in, and relax in the safety of the van, in his company. "This is a meditation. If you can relax with my snoring in your ear, you'll be able to fall asleep just about anywhere." And that I did, curled up in his arms, drifting off with a delicate snore. Or so I was told.

CHAPTER 53

WALKING TO JAPAN

After Carolyn and I returned from our cross-Canada trip, I invited her to co-lead my next pilgrimage with Lucile. The more freedom I found within my marriage, the more I loved Lin, and I knew that despite Carolyn's and my deep connection, I would never do anything to break my Circle with Lin.

In March of 2005, Carolyn and I were on the phone together, planning the upcoming Camino journey. "Hey, isn't your birthday about a month after we get back from Spain?" she asked.

I confirmed her suspicions. "My 65th."

"I thought so! Are you going to celebrate?" she hinted. The thought had never entered my mind. The last big party I'd had was when I turned 40. Sixty-five was a big number, but what did it really mean? Old age pension? Hell, I was still cranking up the stereo and dancing in the living room.

Carolyn continued excitedly about cakes, gifts, guests, and activities. I found increasingly annoying, but she persisted. "Come on, you have to celebrate! You'll be an elder! What can you do that's really, really special? Something you have always wanted—" She stopped mid-sentence, going silent, and I could almost hear the cogs in her brain turning. "Derek," she continued, "What about Japan?"

My immediate reaction was not *yes*, and this surprised me. After all these years, why not go now? I told her I'd have to think about it.

"Think about it? What's there to think about? You'd be fulfilling a lifelong dream! Plus, won't August 6 be the 60th anniversary of the bomb? What better time to go?"

"I'll call you back tomorrow," I said. The anniversary was a compelling reason to go and I could afford to. Still, something didn't feel quite right.

I had folded at least a thousand cranes. My walks had taken me throughout the world and by now I'd told the story of Sadako at least a thousand times. Though walking to Japan had started as a literal goal, with an intention to traverse every continent on Earth, I had let go of the specifics as the dream took its own shape, one step at a time. The image of walking into Hiroshima and placing a peace crane on Sadako's statue had kept me passionate and aware, and had propelled me forward in times of uncertainty. My inner journey had eclipsed the outer journey.

Ever since I first spoke my dream aloud, people encouraged me to jump on a plane and just *go*. "What are you waiting for?" they'd ask. "You can be there in ten hours!" I gave up trying to explain that Japan was a dream for me rather than a goal, that it couldn't be reached in a straight line. I would just smile, knowing I would get there in my own time. I had things to see, people to meet, and wisdom to gain along the way. But still, why wouldn't I want to go now? I even had friends there to visit. So what was up?

That night, when Lin and I crawled into bed, we lay there deconstructing my resistance. "It's funny how I don't feel driven to actually *go* to Japan in the same way I once did," I said.

"That's good," said Lin. "You've let go. So it's a simple choice, really. No obligation; do you want to go or not?"

"Well, yes, I think so. But there is something in it that feels like a loss, not a gain."

"Oh silly husband. It's like you always tell me—it boils down to attachment and fear. You've always loved telling the story of your dream. It has been your motivation. But perhaps you have become too attached."

Of course she was right. It was an ego boost to hear people tell me I inspired them. And I even liked being told that walking to Japan was a crazy idea because it spurred me on even more. But what would keep me going after I'd reached Japan? I was so attached to the dream that I was reluctant to let it become reality, out of fear of losing my motivating force, and what that would mean to me as a peace walker.

Years ago, as a young adult feeling the call of my own spirit, I had a desire to be *more*. Now, at the age of 65, I was proud to see how I had lived this out in so many ways. But I also saw the paradoxical nature of what I had been telling others for a long time. There is always more—and—there is no *more*. In the little picture, yes: as long as we are alive, we can continue to help others, share love, and expand into who we are. This can drive us in positive ways, but also make us strive in unhealthy ways to the point where we can feel we never do enough, and never are enough, despite our inherent value. In the big picture, because we're all connected to everyone and everything that exists, there actually isn't anything more. The few times when I actually grasped this paradox, I felt peace settle into my bones. And this was one of those times.

I could choose to go, or not to go. It was simple. I knew what I wanted.

Lin would have come with me if I'd asked, but it would have required her leaving her patients, some of whom were seriously ill, and this just didn't feel right to me. So of course I asked Carolyn, and was surprised to hear resistance, after being so enthusiastic for me. I was prepared to find someone else, but first I asked her to *try on the new coat*. She took one night—long and sleepless from the sounds of it—and said yes. We never looked back.

In the months before leaving, Carolyn and I held storytelling and peace crane making events. As I talked to children especially, I saw in their eyes the connection they felt to this girl. She, who was so much like them, had lain on her deathbed folding cranes. As we sat making origami, I felt as if Sadako were with us, just out of reach. *Yes*, I told her. *You're the one who inspired my dream.* I might have let go of the need to walk to Japan for myself, but I still wanted to do it for Sadako. *I'm coming*, I said, silently. *I'll be there soon.*

By the time we left, we had hundreds of birds, some even sent to us from abroad, each imbued with tangible wishes for peace. Carolyn packed them all tightly into a tiny box she carried in her small backpack. The birds flew with us on the plane to Japan, where we were met by old friends, Chris and his wife Lieh, whom I'd met on the Sunshine Coast.

The next morning, we walked several hours into Hiroshima. It was hot and humid. I was jet lagged and walking was not easy for me, but my dream was coming true. Memories flooded into my mind of all my past walks. And now here I was. How had this happened? *One step at a time,* I thought, *always.*

On August 6, at 8:15 a.m., we sat in silence with a delegation of over 50,000 people in the Peace Park, only the cicadas buzzing eerily from the trees.

Despite the early hour, the heat was fierce, approaching 40°C, but how could we complain? It was nothing like the heat of the atomic bomb. We thought of the hundreds of thousands of people who had died in the great blast in 1945, many of whose bones lay beneath us. As we sat there quietly, listening to a children's choir, an insect landed on my leg. It was large and yellowy-green (according to Carolyn), with big bulging eyes. A praying mantis, perhaps? It befriended me for the remainder of the ceremony, walking slowly along my leg to peer thoughtfully at the gold paper peace crane perched on my knee. Carolyn and I looked at each other and I saw my thought echoed in her face. We were both wondering, could it be—the spirit of Sadako? It stayed there for the next 30 minutes, until someone behind me saw it and let out a scream, and it hopped away.

A reader began reciting a list of names, the latest casualties of bomb-related illness. Of course, these were just the recent deaths, Sadako's not among them. But with each name I thought of her and wondered about each story, the life held in every unfamiliar name. My face was wet with tears. The total number of deaths attributed to the bomb, including the 140,000 who died immediately (nine out of every ten citizens), was now over 240,000. Many died in the weeks after due to injury by debris, or from burns or blood poisoning, but people were still dying from the radiation's long-term effects, from leukaemia, cancer, and other kinds of cellular and genetic damage.

That afternoon, Chris and Lieh introduced us to an *hibakusha* (an atomic bomb survivor) named Emiko Okada, who had been a child when the bomb was dropped, and had lost most of her family. So far, she had not succumbed to any of the radiation's invisible dangers. Without a hint of bitterness, and with a lightness of spirit, the woman frankly shared her story of survival. This is how she spent her days, her life dedicated to peace.

Later in the crowd, I spied familiar orange robes. With mirrored looks of surprise and delight, I walked towards two of the Nipponzan-Myōhōji monks I'd met on the GPM. Not Sawada or Kijima or Nagase, but still, they were dear to me, and we all pointed and laughed at our white hair and wrinkles. I filled with pride and love and the strange sense of being completely out of time.

After the formal events and more introductions than we could keep track of, Carolyn, Chris, Lieh and I silently circled the Peace Park with our paper cranes, coming to a stop at Sadako's statue. The time had come. We each took a turn ringing the gold bell that hangs in the middle of the statue. Then we carefully laid down our birds. I knelt down in front of the monument and made an offering. It was a small crane that Lin and I had made together. I closed my eyes and the rest of the world disappeared. Now, in addition to the friends who were standing beside me, I felt ALL my friends—my grandchildren, Mary the Peace Pony, the circus children from France, Lani, the Great Peace Marchers, everyone—there with me. And I felt the unmistakable presence of another. *Thank you*, Sadako, I prayed. *Thank you for bringing me here.*

That night we sat under a bridge on the banks of the Ota River with our friends and crowds of strangers, traffic thundering overhead. Hundreds of paper lanterns—yellow, orange, and blood-red—floated by, lit inside by candles. On this day in 1945, the river had been ablaze with burning bodies. With the eerie rumble of cars and trolleys above us, we sat and watched the beautiful lights swirl slowly and silently though the water.

Three days later, at 11:02 a.m. on August 9, Carolyn and I again sat in silence at the Peace Park in Nagasaki. Then we wandered through the city. Although the bomb that fell on Nagasaki was larger and potentially more devastating than Hiroshima's, more people and buildings survived due to Nagasaki's hilly geography.

Following a path up one of these hills, we found a small Shinto shrine and were drawn to a huge ancient camphor tree festooned with cranes. Some time after the tree was destroyed in the bombing, it come back to life, growing around the charred remains, and thereafter became an object of veneration. With a stethoscope, we were able to listen to the tree "breathe". I could hear both a muffled crackling, which I think was tiny insects, and a gentle rhythmic whooshing which must have been osmosis. The sounds left me speechless. What life!

We left Nagasaki impressed by its thriving, bustling energy, like that of Hiroshima. Having survived almost total destruction, the cities live on, their citizens pledging to never let the world forget the horrors of nuclear war.

Next, Carolyn and I picked up a rental car in order to explore the island of Shikoku, the smallest of Japan's four main islands. On Shikoku is a pilgrimage to 88 temples in honour of Kobo Daishi, the founder of the mystical Shingon sect of Buddhism, and the route is said to follow his footsteps. This was the "fun" part of our trip.

On the bus to the car rental agency, a stranger engaged us in conversation, and we made do with his English and the few Japanese phrases that Chris had prepared for us. Upon hearing our plans, the man gave us the equivalent of about $100. It is considered an honour to bestow gifts like this on pilgrims, and though we tried to refuse his gift, he'd have none of it. We bowed and thanked him profusely. We were the ones who felt honoured.

The car rental staff sent us off with very shaky smiles, not visibly confident we'd make it back in one piece. But, off we went in our tiny box on wheels, Carolyn learning how to drive on the left, shift with the right, and I scanning for rare English roadsigns.

On Shikoku, we woke early to walk before the heat. We strolled alone through temple grounds, the only sound our footsteps and the rustle of bamboo. We took narrow paths to grottos with little shrines to unfamiliar deities in the shadowed corners. We wrote prayers for peace on tiny scraps of paper and tied them to trees. We rang large bells and cleansed our hands and mouths with holy water before entering sacred buildings. Inside, we inhaled the musky scent of incense, and stood in awe, gazing at rows of golden lanterns and statues of the Buddha. We visited 11 of the 88 temples and met not one other Westerner. Occasionally we'd bump into a Japanese pilgrim, dressed just like Kobo Daishi himself, in traditional white coat and conical hat, carrying a walking stick.

At the final temple, we had a visitor. Perched on the rearview mirror of our rental car, peering through the window, was an insect just like the one who'd rested on my knee in Hiroshima. It felt like a visit from Sadako, here to congratulate us on our pilgrimage.

The next leg of our journey took us back to Chris and Lieh on the far west coast of the main island. Like a couple of kids with our noses pressed against the bus window, we stared out at hillsides thick with bamboo. Once we arrived and settled in with our friends, we gave a talk and led a peace walk. On one of our last evenings in Japan, we went to the beach, where we finally cooled off in the rolling surf.

Later, over noodles and beer, Carolyn and I raised our glasses to our hosts, who had taken such great care of us. And in turn, Lieh toasted me. "Derek," she said, "do you realize you have walked to Japan?"

"I guess I have!" I replied. "Who'd have imagined it?"

"So, what's next?" asked Chris.

"I don't know. Let me finish dinner first," I chuckled.

It was so hot around the dinner table that Chris and I took our shirts off. My belly felt full, but it was nothing compared to Lieh's (still clothed) belly. Hers had grown exponentially since we'd last seen her because—she'd be having a baby soon! "In my expert opinion," I said, "I bet it'll be a boy."

"Hmm," said Chris. "We'll see about that!"

There was a silence in which it felt like we were all imagining the child to be. And it occurred to me that my grandchildren would be soon old enough to have children of their own. Once again I began to wonder about the future.

It's not an easy time in the world with terrorism on the rise, the nuclear threat still looming, climate change and corporate domination. And the things that could serve to bring us together through technology and media often end up creating separation instead. In all my walking and talking about peace, I haven't stopped nuclear weapons, or the genocide in Rwanda, or the fighting in Gaza. But I have helped friends and strangers. I have made a difference by talking with people, listening to their fears, feeling their pain, and sharing my love and hope. We can all make a difference by working to let go of fear and hatred, by living from the heart. The world's children are our reminder.

CHAPTER 54

FULL CIRCLE

I was quite wrong about Chris and Lieh's baby. Maya is a girl, wise, kind and beautiful. And now she has a little brother, Towa. They make me laugh, and they delight me with their unique blend of Japanese and Canadian qualities. Most of all, the sparkle in their eyes gives me hope for the future.

Lucile has a baby too, Nina, who is growing into an adventurous little girl. She's full of energy and even though she doesn't understand my English and I don't understand her Dutch, we talk and giggle up a storm. Kids and I get along. Perhaps it's because we know how to play, which is really about just surrendering to the moment.

As birth is a miracle, so is death, our biggest surrender of all. And at 9:00 p.m. on May 12, 2007, my precious soulmate Lin returned to the light where she began.

Lin had not felt well for some time. Tests showed non-life-threatening fibroid tumours and expert doctors' opinions backed that up, but her abdominal pain increased to the point where she was sent for more tests. Then came a horrifying moment that I will never forget.

Lin went to the hospital for minor surgery, which was supposed to take an hour. After four hours, I could hear my heart pounding in my chest; I knew something was wrong. The surgeon entered the waiting room looking tired. She sat down beside me, looked right into my eyes and took a deep breath. I saw her begin to speak slowly, but her words blew right through me. I couldn't make sense of them, but her eyes conveyed the message. Lin had a rare form of cancer which had progressed too far to treat. It was terminal.

I felt numb, unable to move, unable to talk. Moments later I was out in the parking lot. I found my car, locked myself inside and wailed, while rain pounded the windshield. When I had no more tears I just sat, numb. Eventually emotions bubbled up: rage, fear, sadness for Lin, sadness for myself. And I felt lost. What could I do but let go? A memory flashed through my mind of being on the cliffside high in New Zealand's Alps on the Peace Trail, when I was nearly frozen with fear. *Don't look too far head, Derek*, I reminded myself. *And don't look back.* There is only now. And only love is what's needed in this very moment. I went back into the hospital and sat with Lin, just holding her.

For the next six months I never left Lin's side. She had supported me faithfully during all my travels and now it was my turn to support her journey. I began by helping her write a blog early in her journey with cancer, where she could share her fears and hopes. In her usual gentle, frank style, she poured her heart out. Now, the world got to know the smart, honest, kind, forgiving woman I adored. The flood of love and prayers kept her spirits high.

The previous summer, we had moved from our house in the country to the small town of Sechelt, where we were two minutes from shops and a hospital. This was a blessing, as it would have been tough for everyone had we still been another hour's drive up a winding road. My daughters Pauline and Christine made it clear they'd drop everything to come, but neither Lin nor I wanted them to face losing their jobs in the city. Lani and Carolyn, who also now lived on the Sunshine Coast, took care of us. Almost every day they came to the house to prepare meals, clean, walk the dog, take phone calls, and give Lin gentle massage and Reiki.

Alternative health treatments were offered up from all directions, thanks to all our friends in the healing community. Sarah and Urszula, two young Traditional Chinese Medicine practitioners who took over Lin's practice, donated their time and expertise. There were short-term improvements, but nothing had any lasting effects beyond her feeling loved and supported. Still, this didn't resign us to a death sentence. Each day held possibility. "It's so great to be alive!" Lin would say. Never once did I hear her say, "Why me?"

Lin was a very private person and could easily get overstimulated and exhausted, especially when interacting with people who were uncomfortable with death. But she tried her best to connect with those who came to see her, especially her brother Dave, Lani's husband Peter, Zachariah and his wife, and Janet, her best childhood friend from England. Sometimes, though, she couldn't handle seeing anyone at all.

Early in the illness, we were able to drive to the local nature reserve to walk our dog. When Lin's energy decreased, we would just stroll out the door and make the ten-minute loop around the duck pond next to our house. Inevitably, Lin lost the strength to get out the door, but we were still able to stretch out on our huge red comfy couch in front of the fire and watch movies. We were constantly adjusting to the "new normal". Just when we thought we had something figured out, it would change. Lin's world got smaller and smaller.

The smaller her world became, though, the more she cherished it. Things we used to think were important—like replying to emails in a timely fashion—were rendered insignificant, and things had once seemed mundane took on new significance, like the view out our bedroom window. I took special care to make it as pretty and restful as possible. Pots of geraniums and fairy lights, with the pond and trees behind, gave Lin so much joy. There were times, as we lay in bed together, when the busy quacking of the ducks sounded like laughter, and we couldn't help but join in with them. Despite her frailty, Lin laughed like never before. She called it *bedpan* humour.

For many years Lin had been an aerobics instructor at the YMCA, bouncing and strutting, yelling encouragement to her students to get up and move their bodies. Not many people knew the gentle and reserved Dr. Linda Ward this way. And now she could only walk as far as our ensuite bathroom. Once, I caught her voice sailing out the door as she sang out of tune, but with gusto, "What a Feeling!" from *Flashdance*. I had to laugh. But never had her voice sounded so full of life to me.

Each day was a gift and together we made the most of it, living step by step, moment to moment, witnessing fear, elation, exhaustion, despair, and ever-deepening love. I said to Lin one day, as I had said on countless occasions, "I think I'm falling in love with you."

"Well, you'd better hurry, then!" she replied. Her audacity stunned me, and warmed me to the marrow.

Each day we spoke the unspeakable. We discussed what might lie ahead on both the spiritual, and the physical blood-and-guts level. We joked about rigor mortis, which took the *morbid* out of it. All our conversations helped Lin to prepare for as graceful and peaceful a transition as possible, whenever that time would come. We also believed it was entirely possible that she'd have a spontaneous remission. There was no reason why all the tumblers in that metaphorical combination lock couldn't all just fall into place and line up a miracle for us. But we couldn't count on it. We talked about letting go and then fell asleep locked in each other's embrace.

Some nights Lin couldn't sleep because of pain and nausea, so we'd talk into the wee hours, recounting our happiest times together. And then gradually the day came when we felt no need to reminisce. Instead, we'd fantasize about meeting again on some other plane. We had to admit we didn't and couldn't know the truth, but both of us felt that there was something more. We agreed that when she died and ended up on some "other side", she would try to give me a sign.

One night, Lin told me she was concerned that I wasn't getting enough sleep due to our every-two-hour morphine injection routine. "Hey, woman," I chided her. "We're in this Circle together. I want to feel your pain and your joy, everything I can!"

In silence she gazed at me, and we snuggled up as close to each other as we could, wanting to crawl inside each other's skin. "Oh Derek," she said, "it's true. I can feel *you* feeling all of *me* right now." She began to cry and a tear fell directly into my eye. At that very moment, I began crying myself. Fifteen years earlier I had fallen in love with the most wonderful woman in the world. *She* and *I* became *We*. Now, *We* were stronger than ever.

"I wish everyone could feel like this," said Lin. "These last few months—isn't this the way we should all be, all the time? Any of us can die at any moment." *Hoka Hey.*

The veil between spiritual and physical planes is a thin one. Normally, even if we believe it's there, we mistake it as opaque and thick. Sometimes this causes us to suffer and to grasp for what's on the other side. But at times like birth—or death—we can glimpse through the veil and are reminded of our oneness, our fragility, and the preciousness of life. Lin was in this place.

Three days before Lin's death, our dog braved the steep flight of stairs that led up to our bedroom, hobbling up one step at a time, despite her hip dysplasia. She'd never come upstairs since we moved in, but she must have sensed something. She curled up by the edge of the bed and Lin could just barely reach down to touch her.

Lin and I didn't talk much by then. She slept most of the time, and I just lay beside her, listening to her breathe. She opened her eyes at one point, and whispered, "I'm ready." But still, her body hung on.

In six months, Lin's body had changed from an athlete's sturdy form into an emaciated shell. I still loved that body, but even more I loved her spirit, which I knew would soon be free. Eventually, her breathing slowed and slowed, and the pause between each shallow inhalation and exhalation got longer and longer. Often I thought I was witnessing her last breath. *No, no, this can't be it*, I would plead, and my heart would lurch as I saw her chest rise ever so slightly once again. But when the time actually came, I somehow knew it and felt no fear.

What I did feel was relief that Lin was now at peace, no longer at the mercy of her body's pain. I felt a flood of gratitude for this amazing woman. I felt no separation. I saw through the veil between life and death, glimpsing indescribable beauty.

After some time I glanced around the room. The clock had stopped, and now the L.E.D. display was blinking "12:00". I left the room and went to tell Dave, Lani and Carolyn, who were sitting downstairs. Later, the women and I bathed Lin's body in lavender water, dressed her in her purple wedding dress, and placed her dried wedding bouquet in her arms. It was obvious that the being we knew as Lin had left her body.

The next morning we all sat at breakfast outside on the patio, listening to the cackling ducks. We laughed along joyfully, feeling Lin holding us in her embrace, still pouring out the limitless love that seemed to come so easily for her.

Lin died as she lived—peacefully. And that peace remained with me. In the days after her death, I would see sparks flit about the bedroom before I went to sleep. Were they energetic traces of the physical being who had ceased to be? Were they a manifestation of her spirit? Was this the sign we had talked about? I didn't know exactly. But if it was true that there is always more, then it was so for Lin, even beyond death.

SILENCE

Begin with silence
Enter naked as the Arbutus tree
Move through life as the ocean
Busy yourself like the kingfisher
Be patient as the blue heron
Return to silence

CHAPTER 55

GRIEF TO GRATITUDE

As always, life's harshest experiences kept teaching me to trust.

As difficult as it was to watch Lin die, the worst for me was yet to come. I had no idea how deeply the pain would cut, how difficult it would be to go on living without her. Grief would be the most brutal test of faith and the most transformative pilgrimage of my life. It would require more letting go than I'd ever imagined.

I'd kept busy through Lin's illness. Now I allowed Lani and Carolyn take care of me. I did nothing but cry for days. I thought surely the source would run dry, but no, the tears kept flowing.

After the initial shock wore off, exhaustion and numbness set in. I was utterly depleted. If I felt anything at all, it was—lost. So I set a course for Long Beach on the far western coast of Vancouver Island, a favourite destination of Lin's and mine.

My first morning there, I sat on the deck of my rented cabin, watching the waves crash, the sound mercifully drowning out the sounds I felt erupt from my throat. I searched for a horizon to settle me, but found nothing. Lin was gone. She was never, ever going to come back. Every experience we had shared, everything we'd uttered to one another, seemed to collapse into one colourless, flat dimension in some far corner of my being. *It's all over.*

With just the endless expanse of ocean for company, I let go into its embrace. And at the bare, scoured floor of my grief, there was a whisper of a question. At first I blocked it out, but like the wind it kept whispering. *What*, the whisper asked, *is the "it" that's over?* Lin's physical life had come to an end, but—her spirit? The love? No. Both were infinite, like the waves that swept towards the cabin. *And look at the pine tree*, said the whisper. *You can once again be that deep-rooted and centred.* I felt it.

At home, my emotional pendulum swung back to despair, of course. Later, I'd find relief, but not for long. I had to trust that in time I would find balance, but for now I was being stretched from one extreme to another, painfully and uncontrollably. Every day I longed to hold Lin's hand, to hear her voice, to laugh, to go shopping, watch movies, and walk in the silent woods. If I could just only smell her delicious scent one more time. The list of longing seemed endless.

Sometimes I felt a dark urge to retreat so far into my grief that I wouldn't come out. It was as if the shadow side of me was beckoning, trying to convince me that if I only crawled far enough into the pain, I might revive those transcendent moments when Lin touched my soul with those deep blue eyes of hers. How seductive this idea was, yet I knew I couldn't let the shadow overtake me. That would surely mean my own death.

Then, I remembered the Long Dance. Lin had come into my life for a period to dance with me, and now I was alone again. But we were still *all one*.

I returned to the online journal that Lin had started, and began posting entries about my grieving process. It was a start.

> *I go back to staring at those rows of black letters,*
> *numbers and symbols, willing them to come*
> *together and convey something meaningful. My*
> *wrinkled, brown spotted hands seem unable or*
> *unwilling to peck out the words that I long for....*

Writing, even when it was about lacking words, grounded me, and it was a way to reach out when I was so raw. I found it excruciating to venture out into the real world, even to the grocery store, knowing I'd likely bump into a friend or neighbour who'd ask how I was, or even worse—how Lin was, not knowing she'd died.

Friends called up, wanting to see me. I was grateful, but both they and I were unused to me being in this position. I was almost always the helper, the listener, and now the tables were turned. Some folks didn't know how to handle that, and unconsciously expected me to be there for them while they processed their own grief as well as their reactions to mine. Many times I ended up exhausted and I realized that, except for Lani and Carolyn, being alone was easier.

One day I found an old photograph of Lin and got lost in her beautiful face. I came to, I don't know many minutes or hours later, curled up in bed. How I got there, I didn't know. My face was wet with tears, and I rocked back and forth, the sheets clutched in my fists. I felt I could pull them over me and never come out. Grief had become a comfort. It was a friend, dependable and safe, unlike the responsibilities and uncertainties of the outside world. But suddenly I saw an image of myself watching TV while sitting on my red couch, where Lin and I had sat together as her world began to shrink. I knew I mustn't let my own world shrink.

It was time for the next step. Putting myself in motion would help catalyze internal shifts. Though I was prepared to strike out on my own, I felt like I needed a psychic bodyguard. And I sensed that I could isolate myself just as easily on the road as at home. I needed company.

I knew Carolyn would drop everything, but did I want her to? There had to be something in it for her besides caring for me. We would go to Europe where we both felt at home, she would take photos, and we would walk through some of the places I'd been with Mary the Peace Pony. Perhaps this would connect me with a time when I'd felt strong and capable and full of dreams.

First we went to England to see Lin's best friend Janet. It was a difficult visit, but I knew I had to do it, to honour their strong connection. Next—Alsace, to visit Mimi and Marcou, who had so generously given Mary a home years ago. Our arrival was a surprise, and the smiles and tears didn't stop for the longest time. Later, we took to the road with no plan. We walked together, slowly, for hours each day, along many of the same routes I'd taken with Mary years ago.

Peace and delight consumed us often. Other times, we'd just look at each other and burst into wracking sobs. Carolyn somehow could hold both my grief and her own and not fall apart.

In Amsterdam we met up with my granddaughter Chamille, who was in Europe on an adventure. And of course we visited Lucile. As we walked around her neighbourhood, my eyes were drawn to a poster advertising an open-air concert the next evening. It was Peter Gabriel, one of my all-time favourites. The next day it rained, but as the show began the clouds disappeared and a rainbow filled the sky. Dancing and singing along at the top of my lungs, in that moment I felt no grief, no loss, only joy, only love. I sang louder.

Inevitably, we had to return home. Everywhere I looked and everything I touched reminded me of Lin. I didn't want to shut out the memories, or purge them, but I didn't want to drown in them either, so I got busy. I cleaned the house. The floors were immaculate, windows gleaming, oven spotless. I inserted colourful liners into the kitchen drawers. One morning before breakfast I took down the delicate bathroom curtains, hand-washing and then ironing them before putting them back up. Then I went out and brought home bouquets of flowers.

On the verge of obsession, it was time to travel again, and I was ready to go solo this time. I planned a pilgrimage for Lin's birthday—our wedding anniversary—to the Self Realization Fellowship gardens in California where we had proposed to each other. I needed to return to the source, to *our* bench, and sit in silence.

I flew to California on a first-class ticket. I boarded the plane, stretched out my legs as far as they could go, and waved my feet in the air. Delicious drinks and snacks kept coming my way. I felt like a kid at Christmas. My heart was warmed, knowing that all of this was a gift from Lin. She had accumulated a ton of points on her credit card, so my flight, hotel and rental car were all paid for.

The luxury felt a bit strange. On my walks I'd often slept in fields, in barns and on porches. I'd gone for days without food. Now I was at the other end of the spectrum and it felt almost too indulgent. But I heard Lin whispering, *Oh for goodness' sake, Derek, you deserve this. This is OUR trip, so enjoy it!*

"Thank you, Lin," I whispered aloud.

On the morning of August 26, I woke at dawn, didn't even bother with my caffeine fix, and got on the highway. There was barely a car on the road. I arrived at the tall black iron gate of the SRF Ashram, clutching a beautiful small bag that Carolyn had sewn, inside of which were some of Lin's ashes.

My legs began to shake as I followed the path to the fish pond. And then I saw the bench. I sat down under the shade of a drooping rubber tree and placed the bag of ashes beside me. I closed my eyes.

Breathing out I am emptying, breathing in I am releasing, breathing out I am giving. Breathing in I am receiving. Thank you Lin, for all our beautiful years together, and for your continuing presence in my life.

I returned home feeling the Earth more solid under my feet. I reached out to friends and my daughters too. Over the years, my relationships with Pauline and Christine had grown so rich. I enjoyed witnessing their transition from childhood to adulthood, and I had become a resource for them in their own struggles with parenthood. I was constantly amazed at their wisdom, and we enjoyed long talks on the phone. I wasn't quite ready yet to be *Dad* again. But they wanted to be there for *me,* so I let them in as much as I could.

Carolyn was coming over almost daily to check up on me and hang out. Before long, the road called to us. We ventured south. I can ramble on about the glowing reds of the arched rock formations in Utah at sunset, or the line of pelicans gracefully skimming the undulating waves off the California coast. That was the outer journey, and words to describe physical realities are abundant. But how do you describe the inner journey, something you can't see, something that slips away from you every time you think you've grasped it?

Whatever and however the shift happened, I was no longer depleted. I had love and ideas and dreams to share. Upon our return home, Carolyn and I began creating. We hosted a meditation circle and movie nights at her house, and gave presentations again in the local community. We were even invited to present at a Camino conference in California. Life was returning to full colour.

Since then my shadow side reveals itself periodically when I feel the urge to lock the door and draw the curtains. Then I see Lin with those big, loving, accepting blue eyes that seem to say, *Derek, it's OK to acknowledge this dark side, but don't forget your light.* She would not want me to shrivel up. I cry, but then the anguish and longing subsides. I am creating a new relationship with Lin based in the present. My grief begins to transform into gratitude.

I imagine the day when I die, leaving my friends and family behind. What would I wish for them? Obviously they'd miss me. But after a while, I would want them to live, I mean really *live*—fully and authentically. I would wish them to become even more for having known me, not less, because of my passing.

I make a promise to Lin and to myself. I will always become MORE. More understanding, more friendly, more humorous, more accepting, more forgiving. I will walk more, laugh more, cry more, see more, listen more, and love more.

What an extraordinary journey it has been. I have held babies as they entered this world and embraced loved ones as they prepared to die. I have had to learn how to take risks and be vulnerable, to accept both the light and the dark. I have walked on fire and felt the heat of my own fear. I have swum with the dolphins and danced with the deer. I have lifted many a rock and leaf, where infinite mysteries were revealed. And having tasted the delights of being alive instead of merely existing, I have vowed to continue living passionately. Yet—I must let go of it all.

My life has been all about letting go of things, places, people I've loved deeply, and ideas—about how the world should be, even about who I really am. I can even let go of walking for peace. But because I can let go, there is always more. In my head, I hear the Buddhist meditation master saying, "*Start again.*"

Derek's return from California was marked by a renewed vow to complete the book, which had been on hold since Lin took ill. When he'd started it years ago, it was in the hope that his future grand-children would read it. Now he was determined to finish it for Lin, the story of her death and his grief journey as the epilogue.

We had some productive spells, but other aspects of life at times overshadowed the book. The nature of Derek's and my relationship continued to change. Being together as a couple was nothing either of us had ever imagined, but it happened very organically.

Derek and Lin had enjoyed the most fulfilling marriage I had ever witnessed, and I felt honoured to be drawn so close to their Circle. The fact that Derek was so deeply committed to Lin made me trust him. I felt safe with this man who was my mentor, collaborator, and best friend. They had become role models for me, and I knew I wanted a relationship like theirs one day.

A week before Lin's diagnosis, I'd sold my house in Vancouver and moved to the Sunshine Coast, to be near them and several other close friends and cousins. I'll never forget that devastating afternoon and Derek's distraught voice on the phone.

If I had still been living in Vancouver, my future might have unfolded very differently. Derek asked both me and Lani to commit to caring for Lin on a regular basis. My decision changed my life. I learned about priorities, loyalty, and intimacy. The four of us created the kind of bond I'd only ever dreamed was possible.

Even though Lin's death was expected and they got to say goodbye, Derek's grief shook him to the core. What I saw was a man making an effort to enjoy life while consciously witnessing and honouring his grieving process and not sweeping it under the rug. What I didn't see was what he told me later, that he'd imagined himself just going out the door one day to never come back, to die walking. At the time, I supported my friend the best I could. Later, he told me I was his reason to keep living.

In the spring of 2008, Derek took me to the stone bench at the SRF gardens. He wanted to show me the place where his and Lin's love had blossomed into commitment. On our walk through the grounds, he reached out and touched a crimson rose. A thorn pricked his little finger, and the blood ran down onto Lin's wedding band, which he wore on his pinky finger. We couldn't help but see this as a sign of his letting go. The following spring, while on another trip, he lost the ring, and never found it.

On the second anniversary of Lin's death, Derek asked our friend Reverend Mark to make a bench in her memory. We installed it at one of their special places on the Sunshine Coast, where they used to sit and watch seabirds and boats go by. Friends joined us for the unveiling.

Derek and I were developing our own very strong Circle, and Lin was a part of it in spirit, as she would always be a part of him, and of me.

In many ways, Derek and I were alike. We loved dancing, playing, exploring. And of course we both loved so much to walk. Although I am a fast walker, I was determined we walk together, despite his slower pace. We'd mosey along for a while and then I'd speed ahead to explore, leaving him sitting comfortably on a bench or rock, meditating, with his face to the sun. "I'll be the one here waiting for you when you get back," he'd say. On my return, before he could possibly even hear my footsteps, he'd open his eyes and glance up at me. Somehow he could always feel my presence. I told him he had supernatural powers, but he chalked it up to my magnetism. We'd laugh and then continue strolling on together slowly, hand in hand, faces in the sun.

After some time, we considered moving in together. As my house was much larger, naturally we presumed he'd shack up with me. I had really wanted to make the most of the space and continue my renovation project, turning the lower level into an artists' retreat and gallery. The view was gorgeous, as was the garden and its fish pond. But one day as I was sitting on the big red couch in the living room of Derek's townhouse, I had a "lightbulb moment". I saw that I could easily live in his space. It would require a lot less upkeep and it would free us up to travel more.

The thing was, I had a lot of stuff. Derek had been amazed by the sheer volume of belongings I had already let go of when relocating from Vancouver to the Sunshine Coast. But I still owned more than would comfortably fit in Derek's place, so for the next few months I slowly and systematically purged. This required taking a serious look at what I had, and thinking about what I actually needed. I kept favourite small items, probably more than many people have, but I gave away antiques and artwork and appliances to family and friends, and with everything I let go of I felt more and more free.

As engaged as I was in this process, I had actually grown to find the Sunshine Coast rather small, having lived in a city almost my whole life. Derek found Vancouver too big and busy, but we agreed that the smaller city of Victoria, on Vancouver Island, would be an ideal place to retire to in a few years. Midway through my transition over to Derek's place, I began browsing online at homes in Victoria, just for fun. A unique townhouse caught my eye and I couldn't stop thinking about it. *Why wait?* I said to myself. But how crazy to even entertain the notion!

Derek and Lin had lived in about eight different homes, and he was weary of moving. Strangely, though, he didn't think this idea was crazy. We caught a floatplane to Victoria and saw the townhouse. It was perfect. We signed the papers that day, and several months later, we were living there.

Friends were shocked, but it felt so right and the transition was smooth. The new surroundings were healing, and gave us lots to do and explore. I made the house beautiful while Derek learned how to use video editing software to create sound effects and green screen backdrops for the silly videos we filmed for friends' birthdays. We wrote songs together. Derek walked more than he had in years. Friends of his said they had never seen him shine like this. He was squeezing every little bit of enjoyment out of life.

The next step in our relationship came naturally, although I did need to spend some time seriously considering marrying a much older man, and what that might mean for our future. But our love was so strong. How could I turn away from it? No, I wanted to be with him for as long as I could.

Our commitment was an outcome of tending to our friendship honestly, day to day. Neither of us required the piece of paper, and I had never desired a ring or white dress or any of the trappings. We'd both been lifelong non-conformists. It was actually Derek who suggested we marry legally, and, as I look back now, I think he wanted me to have that ring, that piece of paper, as proof of our commitment after he was gone.

We proposed to each other one night on a park bench by the sea. We agreed that the most fun and easy way to do it would be to elope. And the location was obvious: the Camino.

Next, we needed to inform family and to explain the elopement, so that no one's feelings got hurt. We prepared ourselves that not everyone would be supportive. Lin and Derek had been such a perfect couple, and I was afraid of tainting that. But almost everyone was thrilled for us and many said they saw it coming. My fears of being rejected by Derek's daughters were unfounded. Ultimately, they welcomed me with open arms.

As it turned out, we didn't just get married once but three times. Or maybe four. First, in May of 2010 we returned to Spain, and after three days of walking alone, I was to meet Derek at our special hilltop spot. I had imagined the sun would be beaming down on us as we caught sight of each other from a great distance, as it had six years earlier. But I woke up that morning to fog and snow. I couldn't see more than about ten metres in front of me. My walk through the valley seemed to take forever, and I feared I had somehow missed our rendezvous point. But then I looked up through the mist, and suddenly, there was the hilltop, and a ghostly figure at its edge. The truth is, my heart juddered and I nearly fainted. There he was!

In a couple of minutes I scaled the cliffside and we embraced in the freezing air. Then, warm from the inside, I took off my rain jacket and infamous pink hoodie, and unfolded the long gauzy pale green dress underneath. Derek reached out and gave me a wilted but exquisite bouquet of tiny wildflowers. Through tears and rain we hugged and kissed and recited spontaneous vows. Derek's fingers were numb from standing in the cold for half an hour, but we managed to exchange rings.

Afterward, we joined Lucile, her partner, and their baby Nina. They'd travelled with us to Spain, and we warmed up in our favourite rustic hilltop inn, dining on hot *caldo gallego* (bean soup) and toasting each other with glasses of *cava* (sparkling wine). Our wedding cake was the traditional *Tarte Santiago*.

A few days later we travelled to San Sebastian, close to the border of France in Basque country. There we met Derek's old meditation master, Dhiravhamsa. He greeted us with a warm smile. Together we all stood, eyes closed, on a golden sandy beach. He clasped his hands and recited an ancient sutra. When he was finished he held our hands together and blessed our rings with his own wishes for our union. We considered this our second wedding, after which we all walked to a café and sat laughing and sharing stories over tapas and red wine.

At home, we settled into our beautiful new house for a week or so and then headed off to the Sunshine Coast for our third, and legal, wedding. It had been raining like crazy for days, but the sky cleared and we walked out onto the rocks near our friend Tina's little cabin by the sea. Tina was our witness, and her partner Mark, an Anglican priest, officiated. We had no guests.

It was important to me, though, to invite our friends and family to share in our new life. So, the following month, on St. James Day (he being the patron saint of the Camino) we held another ceremony, in the courtyard behind our house. Again Reverend Mark officiated. We called it a "house blessing and wedding celebration", but those who attended all said they felt they'd taken part in an actual wedding. So be it: wedding number four.

And then came the living together and working things out, which, though difficult at times, made the whole thing worth it.

We felt like we'd found the key to the fairy tale: not to think too far ahead to the "happily ever after". We knew our time together was precious. NOW was all that mattered.

Early in 2011, we'd just begun a few solid weeks of work on the book after a hectic year or more of moving house, weddings, and settling into our new life. But our writing was interrupted by more important things. Lani's husband Peter, after living for many years with prostate cancer, was now in his last stages of the disease, so we went to see them on the Sunshine Coast. We'd witnessed both his determination to live, and now, his willingness to let go. Derek and I, along with Peter's 23-year-old son, were there when Peter died, Lani at his side.

We stayed on a few days to help out, planning to return several weeks later. Derek, of all people, knew what lay ahead for Lani.

Before we left the Sunshine Coast, we drove over to see our friend Urszula, who had taken over Lin's medical practice with her friend Sarah. The two of them were surely making Lin proud. On this visit, Urszula told Derek that she and her husband were trying to conceive a baby. Derek placed his hands on her belly and told her not to fret. When the time was right, it would happen.

In the following week, Derek decided to make another pilgrimage. I was happy that he was interested in walking again. Because he'd already just been away, and because of his slowing down, we decided he'd simply do a pilgrimage here in Victoria, in segments, over the course of several days. And what would be more apropos than walking from our house to Mile Zero, the beginning of the Trans Canada Trail? This was the spot where Canadian hero Terry

Fox would have completed his historical run across Canada, if he had not died of cancer.

Of course, Derek chose not a straight line but a winding and picturesque route to Mile Zero. Every day for five days, I dropped Derek off for his walk. It felt good to reverse the roles. I'd cruise by later, giving him a wink and whistle. "Want a ride, sailor?" He'd beam at me, gratified and determined. On the home stretch, I walked with him to the statue of Terry Fox, on which an inscribed plaque reads: *Dreams are made possible if you try.*

On March 11, 2011, a tsunami occurred in Japan, triggering the Fukushima nuclear disaster with devastating consequences. We tried to get in touch with Chris and Lieh and their kids without any luck. Derek was concerned for them, and for everyone in Fukushima, including his old friend Sawada's family. And who knew how the rest of the world would be affected by the tidal wave and radiation?

The following week, somehow time stretched out and life seemed especially precious. We made a huge shopping trip for groceries, coming home with a lot of our favourite comfort foods with which we stocked the freezer. Derek decided to complete a few unfinished projects around the house and in the garage, including installing a bamboo fence around our hot tub.

Most Sundays, Zachariah would come over in the afternoon for our weekly soak. The three of us would sit together, sometimes saying nothing, but often engaging in silly Monty Python banter. This time, conversation turned to life and death, which was not unusual, but because of Peter's recent passing it was more in our thoughts. Derek said, "You know, if I were to die tomorrow, it would be really OK. I feel so content right now." It was true. He had reached a place of peace and satisfaction in his life, and everyone had noticed.

"What do you think about life after death, though?" Zachariah asked, ever the skeptic.

"I don't *know*, of course," Derek answered, "but I *feel* that I am spirit, living in a body, learning how to be human, and that is very important to me. And I've experienced things that lead me to believe there is more for us beyond this realm. But I can't count on that. How I behave now should not rest on what does or doesn't happen next." Zachariah and I nodded in agreement.

"I don't want to skimp on enjoying the material world," Derek continued. "Even if this is all just a manifestation our collective soul has dreamed up, I want to live life to the fullest. At the same time, I have to be cautious about attachments. And this means I always have to be willing to let go. That even includes Carolyn," I knew this was true, but I nodded less enthusiastically.

"You see, I had that with Lin," he went on. "When we got together, we knew we had to be willing to let go, or it wouldn't work. When she died, if I had hung on, I would not be in this place of contentment today."

"I'd like to believe I could let go of you, but I'm not so sure," I said. "Perhaps I'd just go to bed with some books for a while and crawl out a few months later," I said, half-jokingly.

The next day Derek and I sat in the hot tub again, quietly. Sometimes we'd look up and comment on the clouds, but we saw nothing but blue now. And, then, only moments later it seemed, I gasped at what I saw in the sky. Derek looked over and saw me staring skyward and joined me. It was an infinity symbol, white on blue, as clear if it had been drawn in chalk. It's the kind of sideways figure 8 a small plane could have made, but we'd heard and seen nothing. "It's a message from Lin!" I cried, excitedly. Neither of us normally looked for signs, but not only was it an infinity symbol, it was a 8—Lin's favourite number. Derek just smiled.

Eventually, we were able to contact Chris in Japan, via Skype. He had moved his family far away to Lieh's parents' home. We were relieved to see them, and Derek entertained the kids with an impromptu puppet show via web-cam.

We resumed our joyful togetherness. One evening, Derek downloaded some music that a friend of his had composed. He turned up the speakers on his computer and danced out into the living room. He grabbed some maracas and I picked up the bongo drums and we danced our bums off, as Derek liked to say.

The next day, driving home from a stroll on the beach, we turned on the car radio. It was playing "Spirit in the Sky" by Norman

Greenbaum. Derek piped up suddenly, exclaiming, "THAT's the kind of music I'd like at my wake!" It was rare for him to be so dramatic. I grabbed a pad of paper and pen from the glove compartment.

"Any other requests?" I asked. Peter Gabriel and John Lennon topped the playlist. "What about your ashes? What should I do with them?" I continued.

"Mount Galiano," he answered. "And maybe the Camino? You'll know when the time comes."

"How about Hiroshima?" I asked.

"Oh, of course," he replied.

"And Redcar?"

"Aww, sweetiepie, you're so thoughtful," he said.

At home we kept talking. Death was not a subject we shied away from. It was an easy, light conversation. That night in bed, gazing into each other's eyes, we recited a long list of everything we adored about each other, going on until we fell asleep in each other's arms.

Two days later, just after waking up, he had a sudden heart attack and died almost instantly. March 18. It was 23 years to the day since his mother Elsie died.

At first, it seemed like the universe, or even Derek himself, had played a cruel joke on me. *This is what you mean by being in the moment? One moment you're alive, then next moment you're not? This is what you mean by letting go?* But it was not a joke. It was real. And it made no sense when I tried to reason my way through it.

When I woke up the next morning, it was clear, though. Derek was gone, but his energy, his love, and his words of wisdom surrounded me in a protective bubble. Our Circle was still very much intact, and remained the most real and solid thing for me.

Several weeks after Derek's passing, the coroner's report showed that he had suffered from a congenital heart condition. It is highly likely that his neuropathy was a symptom of this. I also found out from his family that his mother had died of a heart condition, and his brother Howard had undergone several bypasses and now had a pacemaker and built-in defibrillator.

In hindsight, I could see that there had been signs that both of us had unconsciously ignored. But Derek was a stubborn man, and heart condition or not, he was never keen on the medical establishment, drugs, hospitals or anything of the kind. He died the way he always said he would: at home, with me, and not after some horrible long drawn-out illness. So it was perfect for him, if not for me. But I had no regrets. In a way, every day we had spent together had prepared me for this.

The next few months were surreal. Though I was safe and grounded in the Circle, the rest of the world seemed to morph. My sensitivity to everything heightened, which meant nature's colours grew brighter, and certain friends grew dearer. But at the other end of the spectrum other things were too harsh. Even some of my favourite music seemed too loud, too intense, and sapped of relevance. I walk the city streets feeling split open, raw. Can people see my pain? I look around at other women and men, wondering what pain and loss they may be trying to hide. I realized I am not alone. I had been thrust into a huge, but invisible and silent, confederacy of the grieving.

The thought that books would be a source of solace was laughable now. I didn't want distraction. I wanted to just exist in the Circle. But I had a memorial to prepare for. I began rummaging through the garage looking for photos to scan for a slide show and found some audio cassettes. Fortunately I still had a player. With trepidation I inserted one tape and heard Mary the Peace Pony's hoofs clacking on pavement. I could almost feel Mary's soft hide, and smell the meadows in the French countryside. I played another tape and heard Derek and the children at the circus singing, "All we are saying, is give peace a chance...." Tears streamed down my face. The stories he'd told me came to life. And what a remarkable life.

I found boxes of photos and spent weeks scanning. The slide show became my obsession, and I tweaked the images and music endlessly. Then the day came, Derek's birthday and celebration of life, June 16th, 2011. I'd prepared a playlist based on what I'd jotted down that day in the car, including, of course, "Give Peace a Chance", which made us all cry.

I had asked friends and family to come dressed in silly hats and glasses, and they didn't disappoint. Mark, the priest, was Master of Ceremonies, and came wearing his clerical vestments, which he took off piece by piece as he spoke, revealing a brightly coloured tie-died shirt of Derek's. I could hear Derek right then, saying, *If it's not fun, I'm out!*

We were all touched by each other's stories of the special moments we'd had with Derek, the dreams he helped us dream. We reflected that we'd never met anyone so comfortable in his own skin, and how he had a way of making us all comfortable in our own. We finished with a singalong of "Always Look on the Bright Side of Life", one of Derek's favourites, from the Monty Python film *The Life of Brian*. It's the closing tune, sung by a crucified man. It sounds dreadful, but it's a truly uplifting scene, excuse the pun.

Not long after the gathering, our friends Urszula and her husband Joe called me with some good news. She was pregnant, after trying for some time. They'd calculated that they'd conceived shortly after seeing Derek for the last time, when he'd laid his hands on her belly, saying, "Don't worry, it'll happen." New life was on the way. This was the kind of news that kept me motivated and connected.

Although I'd suffered the loss of my parents and other loved ones, I had no foresight about the degree to which the loss of my partner would affect me. There is no more *us*, *our* dreams, *our* plans. Derek accepted me, all of me, and let me know how cherished I was, even the quirky bits. The loss of our mutual care, affection and affirmation has eroded my self-confidence.

Can I ever be that happy again, as I was with him? I have to trust that I will. But there are times when I think I'm going crazy, almost believing that if I cry loudly enough, Derek will hear me and come back. There are times I want to scream at the next well-intentioned person who tells me that nothing has really changed for me. "Derek is still with you," they say. "Some of us will never have what you two did." *Smug, New Age flake*, I think to myself. *You wouldn't say that if you'd lost your spouse!* Yes, I do believe he is out there in some way, and in me, and yes, there is still so much to be thankful for. But some days I'm scraping the bottom of the gratitude barrel.

I draw strength from Derek's own experiences. I read what he wrote after he lost Lin and I remember I'm not crazy, I am grieving.

Walking to Japan

Like he did, I need to create a new relationship with my beloved, so he can be in my life without me feeling constant loss. So, I let myself feel the pain completely and, as Derek said, it transforms from grief to gratitude. I am released, if only for a time. When it comes again, I let more in and let more go. Then I remember that Derek was 45 when he decided to go on the Great Peace March. I am widowed at 45. When I realize he had his whole life ahead of him at that point, I have hope for myself. As he said, I intend to live—fully and authentically, to become even more for having known him, not less, because of his passing.

It's strange to call myself a widow, but somehow the word gives me comfort. It lets people know that I've been through something momentous. But I am more. So who am I now, on my own? These days, walking is the best way for me to find out. I have taken Derek's ashes everywhere: to Mount Galiano, Hiroshima, the Camino, Redcar, Battersea, to the statue of Terry Fox in Victoria, and to the Sunshine Coast.

Friends, too, have made their own pilgrimages around the world and taken him along. Lucile scattered ashes at the statue of Gandhi in Amsterdam, and Zachariah at Doune Castle in Scotland where one of their favourite movies, *Monty Python and the Holy Grail,* was filmed. Derek still walks in peace, in all of our footsteps.

Sixteen months after Derek's passing, I resumed working on *Walking to Japan.* Sometimes I sit at the computer, thinking, *But I'm no author!* And then I recall my own words to Derek and hear them now in his voice: "Just take a step, and I'll help you."

So I put my fingers back on the keyboard. It feels a bit like slipping my camera over my shoulder, tying my shoes, and stepping out the door.

PHOTO CREDITS

Efforts were made to attribute all photos accurately.

Carolyn Affleck Youngs: iii, xii, 2, 14, 54, 64, 66, 74, 80 (mask D. Youngs), 87, 88, 104, 110, 148, 152, 176, 180, 198, 214, 229, 230, 246, 254, 262, 266/267, 286, 312, 332, 340, 348, 354, 364, 370, 372, 380, & cover photos

Derek Youngs: 18, 46, 108/109, 122, 138, 238, 292, 308, 326, 336, collages pages 1 & 68 (collaged photos various sources)

Keith Thirkell: 188, 206, 238

Marcou & Mireille Valot: 276, 282

Zachariah Crow: 222, 268

Brandon Wilson: 394

Christine Youngs: 304

Elsie Youngs: 156

Lani Kaito: 96

Lucile Kerkmeer: 10

Uncredited: 6, 30, 36, 40, 58, 116, 134, 170

ABOUT THE AUTHORS

DEREK WALKER YOUNGS

Between 1986 and 2011, Derek Walker Youngs devoted much of his life to peace. Born in 1940 during a World War II air raid, his first steps for peace were taken on the Great Peace March for Nuclear Disarmament across the U.S.A. He went on to found the Peace Walker Society, and traversed more than 25,000 kilometres in 25 countries, each day walking in trust and faith, not knowing where he would sleep or find his next meal. He appeared as an international news item in print, radio and television media, and shared his stories of love and learning with people across the globe.

CAROLYN AFFLECK YOUNGS

Carolyn Affleck Youngs, born in Vancouver, Canada, is a photographer, walker, and grammar queen. Her pilgrimages include the Camino de Santiago in Spain, and the 88 Temples in Japan. She has walked all the city streets of Vancouver, and plans to walk across Canada one day. Another day, she'll walk from John O'Groats to Land's End in Britain.

www.peacewalker.com
www.carolynaffleck.com